D0041966

{

brave

girl

eating

}

A FAMILY'S STRUGGLE WITH ANOREXIA

{ brave

girl

eating }

HARRIET BROWN

wm WILLIAM MORROW *An Imprint of* HarperCollins*Publishers*

BRAVE GIRL EATING. Copyright © 2010 by Harriet Brown. All rights reserved. Printed in the United States of America. No part of this book may be used or reproduced in any manner whatsoever without written permission except in the case of brief quotations embodied in critical articles and reviews. For information address HarperCollins Publishers, 10 East 53rd Street, New York, NY 10022.

HarperCollins books may be purchased for educational, business, or sales promotional use. For information please write: Special Markets Department, Harper-Collins Publishers, 10 East 53rd Street, New York, NY 10022.

FIRST EDITION

Designed by Joy O'Meara

Library of Congress Cataloging-in-Publication Data has been applied for.

ISBN 978-0-06-172547-0

10 11 12 13 14   OV/RRD   10 9 8 7 6 5 4 3 2 1

This book is for Kitty, and for every young woman or man who's ever struggled or continues to struggle with an eating disorder: for your courage, your strength, your capacity not just to endure but to overcome. I honor you and your families with every word.

The wreck and not the story of the wreck
the thing itself and not the myth . . .

　　　　—ADRIENNE RICH, from "Diving into the Wreck"

{ contents }

Contents

{ foreword }

by Daniel le Grange, Ph.D.

Anorexia nervosa is a serious disorder with devastating psychological and physical consequences. Almost 75 out of every 100,000 people are diagnosed with anorexia nervosa. More specifically, 0.6 percent of adolescent girls are diagnosed with this illness. We have a tremendous challenge before us to determine *why* it is that young people develop this illness. While we wrestle with this vexing dilemma, however, a more urgent challenge is *what* can be done to reverse anorexia and its array of devastating consequences.

Despite the crisis associated with self-starvation, few treatments have been tested, and anorexia nervosa remains a confusing trial for sufferers, their parents, doctors, and researchers. One intervention that has received considerable clinical attention is family-based treatment (FBT). In FBT, parents aren't blamed for their child's illness; instead, they're viewed as a crucial resource in bringing about their child's recovery. They are encouraged to be in charge of their son/daughter's weight restoration while the therapist acknowledges the enormous difficulties of this task and supports the whole family. Once healthy weight has been restored, some of the developmental issues of adolescence are addressed in FBT.

Brave Girl Eating chronicles the Brown family's ordeal battling Kitty's anorexia nervosa—a remarkable journey that brings to life the almost unbearable struggle that both Kitty and her family endured. Anorexia nervosa brings about profound psychological as well as physiological changes in the sufferer. These changes are often so severe that it is common for parents not to recognize their offspring—to feel "This can't be my child." It is easy to see how perfectly competent, loving parents become bewildered and disorganized as they fail to understand this baffling illness. This confusion often makes them second-guess their natural instinct to reach out and help their child. As a consequence, they become immobilized in the face of the seemingly overwhelming power that anorexia has over their child and over them. The Browns' story is an uplifting drama as the parents' determination and perseverance, as well as Kitty's brave efforts, succeed in wresting Kitty away from the eating disorder.

Understanding and treating anorexia nervosa are daunting tasks. But one thing is certain: food is medicine, and recovery cannot come about unless healthy weight is restored. Put more bluntly, one has to eat in order to get better. Many obstacles block the road to recovery, and in *Brave Girl Eating* the author describes some of these firsthand—for instance, the frustration experienced by both parents and teen when they get stuck in what we call "anorexic debates," where even the most rational adult can be convinced by (or give in to) the teen's insistence on the caloric "value" of a salad without a dressing. These debates demonstrate how malnutrition affects the mind and highlight the irrational power of the illness. As

Brown points out, "The question isn't why but what: What do we do now?"

Brown also shares many of the important lessons she and her family learned throughout their ordeal. Most affirming of parents, and valuable from my perspective, is that families (parents) are not helpless—they just have to (re)gain their confidence. This, of course, is no easy task; in fact, it is perhaps one of the most difficult goals to achieve in battling anorexia nervosa. But with the support of the therapist, parents have to "stand up" and face this illness, with love and caring. Kitty's story demonstrates anorexia's awful power over the teen sufferer and over the desperate parents trying to rescue their child.

Brave Girl Eating highlights some commonly held misinformation about anorexia nervosa. By showing us Kitty's struggle, the author dispels the myth that anorexia nervosa is a choice. She equates it with other serious illnesses and disorders, and we are reminded that "anorexia chooses you!" Kitty's struggle educates all of us about the turmoil and guilt felt by both patient and parents. Confusion and denial are commonplace as the eating disorder challenges every family member, not just the teen. This book also speaks to the frustration and anguish felt by all parents who try to understand and do something when they suspect their child has an eating disorder. These feelings are exacerbated when parents have to scramble to find a specialist eating-disorders team as they navigate the health-insurance quagmire.

It is all too clear that everyone involved in this battle with anorexia nervosa requires support and guidance. While Kitty's family found ongoing support in their pediatrician and other professionals, they did not have access to a local FBT therapist and, instead, conducted the arduous task of weight restoration mostly by themselves.

This absence of direct support and guidance no doubt complicated an already demanding task. I agree with the author that *having hope is a great gift*, and this hope ushered them through many tough times. However, no family who struggles with this awful illness should have to do this on their own.

Notwithstanding many obstacles along the way, Brown and her family have regained their footing, which is evidence of their resilience. Brown has since used her expertise as both a parent and writer to help empower other parents so that they may take center stage in the treatment of their children with eating disorders. *Brave Girl Eating* serves as a reminder that parents are not to blame for their child's eating disorder; rather, they are a reliable resource in the recovery of their children.

Daniel le Grange, Ph.D., is a professor of psychiatry and behavioral neuroscience and the director of the Eating Disorders Program at the University of Chicago.

{ author's note }

Impurities creep into every memoir for the simple reason that memory is fallible and you don't know, when you're living through an experience, that you'll someday be writing about it. (Even if you do know, walking around with a tape recorder doesn't play well in everyday life.) Then of course there's the question of perspective: two people can live through the same experience and remember it very differently—especially members of the same family.

Those issues become even more urgent when a memoir describes the lives of children, especially your own children, who are vulnerable in a variety of ways and who can't in any real sense give informed consent to being written about. It's one thing to expose your own life; it's quite another to expose the lives of your kids. As a longtime journalist and, now, a professor of journalism, I think a lot about what's ethical and what isn't. In this book, I considered the line between openness and exploitation. My intention here is to tell the truth as ethically and as compassionately as possible. To protect my children I've given them false names and disguised some of their physical and other characteristics.

Deciding to tell this story was a process for me and my family. We discussed it over a period of months, weighing the potential for good against the possibilities of harm. I give much credit to my daughter Kitty, who overcame her own preference for privacy out of a wish to help others. She's a brave and unusual young woman.

As for the vagaries of memory, I kept an extremely—one might even say obsessively—detailed journal during Kitty's illness, partly to keep track of her progress and treatment, and partly to keep myself from drowning in anxiety. In the journal I recorded many conversations more or less verbatim, and recapped others. The events I describe in this book are based on my recollections and on that journal. In a few instances I've conflated situations in order to compress the story line, but every conversation and event in this book is true and did happen as described, as far as I recollect.

People who are acutely ill with anorexia and bulimia often read a memoir like this as a guidebook for staying sick—as "thinspiration." For that reason, I have avoided mention of specific weights, numbers, and other details that might be interpreted as "pro-anorexia" or "pro-bulimia" material. It's my intention that this book never be used in that way.

{ brave
girl
eating }

What I Wish Everyone Knew

Close your eyes. Imagine that you're standing in a bakery. Not just any bakery—the best bakery in Paris, its windows fogged, crowded with people who jostle for space in front of its long glass cases. The room is fragrant and you can't take your eyes off the rows of cinnamon rolls and croissants, iced petits fours, flaky napoleons and elephant ears. Every counter holds at least one basket of crusty baguettes, still warm from the oven.

And you're hungry. In fact, you're starving. Hunger is a tornado whirling in your chest, a bottomless vortex at your core. Hunger is a tiger sharpening its claws on your tender insides. You stand in front of the glass cases, trying to swallow, but your throat is dry and your stomach clenches and contracts.

You want more than anything to lick the side of an éclair, swirl the custard and chocolate against your tongue. You dream about biting off the end of a cruller, feeling the give of the spongy dough, the brief molecular friction of the glaze against your teeth, flooding your mouth with sweetness. The woman beside you reaches into a white paper bag, pulls out a hunk of sourdough roll. You see the little puff of steam that flares from its soft center, breathe in its warm yeasty smell. She pops it into her mouth and chews and you chew along with her. You can almost taste the bread she's eating. Almost.

But you can't, not really, because how long has it been since you've tasted bread? A month? A year? And though your stomach grinds against your backbone and your cheeks are hollow, though the tiger flays your belly, you can't eat. You want to, you *have* to, but your fear is greater than your hunger. Because when you do—when you choke down a spoonful of plain yogurt, five pretzel sticks, a grape—that's when the voice in your head starts up, a whisper, a cajoling sigh: *You don't need to eat, you're strong, so strong. That's right. Good girl.*

Soon the whisper is a hiss filling the center of your head: *You don't deserve to eat. You're weak, unworthy. You are disgusting. You don't deserve to live.* You, you, you. The voice is a drumbeat, a howl, a knife sunk in your gut, twisting. It knows what you're thinking. It knows everything you do. The more you try to block it out, the louder it becomes, until it's screaming in your ear: *You're fat. You're a pig. You make everyone sick. No one loves you and no one ever will. You don't deserve to be loved. You've sinned and now you must be punished.*

So you don't eat, though food is all you think about. Though all day long, wherever you are—doing homework, sitting with friends, trying to sleep—part of you is standing in the bakery, mesmerized with hunger and with fear, the voice growling and rumbling. You have to stand there, your insides in shreds, empty of everything but your own longing. There will be no bread for you, no warm buttery pastries. There's only the pitiless voice inside your head, high-pitched, insistent, insidious. There's only you, more alone than you've ever been. You, growing smaller and frailer. You, with nowhere else to go.

The voice is part of you now, your friend and your tormentor. You can't fight it and you don't want to. You're not so strong, after all. You can't take it and you can't get away. *You don't deserve to live.* You want to die.

This is what it feels like to have anorexia.

I've never had anorexia, but I've lived with it. I've observed it closely in someone I love: my oldest daughter, Kitty, who was fourteen when she got sick. I watched as the upbeat, affectionate, empathetic girl I knew became furious and irrational, withdrawn and depressed, obsessed with food but unable to eat. I saw her writhe in terror, heard her beg my husband and me for help, and then, in the same breath, shriek that we were trying to poison her, to make her fat, to kill her. I heard a voice I did not recognize come out of her mouth, saw her face changed beyond knowing. I held her in my arms and felt the arc of every rib, counted the bones in her elbows, saw her breastbone press out through the paper-thin skin of her chest. I felt her body shake and knew that whatever comfort I offered wasn't enough; it was nothing in the face of the thing that was stripping the flesh from her bones and the light from her eyes.

I had no idea anorexia was like that.

Before Kitty got sick, I thought eating disorders happened to other people's children. Not to my daughter, who was savvy and wise, strong and funny, the kind of kid who picked her way easily through the pitfalls of toxic middle-school friendships. She did fit the classic profile: she was a perfectionist, fastidious about how she looked and dressed. She was hard on people sometimes, especially herself. She was athletic, a gymnast; her favorite event was the balance beam—fitting, I thought, for a child who so gracefully walked the line between childhood and adolescence.

But she would never have an eating disorder. She was way too smart for that.

Before my daughter got sick, I thought kids with anorexia or bulimia wanted attention, that they were screwed up and tuned out, bored or acting up or self-destructive. But my daughter was none of those things. She seemed cheerful and well adjusted; she had friends, interests, a passion for new experiences. She wrote her sixth-grade research paper on eating disorders. She knew the dangers. She would never choose to have anorexia. She was safe.

I was wrong about many things, but I was right about that one thing: Kitty *didn't* choose anorexia. Anorexia chose her. And it nearly killed her.

At Kitty's lowest weight, her heart beat dangerously slowly; it could have stopped at any time. Between 10 and 20 percent of people with anorexia die from heart attacks, other complications, and suicide; the disease has the highest mortality rate of any mental illness. Or Kitty could have lost her life in a different way, lost it to the roller coaster of relapse and recovery, inpatient and outpatient, that eats up, on average, five to seven years. Or a lifetime: only half of all anorexics recover in the end. The other half endure lives of dysfunction and despair. Friends and families give up on them. Doctors dread treating them. They're left to stand in the bakery with the voice ringing in their ears, alone in every way that matters.

Kitty didn't choose anorexia. No one chooses anorexia, or bulimia, or any other eating disorder. Intelligence is no protection;

many of the young women (and, increasingly, men) who develop anorexia are bright and curious and tuned in. Families are no protection, either, because anorexia strikes children from happy families and difficult ones, repressed families and families who talk ad nauseam about feelings. The families of anorexics do share certain traits, though: a history of eating disorders, or anxiety, or obsessive-compulsive disorder. Or all of the above.

I've never had anorexia, but I know it well. I see it on the street, in the gaunt and sunken face, the bony chest, the spindly arms of an emaciated woman. I've come to recognize the flat look of despair, the hopelessness that follows, inevitably, from years of starvation. I think: *That could have been my daughter*. It wasn't. It's not. If I have anything to say about it, it won't be.

This is our family's story. Kitty was diagnosed with anorexia in June 2005. In August of that year we began family-based treatment (FBT), also known as the Maudsley approach, to help her recover. That was the start of the hardest year of all of our lives. That year, I learned just how brave my daughter is. Five or six times a day, she sat at the table and faced down panic and guilt, terror and delusions and physical pain, and kept going. And she emerged on the other side. After months of being lost, she came back to us and to herself, and the world took on color and sound and meaning once more.

Between 3 and 6 percent of all teens deal with an eating disorder, whether it's anorexia, bulimia, binge eating disorder, or the all-too-common ED-NOS, or eating disorder not specified. Many more struggle with other devastating illnesses, both mental and physical: Schizophrenia. Bipolar disorder. Depression and anxiety. Autism. Cystic fibrosis. Cerebral palsy. Autoimmune disorders.

We have a long history, in this country and elsewhere in the Western world, of implicating families in their children's illnesses.

As I write, the Academy for Eating Disorders has released a position paper—two years in the making—that acknowledges, among other things, that "family factors" may play some role in both causing and sustaining an eating disorder. But it goes on to say, "Current knowledge refutes the idea that [families] are either the exclusive or even the primary mechanisms that underlie risk. Thus, the AED stands firmly against any etiologic model of eating disorders in which family influences are seen as the primary cause of anorexia nervosa or bulimia nervosa, and condemns generalizing statements that imply families are to blame for their child's illness."

The AED's paper takes a step in the right direction—one that's already been taken when it comes to illnesses like schizophrenia and autism, where the biological underpinnings and mechanisms of the diseases are more widely accepted. We'll get there for eating disorders, too; it's just going to take awhile.

One of the hopeful signs is the slow rise of family-based treatment, which aligns parents with the teenager rather than separating them, as has been the norm. This sea change is not specific to eating disorders, but it's particularly encouraging in that context because of the hundred-plus-year history of blaming parents for anorexia and bulimia. As I write, the Children's Hospital in Westmead, Australia, has just opened two family units, so parents and siblings can stay at the hospital with a child undergoing treatment for anorexia. "It's very scary for an eight- or nine-year-old to be away from home and in hospital for weeks and weeks," says the director, Dr. Sloane Madden. "Treating the whole family as inpatients creates a much more friendly and private environment and is much more similar to what it will be like at home when they are discharged."

I believe we're in the midst of a cultural shift in how we see families across the board. Parents do have an enormous influence on their children, both good and bad. The experiences of child-hood and adolescence can profoundly shape a person's life. But we're also more and more aware of the other forces that contribute, from genetics to biology to the influence of peers and the media. And we know, now, that even imperfect families—and aren't we all imperfect?—can effectively support a child through one of the most hellish experiences of his or her life.

So this book is for the families whose children struggle not just with eating disorders but with depression, anxiety, schizophrenia, autism, bipolar disorder, and so many other illnesses that change the nature of a family's life forever. Know that you're not to blame, you're not alone, and you can make a difference in your child's life.

chapter one

Down the Rabbit Hole

*Starvation affects the whole organism and its results may
be described in the anatomical, biochemical, physiological,
and psychological frames of reference.*

—ANCEL KEYS, from *The Biology of Starvation*

My daughter Kitty stands by my bed. It's Saturday night, close to
midnight, and I'm trying—and failing—to fall asleep. Even in the
dark, even before she speaks, I can tell Kitty's worried. I sit up, turn
on the light, fumble for my glasses. Kitty's hand is on her chest.
"Mommy?" she says, her voice rising in a way that instantly lifts
the hairs on the back of my neck. "My heart feels funny." There's
fear in her deep brown eyes, different from the anxiety I've been
seeing since this nightmare started. A month ago? Two months

ago? I can't remember a beginning, a discrete dividing line separating *before* from *after*. There's only *now*. And *now* is suddenly not
good at all.

"Funny how?" I ask, wrapping my arm around her narrow
back. I could lift her easily. I could run with her in my arms.

Kitty shakes her head. Closing her eyes, so huge in her gaunt
face, she digs the point of her chin into my shoulder as I reach for
the phone to call the pediatrician. I know, the way you know these
things, that this is serious, that we will need more than soothing
words tonight.

Dr. Beth, as I'll call her, phones back right away and tells me to
get Kitty to the emergency room. She'll let them know we're coming, she says; she'll tell them about Kitty. About Kitty's anorexia,
she means. I grab Kitty's sweatshirt, because she's freezing despite
the 90-degree heat. I slip on shoes (a sandal and a sneaker, as I later
discover), shake my husband, Jamie, awake. He wants to come to
the hospital, but someone has to stay home with Emma, our sleeping ten-year-old. "Call me when you know something," he says,
and I'm out the door, the car screeching through the rain-slicked
streets of our small midwestern city.

Six months ago I barely knew what anorexia was. Six months
ago my daughter Kitty seemed to have it all going for her: she
was a straight-A student and a competitive gymnast; she loved
friends, books, horses, and any kind of adventure, more or less in
that order. One of her most noticeable traits, since toddlerhood,
has been her reasonableness. I've seen this quality emerge in her
again and again, even at times when I would have expected her to
be unreasonable—at age two, being told we weren't going to buy a
particular doll; at age five, tired from a long train ride. I've watched
thought battle feelings in her for a long time, and reason has nearly

always won out, a fact that has, over the years, concerned me at times: Aren't toddlers *supposed* to be unreasonable? Don't kids have to go through the terrible twos, the unruly threes, the rebellious twelves?

Which is why Kitty's recent lack of reason when it comes to food and eating has been all the more puzzling. We've talked about it again and again: How her body needs fuel to keep going, especially since she's an athlete. How food is good for her, not something to be afraid of. How human beings are meant to eat everything in moderation. Including dessert.

Even now, I don't truly understand why Kitty can't pick up a fork and eat the way she used to, why she is suddenly obsessed with calories and getting fat. She's never *been* fat; no one's ever made fun of her because of her weight. She has always loved to eat. In one of our favorite family stories, Kitty, age four, ordered a huge bowl of mussels in a restaurant one night and devoured them, licking the insides of the shiny dark shells. The chef came out of the kitchen to see the child with the adult palate and sent out a bowl of chocolate ice cream in appreciation. Which Kitty finished.

I still don't understand, but I'm beginning to know. To recognize the sick feeling in my stomach each time we sit down at the table and Kitty does not eat. I'm beginning to be able to predict how each meal will go: Jamie and I will take turns cajoling, pleading, ordering our daughter to eat, and she will turn aside everything we say with the skill of a fencer parrying a lunge. She will eat a few bites of lettuce, a handful of dry ramen noodles. She will count out six grapes and consume them with infinite slowness, peeling each one into strips and sucking it dry. She will pour her milk down the sink when she thinks we're not looking, allow herself only five sips of water.

And at the end of the meal, she will climb the stairs to her room and do a hundred extra sit-ups, penance for the sin of feeding herself even these scraps. Which would not keep a dog alive.

Which will not keep *her* alive, either.

Kitty sits next to me in the front seat, her lank blond hair scraped back in a ponytail, looking small and lost in the oversized sweatshirt that fit her six months ago. "I'm dizzy, Mommy," she murmurs. I keep one hand on the wheel, the other on her, as if I can keep her from floating away. My brain seems to divide as I drive, so that while part of me is watching the road, hitting the gas and brake, another part is thinking *Don't die. Please don't die.*

The triage nurse is waiting when we hustle into the emergency room. She has my daughter on a gurney, sweatshirt off, hooked up to the EKG machine, within minutes. Kitty trembles in the hospital air-conditioning, goose bumps rising along arms so thin they look like Popsicle sticks. She clutches my hand, the sharp bones of her fingers leaving bruises, as the nurse applies goo and deftly arranges the sensors across her chest.

"Don't leave me," she says, and I promise. They'll have to handcuff me to get me out of the room this time.

I'd left the room a few months earlier, at Kitty's fourteen-year-old checkup, trying to be a good mother, a wise mother, a nonhelicoptering mother. The truth is, I was worried about Kitty's weight. She'd always been on the small side, built lean. When she turned eleven, she'd gained a little weight as her body got ready to grow. It wasn't much, maybe five or six pounds, but Kitty was unhappy about it. That was the first time she talked about not liking how she looked, at least to us. Of course Jamie and I reassured her, reminding her that this was her body's way of getting ready to develop, that she'd be healthy and strong no matter what shape or size she was meant to be.

She was in sixth grade at the time, the first year of middle school, and the emphasis in health class, then as now, was on obesity. The sixth graders were weighed, their BMIs calculated, their fat measured with calipers. They learned about calories and nutrition, all from the cautionary perspective of *too much* rather than *not enough*. So it didn't surprise us when Kitty came home one day and announced that she was cutting out desserts because they weren't "healthy."

I thought it might be a good idea. I applauded her discipline and willpower. Like most women in America, I've had a conflicted relationship with food and eating. Like most women in my family, I'm short and plump and have a sweet tooth. And like most mothers of my generation, I was determined that my kids would be healthier than me. My children would breathe in no secondhand smoke; they would always wear seat belts and bike helmets and eat organic food as much as possible. I baked Kitty's first birthday cake myself, a homemade concoction of carrots and raisins, using applesauce instead of oil and a quarter of the sugar the recipe called for because I didn't want my baby getting a taste for the hard stuff. Our photos from the big day show a sagging Leaning-Tower-of-Pisa construction with barely enough icing to cover the 100 percent whole wheat dough. Very kindly, none of Kitty's grandparents criticized the cake. But nobody ate it, either. Not even the birthday girl. Not even me.

My views had evolved since then. All things in moderation, as Aristotle advised. Still, we probably ate too much sugar; less, in this case, might be more.

If I'd understood what was to come, I would have served dessert at every meal. I'd have bought an ice cream maker, taken up cake decorating. I'd have whipped up brownies and cookies every week. Every day. Hell—I might have opened my own bakery.

Kitty's worries about being fat seemed to dissipate by the end of sixth grade. She grew an inch and put on some muscle after joining a gymnastics team. But at her checkup that December, she weighed half a pound less than she had the year before, despite the fact that she was taller.

"Isn't she too thin?" I asked the pediatrician.

Dr. Beth is a small woman, short, with streaked blond hair and laugh lines at the corners of her eyes. She looked over my daughter's vitals and her chart. She soon had Kitty laughing and chatting about school and gymnastics and friends. While they talked, Dr. Beth plotted her growth on a chart and showed me that Kitty had gone from the 50th percentile in weight to about the 42nd—not a big drop, and probably, she explained, just a blip, a temporary dip in the curve. She'd dropped in percentile that way between ages nine and ten, though she hadn't actually lost any weight that time. Still, said Dr. Beth, this was probably within the range of normal adolescent growth.

"She's just naturally thin," she said. Then she asked me to leave the room so she and Kitty could talk privately. That, too, was a first, a sign of Kitty's growing autonomy. A sign that she had her own life now, and that as her mother, there were things I was no longer privy to.

But sitting in the waiting room, I felt more worried, not less, and I didn't know why. Was I being overprotective? I told myself the doctor knew best. I reminded myself to be proud of Kitty's maturity and good sense. Proud of myself and Jamie, for the hard work of raising her so far. If I felt a pang at the thought that our work was nearly done, that Kitty was growing up, well, that was my problem and my issue, wasn't it?

So why did I feel so uneasy?

Fast-forward four months, to April. Kitty was fourteen years old, with shiny blond hair that fell below her shoulders and dark eyes flecked with gold. She was, as she had been since birth, a compulsively curious person, physically and intellectually adventurous. Her goal was to be a lawyer, and she already knew where she wanted to go to law school: Columbia, because more than anything, she wanted to live in New York City. Which is why it was so much fun to take her to New York that spring, just the two of us. We stayed with friends, shopped, saw a play. And we ate: Indian dinners and sushi, bowls of pasta in alfredo sauce, creamy gelato— far better food than anything we could get back in the Midwest.

When I got the photos back the week after our trip, I thought Kitty looked taller. Or, possibly, a little thinner. In every picture, though, she was smiling broadly, one arm looped through mine. The image of happy confidence.

The triage nurse raises the strip of the paper and studies the zig-zagging lines that hold the answer of what will happen next to Kitty. Then she busies herself tidying up the gurney. "Wait outside," she says briskly to both of us. "The doctor will come get you."

I pull Kitty's shirt over her bony chest and button it, slide her arms into her sweatshirt the way I did when she was a little girl, zip it all the way up again. It's not enough to keep her warm. I wrap my arm around her and she leans on me as we make our way back out to the waiting room. The TV's on, mounted high in one corner of the room, the sound off, and we turn our faces toward it, toward the light and normalcy it represents. The images on the screen might as well be scenes from a foreign film, like the filmstrips shown in grade-school social studies classes, the kind of movies that establish firmly the otherness of the lives on-screen even as the script tries to make them seem just like us. Now we're the others, our lives unimaginably far from the brightly colored lives on-screen. Now we're the ones to be studied. Dissected. Pitied.

On Mother's Day—only two months ago, now—we planned a family bike ride. Emma had recently gotten good enough on a two-wheeler to keep up with the rest of us. And so we set out after lunch on a warm Sunday afternoon. Our route was an easy eight-mile ride; even with lots of water breaks, it shouldn't have taken more than two hours. But almost as soon as we hit the bike trail, half a mile from our house, Kitty began to cry. Not a few sniffles, either, but full-out hysterical sobbing.

We stopped right away. "What happened?" I asked. She'd been fine at home, ten minutes earlier. "What's wrong?"

"I don't know!" she wailed. She wouldn't, or couldn't, tell Jamie or me what was wrong.

After twenty minutes of sitting by the side of the trail, Jamie asked, "Should we go home?"

"I don't want to ruin Mother's Day!" sobbed Kitty, getting back on her bike. Off we pedaled. Five minutes later, the same thing happened again. On and on Kitty wept, and we watched helplessly.

After an hour, we'd made it to a small concrete gazebo in the middle of a playground in a subdivision of McMansions. The gazebo offered the only shade in sight, and we huddled under its small roof, rubbing Kitty's back, trying to get her to drink (she insisted she wasn't thirsty), trying to figure out what had gone so suddenly and bewilderingly wrong. "I don't know," she said, over and over, as tears literally squirted from her eyes and down her cheeks. "I don't know! I'm sorry!"

She didn't want to go home, but she couldn't ride. And so we sat in the gazebo. And sat. The rest of us ate our snacks and drained our water bottles and still Kitty cried. Ten-year-old Emma lay on her back on the picnic table, shredding the season's first dandelion, kicking the top of the table in frustration. I could feel my empathy begin to wane. By now all I wanted for Mother's Day was to be sitting in air-conditioning with a book and a glass of ice water. Preferably alone.

Eventually we persuaded Kitty onto her bike and began to pedal home slowly. As soon as we got there Emma disappeared into the house, slamming her bedroom door behind her. I would have loved to do the same thing. Instead, I wheeled my bike into the garage. "Tell me what's wrong," I said to Kitty, propping the kickstand. "What's going on?"

We sat down on the garage floor, surrounded by stacks of skis and bikes, garden tools, piles of the boards Jamie used to make furniture. Kitty laid her head in my lap the way she used to when she was a toddler. Lately she'd been both insecure and clingy. She reached for my hand constantly, wanting to link arms, walk in step. She hovered when I cooked dinner. Was this normal, I wondered? Weren't fourteen-year-olds supposed to be pulling away? She did spend a lot of time alone in her room, where she'd created a rigorous gymnastics training regimen that involved doing hundreds of push-ups, V-ups, and chin-ups a day. And she was out of the house four or five nights a week at the gym, practicing with her team from six to nine, eating dinner by herself every night around five. When she got home at 9:30, she did homework or fell into bed.

Kitty had always been wired for action. She hadn't slept through the night until she was four. Maybe this was just more of who she was—wide awake, sensitive, tuned in. Sitting on the cool cement floor of the garage, I stroked her hair, noticing that her skin was chilled and dry, even in the heat.

"What is it?" I asked. "What's wrong? You can tell me, you know. No matter what it is."

Her eyes were squeezed tight, as if in pain. Tears streamed down her cheeks. "I'm afraid, Mommy," she whispered.

"Afraid of what?" I asked.

She raised one arm and laid it across her eyes. "Remember I told you that my Spanish teacher has OCD?" she asked. I nodded; the Spanish teacher was Kitty's favorite this year, and we'd been hearing a lot about her idiosyncrasies.

"And remember I told you she has to rearrange the chairs and desks so they're lined up exactly?" Kitty continued. "She says if things aren't lined up, she gets really worried and she can't stop thinking about it until she fixes it."

"Yes," I said, wondering where this was going.

"I think I have OCD, too," she whispered.

This was . . . unexpected. "Why?" I asked.

"Because I can't stop worrying!"

"Worrying about what?"

She shook her head, her eyes still hidden from me, and said no more.

I told her I'd noticed she seemed a little worried lately. And I *had* noticed, because Kitty had never seemed fearful or anxious before. Cautious, yes; she was the kind of toddler who watched and waited rather than throwing herself into a new activity, who studied the stairs for weeks and then one day walked down them carefully, perfectly, one step at a time. But she loved travel, meeting new people, going places. She wasn't shy or nervous; she'd never been afraid of the dark, or burglars, or dogs. I would never have described Kitty as anxious, and anxiety is something I know a lot about, because I've had panic disorder my whole life. But Kitty was nothing like I'd been as a child. At age eight, she insisted on going to overnight camp for two weeks and wasn't homesick at all.

"How about if we go talk to someone?" I asked her now. "About the OCD thing."

Kitty was shaking her head before I finished. "I'm not crazy!" she insisted.

"Of course you're not crazy," I said. "It's not about crazy. Everyone needs a little help at some point."

She said she wouldn't talk to anyone and she didn't need any help. She just needed more Mommy time, that was all. I didn't point out that we'd just spent four hours together and she'd done nothing but cry. Instead I handed her a tissue and said, "If you change your mind—"

She blinked. "I just want to talk to you about it," she said. "Only you. Promise me."

"Of course," I said. I hardly knew what I was saying.

She scrambled out of my lap and ran into the house.

That night Jamie and I went over the conversation again and again. What was really going on with Kitty? He hadn't noticed her counting or arranging things, or showing other symptoms of OCD, and neither had I. But something was making her worry.

Maybe we'd never know. After all, we told each other, she was fourteen, an age one friend described as "the lost year." *Her* daughter spent most of her fifteenth year in her room, coming out only to snap at the rest of the family. Then one day she simply reappeared, her earlier personality restored, and resumed the civilities of family life.

I remembered fourteen. You couldn't pay me enough to be that age again.

Was Kitty going through the kind of adolescent angst that's triggered by hormones? Maybe. She barely had breasts; she hadn't gotten her period yet. Late bloomers are the norm in both our families. Then, too, the kind of intense gymnastics training Kitty was involved in could delay development. But that could be a good thing, couldn't it? I'd written an article years earlier for *Health* magazine on research showing that teenage girl athletes who delay menstruation have a lower than normal lifetime risk of breast cancer, which runs in our family.

In the end, Jamie and I decided, we weren't that worried. Kitty was smart, savvy in ways I certainly hadn't been at her age. She was growing up, that was all. We agreed we'd keep an eye on her, though we had no idea what we were looking for.

And yet. Most parents of an anorexic child can look back on a day when they should have done something but didn't. A day when they first realized something was very wrong but still had no words for it, just a feeling—a prickle at the base of the neck, the hairs on their arms standing up, something in them recognizing danger. For me it was the next day, the Monday after Mother's Day, when Kitty called me at work to ask what we were having for dinner on Friday night, *five days later.* She'd never done anything like that before, and I was, frankly, flabbergasted.

"I don't even know what we're having tonight," I said, laughing. Maybe she was joking.

"I have to know," she said. "Why can't you just tell me?"

I wish, now, that I'd paid attention to the frantic tone in her voice, to the anxiety driving this odd and insistent questioning. What if I'd made an appointment that day to see "someone"? Would that "someone" have seen what we couldn't, yet?

I'll never know, because instead of making a call, I got annoyed. I've never been good at meal planning; I'm the kind of parent who rummages in the fridge and throws something together on the spot. When Kitty wouldn't stop pressing me, when she didn't back down, I said in exasperation, "Spaghetti, OK? We'll have spaghetti on Friday night." And when that calmed her down enough to get off the phone, I forgot about it.

Only I didn't. A few days later I stopped at the library on my way home from work and checked out a video called *Dying to Be Thin*. I didn't go looking for it, and I couldn't have told you why I checked it out. I brought it home and put it on my desk in the living room, where it was quickly covered by a pile of papers. It sat there for weeks, long past its due date, but I never watched it.

Much later, Emma told me that when she saw that video on my desk, she knew Kitty had anorexia. "Why else would you have taken it out of the library?" she asked, with incontrovertible ten-year-old logic.

If only I'd paid attention to my own signals.

As May wore on, Kitty's mood continued to deteriorate. She cried more; she was testy one moment, clingy the next. She kept up with her homework, as usual; she'd always been disciplined about school. Too disciplined; anything less than an A on the smallest assignment could send her into a spiral of anxiety about college and law school. In her chipper moments she couldn't stop talking about her new passion for cooking. "I want to make a dinner party for your birthday, Mom!" she announced one day. My birthday is in October, but that didn't stop her from making elaborate plans— dinner for thirty, place cards, fancy dress. She spent hours reading cookbooks, marking pages with yellow Post-its, making lists of ingredients—lobster, Cornish game hens, heavy cream, tarragon, butter. She called me at the office where I was editor in chief of a magazine to read me menus for the kind of four-course meals you could cook only with a kitchen full of Williams-Sonoma equipment. She flopped down on my bed at night to debate the relative merits of scallops versus shrimp, sweet butter versus French butter. She begged for a subscription to *Gourmet* magazine.

I'd been trying to get Kitty to cook with me since she was three years old, to no avail. Was it possible for a child who had never shown the slightest interest in baking chocolate chip cookies to suddenly care about making a roux? Maybe I'd simply been boring her all these years with my pedestrian suggestions for brownies or spaghetti, and now her gourmet abilities were making themselves known. That didn't exactly *feel* like the right explanation. But then what was going on?

I grew suspicious—of what, exactly, I couldn't say—and then questioned my own suspicions. I'd always been a practical cook, more apt to produce a one-pot casserole than an elaborate menu. Was I threatened by Kitty's new expertise in the kitchen? What kind of mother was I, to be wary of my daughter's new interest? Why couldn't I just support it? Talking about food was the only thing that made her eyes light up. Even gymnastics, which she'd loved for years, seemed more of a chore than a pleasure these days.

The thing was, she didn't actually eat what she cooked. A bite here, a nibble there, that's all. She always had a reason: this dish upset her stomach, she wasn't in the mood for that one. Jamie and

Emma and I ate what she cooked, and it was delicious. But still Kitty's behavior left a bitter aftertaste.

I started watching her. Watching what she ate, and didn't eat. Watching the way goose bumps ran up her arms on a sunny afternoon. How her head suddenly looked too big for her body.

At her eighth-grade graduation in early June, Kitty wore a blaze-orange halter dress she'd borrowed from a neighbor. From across the crowded gymnasium, I saw my daughter with different eyes, away from the usual context of our lives, and what I saw made my heart begin to pound. In an auditorium crowded with eighth graders, she was by far the thinnest girl in the room.

As the other parents in the bleachers clapped and cheered, Jamie and I sat alone. It was as if someone had turned off the sound. When I dared look at my husband, I saw my own terror mirrored in his eyes. We didn't say a word; we didn't have to. The next morning I called Dr. Beth's office and took the first appointment offered— for the end of June, three weeks away.

If I'd said it was an emergency, we could have gotten in earlier. But I felt oddly fatalistic about the appointment. We would take the time they gave us, and until then, I told myself, I would stop worrying about it. Stop thinking about it. I knew, then, on some level; but I still didn't want to know. I was engaged in the magical thinking of denial. *If I don't get upset about this, it won't be a big deal.* I'm a writer; putting things into words is not only what I do, it's how I think and feel and process the world. But I didn't think in words about what was wrong with Kitty, and I certainly didn't say them out loud.

Over the next three weeks, Jamie and I behaved like travelers stranded on a small and isolated island. We knew the big ship would come, and that once it did, everything would be different. We were scared of the change that was approaching and also anxious for it, and so for those three weeks we lived in limbo, in the time between *before* and *after*.

Usually, I talk to Jamie about everything. In our relationship, I'm the garrulous one; talking to him helps me figure out what I think and how I feel. And over the twentysome years we've been together, my naturally taciturn husband has come to appreciate and participate in the process of hashing things out aloud. But I didn't talk to him about Kitty now. I could see some of my feelings mirrored in his face—fear and distress and hope—but he did not bring them up, and I didn't ask. I longed for the day of the appointment, when Kitty's doctor would put a name on what was happening to our child. When she would tell us what to do. And I feared it, the moment when I would have to say the word I'd been avoiding in my head all these weeks.

But I knew what was going on now. I couldn't help it. I saw that Kitty was starving herself. I just didn't know what to do about it. I cooked her favorite foods and watched in frustration as she pushed them away, or took two bites and insisted she was full. I got mad. I yelled. I wanted to both shake her and wrap my arms around her. I wanted to scream, "I don't understand!" And I didn't.

In mid-June we took a family vacation to Door County, a peninsula that extends into Lake Michigan like the thumb on a glove. The bed-and-breakfast we stayed in was freezing and rustic. Kitty spent the week wearing every piece of clothing she'd brought, her teeth literally chattering. Because we were eating in restaurants, for the most part, we didn't feel like we could make a scene about what or how much she was eating, and so she ate even less than before. We were all relieved when it was time to go home.

I kept waiting for her to fall apart, for her hunger and malnutrition to catch up with her. But Kitty kept up her demanding schedule: gymnastics practice four nights a week and days spent working at the gymnastics day camp. Her functioning confused me; how bad could things be, really, if she was able to manage all that? Maybe, I thought, Kitty just didn't need as much food as other people.

Looking back, I recognize that it wasn't just Kitty who was under the sway of an eating disorder; Jamie and I were too. Our thinking was also distorted, by fear and anxiety, confusion and hope. That's one of the strangest things about eating disorders: they affect not just the person who has them but everyone around that person too. They're so insidious, so counterintuitive, that the brain just can't make sense of them. It's like the visual phenomenon called *edge induction*, where the brain fills in visual gaps in a scene or landscape that's poorly lit or hard to interpret. On some level, we see what we expect to see, or what we want to see.

I knew even then what I wanted to see: that Kitty was all right. That she didn't have a problem.

I just couldn't make myself believe it.

By the end of June the summer had turned hot and humid, the kind of weather that constricts your lungs and slows everything down to a dreamy, underwater pace. Our house had no air-conditioning, but Kitty wore a jacket and long pants, even to bed. We were all fractious and tense. More than once Emma ran from the dinner table, hands over her ears to block out the sound of us arguing over what Kitty was and (mostly) wasn't eating. These were battles, now, and we lost every one. We never got Kitty to eat even a bite more than she'd allotted herself.

Once upon a time, family dinners had been a ritual I looked forward to, a time when we came together to talk and laugh. Now I dreaded them. I developed a Pavlovian response to the approach of the dinner hour—headache, churning stomach, sweating palms—and by the time we actually sat down at the table, I couldn't eat either.

I was glad when Kitty was at the gym, even as I worried about her. I went to sleep worrying and woke up worrying, and by the day of our appointment with Dr. Beth, my anxiety was nearly as high as Kitty's. Hers was now undeniable. She fretted for an hour over what to wear to the office, what would happen there. "Dr. Beth is going to help us help you," I told her, over and over, and hoped to God it was true.

As we waited in an examining room, Kitty clutched my hand and I held on, feeling as though we were on a raft heading out to sea and Dr. Beth had the life preserver. She came in with her usual smile, took Kitty's pulse, looked at her chart, and sat down across the room from us. "Now tell me why you're here today," she said with her characteristic directness.

"I think Kitty has anorexia," I said.

There it was, the terrible word, out in the world. Pandora's box, opened now, never to be closed again.

I ticked off the symptoms. Kitty was way too thin. She avoided eating. She cried a lot. And now there was something else, a sour smell I'd noticed in the last week or two. A smell that reminded me of our elderly cat shortly before she died of kidney failure. Ketosis—the smell of the body digesting itself.

Dr. Beth turned to Kitty. "What do *you* think?" she asked. Eyes closed, my daughter moved her head a fraction. It was the first time she'd acknowledged that she had anorexia. And it was the last time, for more than a year.

There was no leaving the room this time. Dr. Beth examined

Kitty, talking soothingly as she listened to Kitty's heart, took her temperature, felt her glands and belly. Kitty's heart was beating only forty-two times a minute (normal is sixty to eighty). She weighed six pounds less than she'd weighed the previous December, and she'd grown half an inch. Suddenly she was at least twenty pounds underweight.

After Kitty pulled her sweatshirt back on, Dr. Beth took one of her ice-cold hands. "I know this is hard," she said. She looked at Kitty, but she was speaking to both of us. "I know you don't feel well, and you're scared. I won't lie to you. Anorexia is a very serious disease, and there's no quick fix for it. But I promise you, Kitty, that a year from now, you'll feel better."

Of all the gifts Dr. Beth gave us over the next year, this was the greatest: she gave us hope. Her words kept us going through the nightmare that was still to come.

She spent a long time talking to Kitty that day, reiterating why and what she had to eat. She encouraged her, talked to her about what was happening in her body, how much better she would feel if she ate. She held Kitty's hand, stroked her shoulder, smiled into her eyes.

Afterward, while Kitty waited in the exam room, Dr. Beth talked to me in the corridor. She had two pieces of advice: try to get Kitty to eat, and find a therapist, fast. What she didn't tell me, what I read for myself later, was that the average length of time for recovery from anorexia is five to seven years. That most people with anorexia bounce in and out of hospitals, recovering and relapsing. That anorexia is the deadliest psychiatric illness; close to 20 percent of anorexics die, about half from starvation and the other half from suicide. Nearly one-fifth of all anorexics try suicide; many succeed.

There was relief in having Kitty's illness out in the open—on the table, so to speak. But I still couldn't see the path to recovery. I was numb and terrified; I felt like a block of stone with a tiny crack in one corner. The crack would widen, with stress and time, and the stone would come apart. The only questions were when and how.

Dr. Beth sent us downstairs to the lab for blood work and to check Kitty's vitals, including her heart. She said she wasn't too worried because Kitty was a gymnast, and athletes have slow heart rates. I was reassured by her words, though later I learned that anorexia can cause cardiac arrhythmias and heart attacks.* I wondered, later, if Dr. Beth, too, was in denial about how serious Kitty's illness was. Or maybe she was simply trying not to overload us with terrifying news.

The lab technician lifted Kitty's sweatshirt, and for the first time in weeks I saw my daughter's naked chest. The sight made me want to howl. Her skin stretched tightly over her sternum. I could see the arching curve of each rib, each nick and indentation of her collarbone. Her elbows were bowling balls set into the middle of her matchstick arms. She looked like a concentration camp victim, right down to the hollow, hopeless look on her face. My bright, beautiful daughter lay broken on the table, her eyes dull, her hair lank. I could not bear it.

And then the tech smiled at Kitty and exclaimed, "You're so nice and slim! How do you keep your figure?"

If I'd had a gun in my hand, I swear I would have pulled the trigger.

My daughter closed her eyes and turned her face to the wall. This wasn't the first compliment she'd gotten on her slenderness,

---

* The only way to tell an athletic heart rate from a true bradycardia is to measure the size of the heart: an athlete's heart gets bigger, whereas the heart of someone with anorexia shrinks.

just the most inappropriate. That spring, strangers stopped us on the street all the time, wanting to tell Kitty how attractive or darling or stylish she was. In a shop one afternoon where I was trying on clothes, the saleswoman turned to Kitty and said, "Aren't *you* lucky—you got the thin genes!"

Every one of these comments made my skin crawl. Yet how could I protest, when people were just, as the tech insisted later, trying to be friendly, offering a compliment? What could I say, when I, too, liked to be told that I looked thinner, prettier, sexier?

That night, after Kitty's diagnosis, I spent hours online and came away bleary-eyed and confused. The next day I called a therapist I knew, retired now, but who'd treated eating disorders for many years, and asked for her advice.

"Anorexia and bulimia and cutting, problems like that, are always about the great crisis in a teenager's life, the onslaught of sexual feelings," she told me. "Anorexia is a way to stay small, to not grow. It reflects a teenager's conflict about growing up. It's not about the food."

Just about every parent of an anorexic hears this somewhere along the line: *It's not about the food*. And the next comment is usually something like *So don't make an issue out of her not eating/binging/purging/fill in the blank*. It's a hell of a mixed message. Kitty's illness wasn't about the food, but we had to try to get her to eat. It wasn't about the food—but she was starving to death.

Though I respected my friend the therapist and her years of experience, her words made no sense to me. With each day that passed Kitty was disappearing, mentally as well as physically. She was hysterical, emotional, fragile. She couldn't think straight, couldn't sustain simple conversations, let alone express or "work through" feelings. If it wasn't about the food, then why was she so irrational about eating? Why, then, would a relatively innocuous comment from one of us—"Kitty, have another bite of pasta"—send her rushing from the kitchen, screaming and crying?

If it wasn't about the food, what was it about? I didn't care. What I really wanted to know was, How was Kitty going to get better? She needed to eat. *That* was clear to all of us. What wasn't at all obvious was how to make her do it. I felt both helpless and utterly responsible. If only I could find exactly the right words, the right tone of voice, surely she would see the truth. Surely, then, she would eat.

I started reading everything I could find about eating disorders, beginning with *The Golden Cage* by Hilde Bruch, long considered one of the classics on anorexia. Bruch portrayed anorexics as attention-seeking and manipulative, purposefully self-destructive. And she painted a devastating portrait of the "anorexic family," one where parents (especially the mother) were critical—expecting outward perfection, quick to pick apart a child's looks and weight, highly controlling—and also emotionally negligent, shutting down any expression of a child's true feelings, forcing the appearance of conformity and pleasantness and refusing to acknowledge difficult emotions.

I felt sick, reading this. Was it true? Was Kitty seeking attention? That didn't feel right. On the contrary—Kitty avoided being the center of attention. She was a classic "good girl" whose fear of screwing up led her to be too pliant, if anything.

Were Jamie and I critical of our daughter's appearance? Did we shut down her feelings, give her the message that she had to conform to our ideas of who she should be? I would have copped to any family dynamics, no matter how bad, if it meant finding a way to fix Kitty, but I didn't recognize our family in Bruch's book. We had our issues, certainly, but overly controlling and hostile? Again, it didn't feel right.

I grew up in a house where how people looked was the major topic of conversation. Where my mother weighed herself daily, recording the number on a chart that hung on the bathroom wall. Where the highest compliment you could pay anyone, anytime, was "You look so thin! Have you lost weight?"

I'd worked hard not to perpetuate this obsession with appearance. I was careful to praise Kitty for her intelligence, her empathy for others, her sly wit, her love for books. One of our often-told family stories was about an encounter we had in an airport when Kitty was just learning to walk. She was dressed in blue pajamas, handed down from a male cousin, and a woman sitting beside us said, "Ooh, what a big strong boy you've got there!" When I told her that Kitty was a girl, she immediately cooed in a high-pitched voice, "What a pretty little girl!" Jamie and I rolled our eyes. For years we've used that story as an example of obnoxious gender stereotyping.

So no, I didn't recognize myself in Bruch's characterization; nor did I recognize our family. But I was coming to mistrust my perceptions. Maybe, I thought, I was in denial about this, too. Each time Jamie or I urged Kitty to eat a little more, to take another bite, I felt not only the anguish of watching Kitty shake her head, push away the plate, disappear bit by bit; I also felt the shame of trying to get her to eat, of *needing* to try, of not being able, as the books said, to just ignore Kitty's eating, talk about other things, steer clear of the subject.

Dr. Beth said we needed a therapist as soon as possible. I called our health insurance company's referral line and, after much wrangling, got the names of three therapists. One didn't see adolescents.

One wasn't taking new patients. The last couldn't see us for five weeks. I made the appointment and put our name on her cancellation list. In the meantime, we were back in all-too-familiar terrain, trying to get Kitty to eat. Mealtimes were intensely unpleasant and unproductive. "Dr. Beth says you need to eat," Jamie would say as she pushed away her nearly untouched plate.

Kitty's responses were always the same: "I'm full!" "I had a big lunch!" Or, more and more, "Just leave me alone!"

But we were more stubborn now than we'd been a month ago. "Come *on*, Kitty," I would say. "Are you *trying* to kill yourself?" Anorexic behavior is the very essence of self-destructiveness. Humans have to eat; I couldn't understand how Kitty didn't see that. Fear and frustration made me desperate, and the more distressed I got, the more Kitty dug in her heels. "Why don't you just eat?" I shouted one night. "I don't understand! You're a smart girl! You know you have to eat!"

The look that passed across her face was nothing I recognized. It was the look of a cornered animal, something with fangs and claws and wild medusan hair. The next second we were back to what passed for normal these days—me wheedling, pleading, and ultimately shouting, and Kitty refusing. Refusing food. Refusing, now, even milk and water. She would take only a few sips of vitaminwater, then insist she wasn't thirsty, she was fine, she was tired, she was going to bed. As we went around and around in the awful circle that had become our lives, that other look haunted me. Had I imagined it? I was exhausted, not sleeping, anxious and antsy and haunted by what Kitty did and didn't eat. Had I hallucinated? Was I now projecting my anger and fear onto my daughter?

That must be it, I told myself. I was losing it. I should try to chill. Still, the vision of my daughter's face, distorted and alien, rose up at odd moments. I dreamed about it one night—a mask of fury superimposed over her familiar and now terribly sad eyes. I could not forget it.

Every day was fraught now, strewn with minefields and tears. The most ordinary activities were emotional mountains we could not scale. Every trip to the grocery store with Kitty had become an agonizing series of negotiations. And she always wanted to come along. Each time I reached for a gallon of milk, a box of cereal, a piece of fruit, Kitty would argue: we should buy skim milk instead of 1 percent, packets of ramen noodles instead of soups, fish instead of chicken, pretzels instead of corn chips, Special K instead of Cheerios, frozen yogurt instead of ice cream.

I didn't want to buy those things. I wanted to buy food full of calories to heal my starving daughter. But if Kitty promised to eat the frozen yogurt, maybe I *should* buy that instead of the ice cream, which I *knew* she wouldn't eat. Because, after all, it wasn't about the food.

I became obsessed with getting calories into her. Kitty said it was easier to eat in front of the TV, so we ate in front of the TV, something we'd never done before. Kitty said it was harder for her to eat in front of other people, so we stopped our casual potlucks with neighbors, didn't go out to restaurants, and told Emma she couldn't invite friends over.

I bought the ramen noodles, the Special K, the pretzels and air-popped popcorn, the light bread, thinking *Something's better than nothing.* None of it made a difference. Kitty still didn't eat, and her excuses for not eating grew less and less persuasive. She knew that we knew, now, that none of it was true: the food was neither too hot nor too cold, neither too spicy nor too bland. Her stomach *was* upset, but it was always upset now. She refused Tums and wouldn't tell me why, but I thought I knew: each Tums contained ten calories. She knew that we knew that she wasn't full, she hadn't eaten at a friend's; in fact she had stopped talking to her friends weeks earlier. "I'm too upset to eat," she said one night. We were sitting at the kitchen table, where it seemed we now spent the worst hours of our lives. Two fans blew hot air across the table, which was piled with sweet corn, chicken sausages, and tomatoes from the garden, none of which Kitty had tasted.

"We're *all* upset," I pointed out, my voice rising. She said I didn't understand. I was pressuring her, which made it worse; my anxiety was making her anxious, too anxious to eat. Tomorrow would be different, she promised. She begged me to understand, to be compassionate. "I'll try harder!" she swore, and I wanted to believe her. But when tomorrow came, she ate three grapes, half a fat-free yogurt, a single slice of low-calorie bread.

Worse, I could see what it cost her to do even that. The façade of hostility slipped sometimes, revealing a deep, relentless anxiety that made my heart ache. "Mommy, is it OK?" she would ask, racked with guilt over a forkful of broiled chicken, and I would reassure her: *Of course it's OK, your body needs food and milk and nutrition. Food is good for you,* I would say. *Everyone needs to eat, including you. If you don't eat, you'll die.* These conversations took on a ritual feeling, a kind of stylized call-and-response that reminded me of the way a toddler will run two or three steps away and look back at her mother, seeking reassurance. Only nothing I said or did made eating easier for my daughter. In fact, my words seemed to have the opposite effect: the more reassurance I gave Kitty, the more fearful we all became.

One night in early July she lay down beside me in bed, sobbing, and it was as if her tears unlocked the words she'd been holding back. "I don't want to die, Mommy, but I feel so guilty," she cried. "I ate a whole Popsicle and I wasn't even hungry. I ate a piece of fish. I'm a greedy pig, Mommy. I ate and I wasn't even hungry. I know it's wrong to feel these things, but I can't help it, it's how I feel."

I gathered her in my arms and rocked her, my teeth chattering with fear. "I'm not going to let you die," I promised. "You're going to be OK. I'm going to keep you safe."

But how could I keep her safe when I couldn't get her to eat a single french fry?

Kitty often cried herself to sleep now, with one of us sitting beside her, holding her icy hands, rubbing her back the way we had when she was a toddler. In bed later, Jamie and I looked at each other in despair. The therapist we'd finally found, Dr. V., would help. We had an appointment in three weeks, and then we would know what to do. Dr. V. would have the answers.

I tried to forget that I'd felt that way about seeing Dr. Beth, too.

That night and every night after for a long time, I went to sleep thinking of the sharp angle of Kitty's elbows, the shape of her bones under skin. I saw against my closed eyelids her hollow face, her enormous eyes, the unnatural point of her chin. I could not bear to see these things. I could not stop seeing them.

In the meantime, our health insurance refused to accept a diagnosis of anorexia from Dr. Beth because, as the "consultant" told us, only a psychiatrist can diagnose a mental illness, and anorexia nervosa is listed in the *DSM-IV*, the bible of mental illnesses. Once more I started on a seemingly endless round of phone calls. The only psychiatrist who could see us within six months—*six months*—was a psychiatric fellow in her last year of training whom I'll call Dr. Newbie, who had an opening the following week.

Our first visit was not auspicious. Kitty stayed curled in a fetal position, her head in my lap, while Dr. Newbie asked question after question. Her diagnosis, after forty-five minutes, was depression and eating disorder not specified, commonly known as ED-NOS. She prescribed fluoxetine (the generic form of Prozac) and weekly visits, both of which we dutifully began, neither of which seemed to help. Dr. Newbie was kind but more or less clueless; she spent most of our sessions telling Kitty she had to eat, which we were already doing at home. The fluoxetine gave Kitty headaches and upset her stomach, making it even harder, she said, to eat.

Worse, what I didn't understand then was that our mental health coverage was limited to $1,800 a year. Seeing Dr. Newbie, it turned out, cost us $200 a pop, using up our precious benefits on an exercise in futility.

Nothing seemed to help Kitty's anxiety and guilt around eating. Though we rarely cook red meat, one night I made lamb; Kitty's lab reports showed that she was anemic, and lamb is rich in iron. After an hour of cajoling, arguing, and yelling, she choked down two bites of meat. Afterward she ran into the backyard and curled up in the grass, where Jamie and I could see and hear her through the kitchen window. "Oh my God," she cried, arms wrapped around herself, rocking in the grass. "That must have had three hundred calories in it! Oh God!" We sat at the table and listened to our daughter's agony, and did not know what to do.

I hoped the therapist would help. On the day of our first appointment in mid-July, she came out to the waiting room and said hello in a high-pitched, syrupy chirp that immediately set my teeth on edge. The old Kitty, a precocious observer of human nature, would have rolled her eyes at me. The new, withdrawn Kitty didn't even blink.

Dr. V. tried to get Kitty to come in alone, but I was done with staying in the waiting room. So in we went, to Dr. V.'s blandly beige office, where she commenced interrogating Kitty in the same gooey tones. I didn't care how idiotic or patronizing she sounded, as long as she could tell us what to do and how to do it. If she'd come up with a workable plan, I would gladly have given her all our disposable income for the next ten years. If I'd trusted her, even a little, we would have been in her office twice a week. Alas, no plan was forthcoming, and trust was not an option after Dr. V. informed me that anorexia "isn't about the food" and was typically caused by "the mother's unresolved conflicts."

"Now, Mom, don't be the food police!" she admonished me as she ushered us out of the office. I wanted to bite her head off. How in the world could Dr. V. be considered an expert on adolescents when she talked to Kitty as if she were two years old? She hadn't a clue how to relate to a teenager.

"What did you think?" I asked Kitty in the car. She shrugged apathetically, but I thought I caught the tiniest hint of something—amusement? sarcasm?—in her dulled gaze. It cheered me immensely, which I needed when I imagined coming back to Dr. V.'s office week after week, offering up our family's dysfunctional moments as Kitty grew thinner and weaker and paler. Dr. V., it was clear, was not going to save Kitty. But if she couldn't do it, who could?

That night, Emma ran away from home. She didn't go far—only to the end of the block—and she was easy to find, because she stood on the street corner and screamed, "I have the stupidest, most lousy parents in the world!"

Man, was I jealous. I wanted to stand on the corner and cuss someone out too. I just didn't know who.

. . .

In the second week of July, the weather turned even steamier, with three-digit temperatures nearly every day. One of those days was our city's annual opera in the park concert, which we went to every year, eating a picnic dinner on a blanket in the grass.

Kitty spent that entire afternoon in our sweltering kitchen, frying chicken and making carrot cake, the oven and range going full blast. The room was like a sauna, but she wore a long-sleeved gray sweatshirt over a T-shirt, heavy jeans, fuzzy socks—and still she did not sweat. Nor would she drink, even when I followed her around with a glass of ice water, begging her to take a sip. "For God's sake, it's a hundred degrees in here," I said.

"I'm not thirsty."

"Promise me you'll at least eat some of what you're cooking," I said, my voice raised in frustration.

Kitty looked at me calmly. "Of course I will," she said.

Of course she didn't, not really. She peeled every speck of fried coating from a drumstick and picked at the meat. She produced a small bag of red grapes and ate three, turning down the carrot cake, the potato salad, the apple juice. "My stomach hurts," she said. "I'm not hungry."

I got angry. Furious, actually. Furious enough to turn my back on Kitty in her sweatshirt, zipped up to the neck. I sat at the opposite end of the blanket, denying her contact, avoiding her icy hands, her now nearly constant need for physical reassurance. *Fine,* I'd thought. *OK. You want to starve yourself to death? Go right ahead.*

The chicken and carrot cake were, no doubt, delicious. I don't know, because none of us ate a bite. I went to bed angry, feeling like things were about as bad as they could get.

And that's when Kitty came to me in the dark, her hand on her chest, her voice full of fear.

. . .

I **can see from** the look on the nurse's face that the news is not good. She ushers us back to the emergency room cubicle, where an earnest young doctor shakes my hand and opens Kitty's chart. He seems to be a long way off, his voice tinny and low as he explains there's a problem with Kitty's EKG. The electrical impulses that initiate each heartbeat are coming from the wrong part of her heart, a sign that her body is stressed. She's also dehydrated, and her heart rate is too low, only thirty-five beats per minute. The number penetrates the gray fog that's descending over my whole body. Kitty's heart rate has dropped since our visit with Dr. Beth two weeks earlier. This isn't good.

"I'm going to admit her," says the doctor. He rubs his eyes as he speaks, as if the very sight of us makes him weary. I suppress the urge to apologize, barely, but it persists as I fill out the paperwork, as we wait for a bed to open upstairs, Kitty shivering in my arms now, fear shining from her huge brown eyes.

By the time we're ushered upstairs to the pediatrics ward, the sun is rising, lightening the pale green walls, the hospital bed, the chair beside it. A nurse opens the door, taking us in with a professional flick of her eyes—Kitty, curled in a ball on the bed, her eyes closed; me pacing, my hair uncombed, my eyes red, literally wringing my hands. She sets to work, helping Kitty into a hospital gown and into bed, talking to her in a soothing voice as she inserts the IV line that will help rehydrate my daughter. Normally Kitty would put up a fuss; needles are the one thing she's scared of. But this morning she lies listlessly in bed, eyes closed. She's asleep by the time the line is in.

The nurse tidies up and leaves, the hospital door closing soundlessly behind her. I sit in the chair beside Kitty's bed and watch clear liquid drip into her arm. Her face is chalk-white; her jaw is clenched in sleep. I take one of her freezing hands between mine and hold it, trying to warm her with my own heat.

There's relief in being in the hospital, after the weeks of going it on our own. It's cool and clean, and, best of all, someone else is in charge. My job is to sit at Kitty's bedside and talk to the endless parade of residents and interns, who want to hear her history over and over: How tall is she, how much does she weigh, when did you notice a change in her eating, when did she lose weight? I tell them she lost only a couple of pounds. I tell them she was fine until two months ago. I tell them our family is not dysfunctional, that we are reasonably happy, that Kitty has never been abused.

Actually I don't tell them that. I want them to believe it, but I see that they don't. I watch their young, transparent faces as they make notes in Kitty's chart, notes I am not allowed to read but that no doubt say things like *Mother in denial*. I don't care. I'll accept any judgment they want to offer, if they will make my daughter well.

I don't get it yet. I still think someone can make my daughter well. That this is a process that will take days, that there's some incantation that will reverse the damage, turn back the clock, remove the curse, and that, like Sleeping Beauty, Kitty will open her eyes and be magically healed.

If only.

After twenty-four hours with the IV, Kitty is rehydrated, but her heart rate is still too low. She's too dizzy to sit up by herself; it takes two of us to help her to the bathroom. She hates the hospital meals, and I don't blame her. The kitchen sends up mountains of steamed broccoli, little cups of Jell-O, bowls of consommé, all of it unappetizing, none of it with enough calories to sustain a caterpillar.

Although she's not on call, Dr. Beth turns up at the hospital that first day, a Sunday, and spends hours talking to the doctors on the ward and sitting with Jamie and me. She is our lifeline, our reminder of the world of sanity and light. And so, late the next afternoon, when the resident tells me that Kitty's heart rate isn't coming up and he wants to transfer her to the ICU, it's Dr. Beth I call in a panic. As the nurses wheel Kitty's bed to the ICU, I trot along beside them, arguing. Isn't this a bit extreme? Aren't we overreacting just a little? Can't we give her more time? She's a reasonable girl. She's going to come around, I know it. The ICU is for people who are really, really sick, isn't it? My daughter's not that sick.

But of course, she is.

Jamie arrives in time to hear the doctor in charge of the ICU tell the nurse, "Get an NG tube."

"A *what*?" I say.

The doc looks up, his eyes impatient. "A feeding tube," he says, drawing the word out as if he thinks I can't hear him. And maybe I can't. "It goes up her nose and into her stomach," he adds briskly. "We'll feed her that way if she won't eat."

"No, Mommy!" cries Kitty from the bed. "Not the tube! I want to be able to taste my food!"

It is a moment of the highest imaginable absurdity. I want to say, "But you're not eating anything now!" Later, I understand her reaction. The need to eat is hardwired into our brains and bodies. Anorexia can keep a person from eating, but it can't turn aside that primal force. Hunger denied expresses itself in other ways—in Kitty's case, in the compulsion to taste and savor every shred of food she consumed.

I bargain with the doctor. "Give her an hour," I beg. "If she eats something in an hour she doesn't need the tube."

The doctor raises an eyebrow. Clearly, he thinks I'm a deluded and interfering mother. Clearly, he doesn't believe Kitty will eat. But reluctantly he agrees that if she downs a whole protein milk shake in the next thirty minutes, and *then* eats a plate of spaghetti an hour later, he will hold off on the tube. For tonight.

The ICU nurse, who is the kindest person I have ever met, brings a chocolate protein milk shake and a straw. She helps Kitty sit up, arranges the pillows behind her, pulls a tray over, and puts the milk shake on it. Kitty reaches for the milk shake, holds it in one hand, lifts the straw to her lips. She's crying silently now, tears slipping over the sharp cliffs of her cheekbones. Her hands tremble. Her whole body trembles. For five minutes, ten minutes, fifteen minutes she sits, holding the milk shake and crying, while Jamie and I murmur encouragingly.

I have fed this child from the moment she was born. I have fed her not just with food but with love. The thought of a nurse, even this one, pushing a bolus into her stomach through a tube makes me want to vomit. I try to arrange my face into a neutral expression. I try to be ready for the sight of the rubber tube threaded up my daughter's nose and down her throat.

But Kitty eats. One shaky, terrified bite at a time, crying steadily, she consumes the shake. Between bites she talks out loud to herself. She seems beyond caring that we can hear, or maybe she's so deep in her own nightmare that she doesn't know we're here. "Come on, Kitty, you can do it," she says. "You don't want to go back to that scary place." Jamie and I are crying now too, as we understand for the first time exactly how courageous our daughter is. Each time she lifts the spoon to her lips, her whole body shaking, she is jumping out of a plane at thirty thousand feet. Without a parachute.

Thirty minutes later exactly, Kitty finishes the milk shake. And an hour later she eats the plate of spaghetti, one agonized bite at a time. The nurses praise her extravagantly, rubbing her hands, her back. It's more than Kitty's eaten in days. Afterward she falls asleep. Jamie goes home to collect Emma from the friends who have been taking care of her. I sit in a chair beside Kitty's bed, exhausted but unable to sleep. Every time I start to nod off, Kitty's sunken, terrified eyes rise up before me. Seeing the shape of her ulna revealed against the white hospital sheet feels strangely pornographic, like seeing part of someone's brain pulsing and exposed. It's a reminder of my daughter's vulnerability, and it feels unbearable, because there is nothing I can do to protect her from the thing that is eating away at her. And how ironic—she's being eaten alive, literally, by the fear of eating.

There is no privacy in the ICU; a glass wall separates us from the rest of the unit. I see the nurses filling out charts at the station, doctors hurrying back and forth. I see other parents with bloodshot eyes and ravaged faces. As night falls I sit, and I watch, and I wait for whatever will come next.

{ chapter two }

Home Again, Home Again

Hunger is experienced not just in abdominal ache
but as a heaviness in the limbs, a yearning in the mouth.

—DREW LEDER, *The Absent Body*

Five days later, Kitty is discharged from the hospital. I'm anxious about bringing her home, because as awful as the hospital has been, at least we weren't alone with the anorexia there. It wasn't just Jamie and me at the kitchen table, locked in mortal combat with our starving daughter. Kitty's eating about a thousand calories a day now—not much, nowhere near enough, but probably twice as much as she was eating before the hospital. What will happen now that we're going home again?

On our way home we stop for groceries, the first of the nearly daily shopping runs we'll make over the next year. Kitty rests in the car with Jamie while I blow through the store at top speed. Just last week I wished I could shop without Kitty's intrusive presence. *Be careful what you wish for.*

As I steer the cart through the produce section, I'm reminded in a curious way of what it feels like to begin a diet: the special preparatory shopping trip, the sense of hopefulness undercut with past experiences of failure. The sense of wiping the slate clean. The feeling that this time, things will be different.

Will they, though? I want to believe Kitty's hospitalization will change things, though I don't, yet, understand how. I can't see my way from where we've been to where we need to go. And I'm a person who needs to be able to see the path ahead, to see what I'm up against and what I have to do, no matter how tough. Right now, not only is there no clear path, there's no suggestion of one—just a seemingly infinite slog through the darkness that has swallowed up our daughter.

If she was ill with something else—if she had diabetes, or pneumonia, or strep—her doctors would prescribe medicine, bed rest, fluids, and we would give her all those things. But this—this is like battling a many-headed monster in the dark. It's like fighting darkness itself, a darkness that is inside my daughter, that's somehow part of her. To fight *it* feels like fighting *her*.

Dr. Beth has explained to us that we need to increase Kitty's calories by about three hundred every couple of days. And that's why I'm here, to prepare for the battles that are coming. I rip up my shopping list and any concept of a budget and speed-walk down the aisles, piling the cart with cookies, Muenster cheese, alfredo sauce, ranch dressing, buttery crackers, ice cream, potato chips, candy bars—all the foods Kitty used to love. Before anorexia, I didn't buy much processed, packaged food. I was a conscientious and health-conscious mother in twenty-first-century America, where we all understand the words *healthy food* to mean *low-fat, low-calorie food, and not too much of it*. Standing in front of the Pepperidge Farm display now, I have the sense that the world as I know it is tipping, elongating, growing as strange as an image in a funhouse mirror. I grab an armful of Milanos and keep going.

At the far end of the store I stop at the shelves of high-protein and high-calorie supplements, which Kitty drank in the hospital with every meal. I tried one once; they taste nasty, a revolting cocktail of chemicals and artificial flavors. But each Ensure Plus packs 350 calories, more than a quarter of Kitty's daily requirement right now, and Kitty has perfected a way to drink it: she holds her nose and pours it down in less than five seconds. I load the cart with chocolate-flavored Ensure Plus and move on.

Kitty's asleep in the backseat when we get home. As a toddler, the only way we could get her to nap was to drive her around until her eyes slid shut and her head drooped. Then we'd carry her into the house, car seat and all, tiptoeing so as not to wake her. Now Jamie unbuckles her seat belt, scoops her into his arms, and carries her upstairs to her room. He looks at me, and I know what he's thinking: it's been years since he could lift her this easily.

I call the friends who are keeping Emma today to let them know we're home and to talk to Emma, who says she's been invited for dinner and wants to stay. Over the last few weeks, she's found ways to avoid all of us as much as possible, and I don't blame her. Emma's world has been turned upside down. She's watched her sister suffer and starve and her parents morph from reasonably functional adults into obsessed, irritable wrecks. I wonder if we should send her to stay with my sister for a while, to get her out of the house. Not yet,

I think. If things get really bad. Then I laugh to myself. How much worse can they get?

I tell Emma of course, we'll pick her up later, and then I take my time putting away the groceries. I stow the Ensure in the basement pantry, tucking the small square bottles behind cans of chickpeas and lentil soup. Their sell-by dates read two years from now. Where, I wonder, will Kitty be then? Where will we all be?

On our first posthospital appointment with Dr. Beth, three days after Kitty comes home, she's still shaky and dizzy, but at least she can walk now, leaning on one of our shoulders. The nurse has her pee into a container in the bathroom and put on two hospital gowns, and then weighs her, standing her backward so she doesn't see her weight.

Dr. Beth is gentle with Kitty when she comes in, taking her vitals, talking to her in the kind of low, soothing voice you might use with a frightened animal. After the exam, as Kitty is dressing, I ask the doctor what we should do next.

"I've never had a patient this sick before," she says, and I feel a now-familiar frisson of guilt run up my spine. Dr. Beth tells us that other families send their children to hospital inpatient units or residential clinics. The nearest clinic is at Rogers Memorial Hospital, an hour away. Lots of teens from our town wind up there, she says. On the plus side, Kitty would probably gain weight there. She'd be in competent hands. We'd have a breather, a break from the relentless drama and terror of anorexia.

On the other hand, says Dr. Beth, Kitty might learn to be a better anorexic at Rogers. I don't understand what she means.

"Right now, Kitty's being fairly straightforward with you," she explains. "But kids teach each other all the tricks in places like Rogers."

What tricks, I want to know. Dr. Beth ticks them off on her fingers: Water loading, the practice of guzzling dangerous amounts of water before a weigh-in. (That's why Kitty's urine is analyzed before weigh-in, to make sure it's not too diluted.) Sewing weights in their underwear. Making pessaries out of coins. Stuffing food in their cheeks at the table and then spitting it into a napkin when no one's looking.

I try to keep my face blank, but inside my head a voice is screaming *No!*

Not my daughter. Not Kitty, whose face, until recently, I could read like my own. Who can't bear the feeling of having done something wrong. Whose sense of right and wrong has always been overdeveloped—for years Jamie and I have been trying to break her of the habit of apologizing fifty times a day. Who still, until recently, left me little notes saying "I love you, Mommy." That Kitty would never do the things Dr. Beth describes. If we send her to Rogers, will that Kitty vanish forever?

Dr. Beth goes on. There are residential clinics all over the country; there's a place in Utah that's supposed to be very good, if you can get in.

Utah? Jamie and I look at each other. We don't know anything about eating disorders, but we know that Kitty needs us. And we need to be with her. She panics when we're out of her sight for more than a minute, and, at the moment, so do we. How can we send her to Utah? How can we send her anywhere?

"What if it's her best chance for recovery?" asks Dr. Beth.

That's the million-dollar question: What will give Kitty the best shot at recovery? Is a faraway clinic her *only* chance? Are we irresponsible to want to keep her close?

I'm a journalist; my usual coping mechanism is to gather information. I'd begun reading up on anorexia, and the statistics terrify me: A third of all anorexics stay sick forever. A third to about a half will truly recover. The rest stay on the brink of illness, living diminished lives: they have trouble keeping friends and holding down jobs; they cycle in and out of hospitals. They spend years on the outside looking in, unable to live fully or wholly.

That's not what I want for my daughter.

And there's no consensus on what true recovery means. Everything I read suggests that anorexia, like alcoholism or drug addiction, is a disease with no real cure, a disease you have to "manage," one day at a time, for the rest of your life. Once an anorexic, always an anorexic.

I refuse to believe that.

But I don't know what *to* believe. I can't read the dozens of books and articles piling up on my desk. They paint such bleak portraits: Anorexics are dying for attention; their parents neglect their true needs, so they take drastic measures to get what they need. Or: Anorexics are dying for control; their parents are so dominating that controlling what they eat (or don't) is the only way they can express their normal adolescent need for autonomy. Or: Anorexics are conflicted about growing up and becoming sexually mature, so they try to keep themselves small and childlike by starving. Choose A, B, or C—the message is the same: anorexics (and their families) are seriously fucked up.

Maybe I'm in denial, but our family doesn't seem particularly pathological. We've got our issues, like all families. I've had panic disorder since I was a child, which I manage through therapy and medication; Jamie grew up in an alcoholic family where emotional self-expression was not encouraged. We bicker sometimes. We're grumpy sometimes. We're far from perfect. Still, I don't recognize us or Kitty in the literature. Each time I read another chapter, another article, I feel worse, not better. Reading has become another exercise in self-flagellation, and I don't need any more of that, thank you very much.

And so I stop reading, and Jamie and I move through the hours in a stupor of barely suppressed terror and confusion. We're back in the same boat we were in before Kitty was hospitalized, only now she's eating a little more. The hospital scared her. It scared all of us. But I can see that it won't be enough.

Dr. Beth calls the day after our appointment with an idea: she's talked to the head of a new adolescent psychiatric hospital in town, and although the hospital doesn't treat eating disorders per se, the director has agreed to what's called a partial hospitalization. Kitty can spend eight hours a day at the hospital, going to classes and group and individual therapy, but come home at night. It might be a good compromise.

The next afternoon, I help her into the car and we drive across town to see the hospital for ourselves. A storm breaks as we pull in, complete with thunder and lightning and pea-size hail, which pelts us on our dash from the parking lot to the building—a fitting demonstration of Sturm und Drang.

The receptionist buzzes open the front door; every door in the hospital, it turns out, is kept locked. We wait in a growing puddle for the therapist who will take us around. Dr. N. is young and friendly, greeting the teenagers we see as we walk slowly through the building. Most are oddly dressed—bathrobes over blue jeans, hair unbrushed, eyes dazed or combative or both. Kitty squeezes my hand and I squeeze back.

Dr. N. leads us to a small conference room for the intake interview. Kitty, she tells us, will come to the hospital at nine each morning and stay until five. She'll have individual and group therapy; the group will comprise other teens struggling with illnesses like depression and bipolar disorder. Kitty can also attend the hospital's "school." "Like right now," she says, turning to my daughter, "the eighth graders are learning about volcanoes and building birdhouses. You can sit in on a class if you'd like."

Kitty physically recoils, and for the first time in weeks I feel like laughing. One of her long-standing complaints about school has always been the slow pace and endless busywork, especially in middle school. Spending the rest of the summer building birdhouses and learning about volcanoes is about the last thing she'd want to do.

Besides, the other kids here are *really* messed up. Kitty's not like that.

But isn't she? Isn't she, in some profound way, like the other teenagers, with their disoriented eyes and odd behaviors? Yes and no. Eating disorders affect a person's thinking and cognitive abilities, but only around certain subjects. Kitty can rattle off a quadratic equation, speak eloquently about World War II, play a violin solo. Her intelligence is unaffected by anorexia—until the subject of food or eating or body image comes up; then she'll eat two bites of turkey and spend an hour sobbing because she's eaten so much and she's going to get fat. When this happens, as it does every time she eats, I want to say, "Don't you get it? You need to eat or you'll die."

I'm only just starting to understand that she really *doesn't* get it. That her perceptions are genuinely out of whack. Much later, another therapist describes anorexia to me as a kind of "encapsulated psychosis": someone with anorexia suffers under a set of delusions just as powerful as the delusions of a schizophrenic—but only when it comes to food, eating, and body image.

Dr. Walter Kaye, director of the Eating Disorders Program at the University of California–San Diego and one of the leading researchers on the biology of eating disorders, once found a way to make this dissonance clear to his students. He invited two anorexic women to class and asked one of them to describe how much she weighed and how she looked. The woman said that she weighed seventy pounds and that she looked fat. Then he asked her to describe the other woman. "She said, 'She looks terrible; she's so thin; she looks like she's going to die,'" Kaye tells me. "And I said, 'But look, you're seventy pounds and she's seventy pounds and you're the same height. How do you put this together saying you're too fat and she's too thin?' And she just looked at me and said, 'I don't know, but I feel too fat.'"*

That's how Kitty feels too.

Dr. N., meanwhile, is talking about rules. There seem to be a lot of them, especially with regard to eating. Kitty will eat breakfast and lunch here, so we all have to know, for instance, that no long sleeves are allowed at the table. "Sometimes they hide food there," she says matter-of-factly.

They? I think. There aren't any other eating-disordered children here. Who is she talking about?

---

* A 2007 study comparing anorexic women with control subjects showed a fascinating difference in how they process images of themselves and others. Using functional MRI scans, researchers Perminder Sachdev, Naresh Mondraty, Wei Wen, and Kylie Gulliford looked at which areas of the brain lit up when both groups were shown images of themselves and others. When looking at images of other women, anorexics and controls responded similarly. When looking at images of themselves, though, several areas of the brains of anorexic women did not "light up," most notably the insula, two small neuro organs where physical sensations—tastes, smells, hunger, craving—are transformed into emotions like disgust, pride, guilt, love, and deception.

"No clothes with drawstrings," continues Dr. N., ticking off points on her fingers. She eyes my daughter's shoulder-length hair. "She'll have to cut her hair or pull it back." *So they can't hide food in their bangs?* I wonder.

Dr. N. goes on: "You'll open your mouth after every bite so we can make sure you're not stuffing food into your cheeks. No bathroom for an hour after each meal. Oh, and you get thirty minutes to eat. If you don't finish, you'll drink Ensures to make up the calories."

A clap of sudden thunder shakes the window; lightning cracks across the steel-gray sky. If this were a horror movie (and it's starting to feel like one), the next flash of lightning would reveal the therapist's bloody fangs. Or maybe the door would swing open to reveal Nurse Ratched in a starched white cap, syringe at the ready.

I'm not the only one feeling the melodrama. When Dr. N. steps out of the room for a minute, locking the door behind her—locking us in, or locking others out?— Kitty grabs my arm. "Don't make me go here," she begs.

The therapist returns with a folder full of paperwork, which I toss into a trashcan on our way out.

When Kitty was a baby, Jamie and I both freelanced—him in photography, me in writing and editing. For most of Kitty's first year, she went to work with one of us. She was popular at magazines and photo studios all over New York City. I became adept at typing and marking proofs with one hand while nursing her with the other. Jamie mastered the front carrier and entered the often-lonely world of hands-on fatherhood. Our parenting strategy—born out of both necessity and the instinct to keep her close—worked when she was an infant.

We're hoping it works now.

· · ·

In some ways, our lives now feel similar to those early parenting days. Jamie and I divide and conquer, one of us taking Kitty and the other handling Emma, which means we rarely have the time or energy for a sustained adult conversation. We both have the same sense of heightened experience, trauma waiting around every corner, the same sense of helplessness and ignorance. Kitty cries nearly nonstop. Her tears turn to rage whenever we confront her with food. Our cajoling moves more quickly now through explaining and pleading and into yelling—for all the good it does. Arguing with Kitty about food is like debating someone in a foreign language: no matter what we say and how we say it, she seems not to understand. She refuses to eat more than the bare minimum she ate in the hospital, and sometimes not even that. Stony or tearful, her opposition remains steady. She will not eat and she will not eat.

Daytimes are a bit easier than nights, especially when Kitty comes to work with me. My office has a door, and I use it, telling my colleagues that Kitty isn't feeling well. I feel a sense of distance from them, as if I'm standing at the edge of a precipice, watching the world as I know it fall away. I need to be near Kitty as much as she needs to be near me. She eats the lunches I pack, watching DVDs on a laptop behind my closed office door as I try and mostly fail to work.

By calling everyone I know and following every lead, I've found another therapist, Ms. Susan, whom we all like. Ms. Susan is a clinical specialist in psychiatric mental health nursing—a nurse psychotherapist, as she puts it. Her office, in a business park ten minutes from our house, is small and friendly, with soft lighting, candles, and a comfortable couch big enough for Kitty to stretch out on, her head in my lap. After our disastrous meeting with Dr. V., I feel a certain amount of anxiety about therapy, but Ms. Susan speaks in a low, musical voice, makes eye contact with Kitty, and speaks to me easily. Her calm feels contagious.

In our first session, she asks Kitty what anorexia feels like to her, and Kitty actually responds. "It's like a voice in my head," she whispers. She's lying on the couch next to me, her head in my lap, so it's hard to hear her words.

Ms. Susan doesn't press her, just says, "Lots of people describe it that way, like a voice in their heads that can get pretty scary. That will get quieter and eventually go away as you recover."

I can feel Kitty's relief as much as my own. Ms. Susan, too, thinks Kitty can recover.

Ms. Susan tells us Kitty will improve with time and food. She also says that she runs a twice-weekly lunch group with a group of young women who are recovering from a variety of eating disorders. Kitty lifts her head from my lap and asks, "Can I go?" It's the first sign of interest she's shown in weeks.

Ms. Susan smiles, and her whole face lights up. "We meet on Tuesdays and Fridays," she says. After the session, she sends Kitty out to the waiting room so we can talk for a minute. "I've seen a lot of teenagers with eating disorders," she says. "Your daughter is unusually open. It's rare for someone this age and who's this sick to have any insight about the illness."

Really? I think. Kitty doesn't seem terribly open to me. But over time I come to realize that Ms. Susan is right. Most teens with anorexia turn away from their families, a process that's encouraged by most therapists and treatment providers. Kitty turns toward us, and toward the people she trusts—Dr. Beth and Ms. Susan. Which doesn't mean that her recovery is easier than others' recoveries, or that the voice is somehow less powerful in Kitty's mind. But it does mean that she accepts our help on a fundamental level.

I hope this will carry us through the worst times and help us repair our family once the anorexia has gone. I can't stand the idea that we might ruin our relationship with Kitty in the process of helping her recover. But I accept the risk. It's better than the alternatives, way better.

I thank Ms. Susan for the encouraging words and arrange to bring Kitty to the next lunch group. We leave with a few weeks of appointments set up.

These days of keeping Kitty close represent an oddly peaceful interlude in the surreal world we now inhabit, Jamie and Emma and I and this new Kitty, with her pointed chin and enormous eyes and will of iron. I try to remember my daughter as she was just a few months before, dancing through the house, laughing and affectionate, talking on the phone or going out with friends. Already this new Kitty, gaunt and tense and slow-moving, seems normal. Human beings can adapt to anything, from infinite riches to the horrors of Auschwitz. I don't want to adapt to the way things are now. I want to scream, howl, tear the hair from my head in mourning and rage at what's happening to my daughter. I can hardly muster the energy to cry.

A few days after Kitty comes home from the ICU, a neighbor drags me to a support group meeting she's read about, for friends and families of people with eating disorders. In the hospital meeting room we find no other parents, only two young women in recovery from eating disorders themselves. I don't want to talk to them; I want to avert my eyes, put my fingers in my ears, and chant *la la la* so I don't have to see or hear them. I want to run to the car without looking back.

But that would hurt their feelings. They're here to help us, after all. And so we stay and talk to Abby, a lank-haired college sophomore whose smile does not reach her tired eyes, and Sarah, a high school senior who fingers the end of her curling ponytail. I glance across the table, trying to see, surreptitiously, how thin they are: Abby is skinny, too skinny, but not as thin as Kitty. Sarah wears a bulky sweatshirt and pants, so it's impossible to see what her body looks like.

Sarah tells us she's been dealing with anorexia for four years. She's just come home after several months in a hospital eating-disorders unit, where she landed, she tells us with disarming frankness, because she tried to kill herself. "Actually, I tried a couple times," she says, lounging in the plastic chair.

I sit beside my neighbor, nearly mute with fear, imagining my daughter with this air of weariness and quiet despair. My daughter trying to kill herself. My daughter succeeding.

I turn to Sarah; I can't bear the look of exhaustion in Abby's eyes. "What's it really like?" I ask. "What does it feel like?"

Sarah swings one foot, considering. "It's like having an angel sitting on one shoulder and a devil on the other shoulder," she says earnestly. "And it's like they're fighting all day long." Her foot goes back and forth hypnotically under the table. "And it gets so bad I can't concentrate on anything else, you know? It's like I'm watching a movie, only I'm in the movie too. The angel says, 'Eat this chicken, you know you should!' and the devil says 'Don't eat it, you're already gross and fat and disgusting.' Honestly, I don't remember very much from when it was really bad. Just that feeling." She twirls a strand of hair around one finger and grins, and suddenly she's an ordinary teenager with a dimple. She might be talking about a bad date or a bummer of a math test.

My neighbor and I walk out the revolving door an hour later. I feel like all the words have been drained out of me. The night air is humid and thick and seems to press on my chest, making it hard to breathe.

I never talk about the evening again. But I think about it often, imagining the angel and the devil on Kitty's shoulders. Kitty's head twisting from side to side as if she's watching a tennis match, her shriveled body jerking as if she's in the grip of something electric. I try to feel what she's feeling, my own head twitching, my mind jagged and disconnected, and wonder if I'm getting a glimmer of what she's going through—not just what we can see from the outside, which looks nightmarish, but her inner experience. I can hardly bear it: my firstborn, the child of my heart, suffering like this.

I have to bear it, though, because she has to bear it. More than anything I want to make it better. That's been my role and Jamie's role for fourteen years—to make it better for Kitty, whether "it" was a skinned knee or hurt feelings. And we've always been able to. Until now.

Later that night I lie awake for hours thinking about Kitty in the ICU, hooked up to monitors and wires. How did this happen to our daughter? What have we done, and how can we undo it? No, that's not right. What have *I* done? Because my husband has no issues with food. He eats when he's hungry and stops when he's full. He's never counted a calorie in his life, and, as far as I can tell, he doesn't care how much he or anyone else weighs.

I, on the other hand, grew up in a household obsessed with food and weight. I went on my first diet at fifteen, the first of many where I would lose, and then gain back, the same twenty-five or thirty pounds. Maybe Kitty's fear of fat is really a fear of being like me? Maybe if I were thinner, she wouldn't have to be so thin?

Or maybe it's my own obsession with food and being thin that's infected her. I've tried, I've really tried, to be a good role model for Kitty and Emma. I've tried never to make disparaging comments about my own body (or anyone else's). I've tried not to say things like "I feel fat!" I've tried, but I know I've slipped up. I know I've failed. And maybe my own ambivalence about my body lies at the root of Kitty's illness.

Or maybe that's an unbelievably egocentric perspective. Maybe Kitty's illness has nothing to do with me.

To be honest, I'm not sure which scenario I prefer. If she's sick because I screwed up, maybe I can do better, and she'll get better. But if Kitty's anorexia has nothing to do with me, then I'm powerless to fix it.

Of course, maybe I'm powerless anyway, regardless of what's caused Kitty's illness. And maybe that's exactly what I cannot bear.

The week after Kitty comes home from the ICU, I buy every book I can find about anorexia, mostly first-person accounts. I read only a few pages of each before stuffing them into the back of my closet. Despite the bright covers, the implied triumphs, the books radiate despair. Or maybe that's what I'm seeing now, because of Kitty. The young women (and they are all written by women) are dealing with so much more than anorexia: abusive or neglectful grown-ups, hostile peers, drugs, alcohol, cutting, thoughts of suicide.

I can't believe that's where Kitty is heading, or maybe already is. OK, she's sick; she's *very* sick. She spent two days in the ICU, where she might have died. I've been slow on the uptake, but I get it now. I've been watching her behave in baffling ways—self-destructively, counterintuitively, without logic or reason.

But Kitty's not like the teens we saw at the psychiatric hospital and she's not like the authors of those books. She wasn't troubled or oppositional or defiant as a child. She doesn't smoke or drink or cut herself.

I know how Kitty reacts to pain and to pleasure. I know her ups and her downs, what pisses her off and what lifts her up. I often know what she's thinking; we've always been able to read each other. We still can, most of the time.

I don't think I'm kidding myself about these things. I don't think I'm one of those mothers who believes she's close with her child when actually the child loathes her.

On the subjects of food and eating and fat, Kitty's delusional. Obviously. On every other subject, though, she's the same girl she's always been, sharp-witted, insightful, quick. She's a perfectionist, yes; an overachiever, definitely. But she isn't crazy, for God's sake. She has an illness, like diabetes or pneumonia or meningitis. With the right treatment—if only we can figure out what that is—she'll get better. She isn't losing her mind. She isn't standing at the top of a slippery slope of self-destructive behaviors.

These are the conclusions I draw from observing Kitty. To me they seem reasonable; given the history of eating-disorders treatment, though, they're downright revolutionary. Back in the 1600s, people thought you could catch a mental illness by touching someone who had one. We haven't come very far from that idea. We treat people with mental illnesses like lepers, stepping over them in the street when their disorders lead to homelessness, poverty, drug addiction; we shun them when they turn out to be people we know. A few psychiatric disorders have lost a little of that stigma—for example, people talk more openly now about depression and bipolar disorder. But with few exceptions we still don't want to hear about the most severe cases of depression, or about the inner lives of people with schizophrenia or personality disorders. Once the label is slapped on, you enter a world made nightmarish not just by whatever disorder you've got but by the stress of being marginalized in a society that fears and loathes any hint of mental differences.

Classifying eating disorders as mental illnesses piles even more stigma and judgment onto sufferers. This categorization shifts assumptions around cause and treatment from the realm of the physical to the psychological. And it paints someone like Kitty all one color—the color of mental illness; whereas I see her as a complex person whose thinking and behaviors are distorted in certain crucial areas, but whose mental processes are working fine in others.

Semantics? Maybe. But the words we use to think and talk about the world often shape the way we see it—literally. I decide right here, standing in front of my closet, that I will never refer to or think of Kitty as mentally ill. She has an eating disorder. She, Kitty, the whole person. The eating disorder is a small part of her. It doesn't define her, even now.

One afternoon about five days after Kitty comes home from the ICU, I'm sitting on the end of her bed, holding a frozen protein shake, the kind she ate in the hospital. Kitty sits propped up on pillows, crying. "Come on, Kitty," I say encouragingly, moving the spoonful of chocolate shake closer to her. I want her to take the spoon and feed herself, but so far she hasn't. In the last half hour I've managed to get three spoonfuls into her mouth. The shake has long since melted; chocolate now stains the front of my pants and Kitty's blanket. My hands aren't all that steady these days.

I'm waiting for Kitty to be able to eat, but she says she can't eat, she can't drink. She says her throat is closing, she's a horrible person, she's going to get fat, she's the worst person in the world. She says she's never felt this way before. "What way?" I ask, still holding the spoon.

Kitty's hand shoots out, knocking the spoon to the floor. "I'm sorry!" she cries. "I can't help it! It's pressing on me!"

"What? What's pressing on you?"

But she's done with words, she's curled up on her pillow, sobbing, as the milk shake melts in its paper cup. I sit on the end of her bed, stroking her foot, waiting for the tears to pass.

I've spent so much time over the last few weeks waiting. Waiting for Kitty to have her IV changed. To cry herself to sleep. To finish chewing, with exquisite slowness, an infinitesimal bite of bread or egg or tomato. Waiting for that tiniest of bites to pass between her lips, down her throat, into her stomach. For the calories in that bite—two? five? fifteen?—to seep into her bloodstream, to circulate through her body and into her brain. To make her better. I'm so tired, I'd love to curl up on the end of her bed and sleep myself. But then where would we be? Still right here, with Kitty starving.

I force myself to sit up, let a little edge slip into my tone. "Kitty," I say firmly, "you have to drink this milk shake. The doctor said so. Come on now, sit up. I'll get you a straw. It's melted anyway."

Amazingly, Kitty sits up. She lifts her tear-streaked face toward me and I nearly drop the spoon. I know my daughter's face far better than I know my own. I've stared at it, examined it, admired it, loved it for fourteen years. I know every look in her repertoire, every expression. But I've never seen this face before. Her eyes have gone blank; her mouth turns downward in almost a caricature of a pout. Her tongue pokes out, and for a second I think she's sticking it out at me. Then I realize with horror that it's flicking like a snake's forked tongue.

Then she opens her mouth, and her voice, too, is unrecognizable. She speaks in a singsongy, little-girl tone, high and strange and chillingly conversational, the creepy voice of the witch in a fairy tale. "I'm a pig," she says, not to me, exactly; it's almost like she's talking to herself. "I'm a fat pig and I'm going to puke. I'm going to puke up everything because I'm such a pig."

I can't say anything because my teeth are chattering. The hairs on the back of my neck stand up as the words pour from Kitty's mouth. No, not from Kitty's mouth, because this is not Kitty. It's not my daughter who looks out of those dead eyes, who rocks on the bed, her bone-arms wrapped around her flat chest, who says the same words over and over as if her brain was reduced to a single thought. Somehow I'm up and off the bed, calling for Jamie, and then the two of us listen in horror and incomprehension as Not-Kitty spews a sickening litany of poisonous, despairing threats.

I don't know how long it goes on. A long time. I pray that Emma, in the next room, stays asleep. Over and over Jamie or I put our arms around Not-Kitty. We speak quietly in her ear, we shout, trying to break the hypnotic trance, trying to get her to see us, hear us. But it's as if we're talking to a ghost. No matter what we do, Not-Kitty keeps rocking and talking, her tongue flicking in and out.

Hours later, her eyes close suddenly and she doesn't so much go to sleep as fall out of the world. The veins in her neck stand out, as if even exhausted and unconscious she's straining against something. That's how it seems to us: as if the Kitty we know is being held hostage by—what, exactly? We don't know.

We creep out of the room without speaking, taking the long-melted milk shake with us. We lie together in bed, trembling. Was I wrong about Kitty? Is she, in fact, deranged, possessed, mentally ill beyond our ability to help her? The next time she opens her eyes, who will we find: our daughter, or the demon who now seems to possess her?

In the morning, unbelievably, Kitty is back to her normal self, or rather back to the version of normal we're getting all too used to. She eats breakfast without complaint and goes off to work with Jamie. I'm too rattled to go in to the office. Thank God for a boss who understands about families, because I need this job. *We* need this job, not just for the salary but because it supplies our health insurance. Such as it is.

That night, Emma's theater camp gives a performance of *Midsummer Night's Dream*. Kitty doesn't want to attend, but we insist. We're trying to maintain some vestige of normal family life, especially for Emma, who stood with us at her sister's bedside in the ICU. Who sits at the dinner table, hearing the poisonous words that pour from her sister's mouth. Whose life has already been profoundly altered by anorexia.

Jamie takes Emma to the theater early, and Kitty and I arrange to meet them there. In the car on the way over, Kitty tells me she feels funny again—dizzy, tight in the chest, floaty. It's been another hundred-degree day, suffocatingly humid; we're all feeling a little ill. In her fragile state, Kitty's probably dehydrated and overheated.

I could turn the car around and take her home, but I know how disappointed Emma would be. And suddenly I'm angry—no, *enraged*—at the idea of upsetting Emma. She's important too, damn it, and I'm not going to let her down. I pull in to the parking lot, grab Kitty's hand, and half-pull her into the building, where I jam change into a vending machine. "Drink this," I say, handing her a twenty-ounce bottle of fruit punch.

"I'm not thirsty—" she begins, but I interrupt her.

"This is not negotiable," I say, my voice tight. "You will drink this, all of it, and then we will go inside. And if we need to go back to the hospital, we'll do it after the play is over."

Kitty's mouth opens in surprise and hurt. Tears spring into her eyes and roll down her cheeks. Remorse prickles in my chest; I ignore it. "Drink," I say. She drinks, all of it, as we stand outside the theater, watching families stream in, laughing and talking, going about their lives on an ordinary summer night.

By the time Kitty finishes, my anger has dissipated, leaving me both appalled at my behavior and encouraged by its results. I take the empty bottle from Kitty's shaking hand and put my arm around her shoulder. "You did good," I tell her. I put two fingers on the artery in her neck, the way the nurses in the hospital taught me, and take her pulse: forty-one beats per minute. We'll call the doctor. But not until after Emma's show.

In the auditorium, I wind up sitting next to an old friend, Lisa. Kitty took dance classes with her at ages four and five. I wonder if Lisa knows what's going on with Kitty. We haven't kept it a secret, but we also haven't broadcast the news. I'm grateful when the lights dim and the show begins, and I can sit in the dark, my face hidden, and focus on something other than anorexia for an hour.

The show is a success, and Emma, a fairy swathed in bright gauzy scarves, has a moment in the spotlight playing the harp. She's been taking lessons for six months, and it's thrilling to see her absorbed in the music. And a relief to hear her pull it off without a wrong note. Jamie snaps photo after photo from the audience. At the end of the show, as the cast take their bows, Kitty and I slip away; Jamie will wait for Emma and bring her home, where we'll celebrate her stage debut.

Before that, though, I call the pediatrician's office and find that Dr. Beth, bless her, has left instructions for just this scenario. I ply Kitty with Propel and ice cream and rub her back until she falls asleep. When Emma and Jamie get home, the three of us eat chocolate ice cream and giggle at Emma's backstage stories. For a little while we are a family again, though we each feel Kitty's absence.

Later, as Jamie sleeps beside me, I think about what I learned tonight. The last three months have been one long and painful lesson in inadequacy—our inadequacy in the face of our daughter's mortal danger. Tonight, out of fury and despair, I stood up to the eating disorder and won, at least for a moment. Tonight I learned that I'm not helpless. *We're* not helpless.

chapter three

There Will Be Cake

*Studies indicate that . . . dramatic calorie restriction can
result in an impairment of competence. . . . Investigators
have noted that patients, often with no previous history of
psychiatric disorder, may manifest megalomaniac and
persecutory delusions, auditory hallucinations,
somatisation, dissociation, suicidality, and confusion.*

—D. M. T. FESSLER, "The Implications of Starvation
Induced Psychological Changes for the Ethical Treatment
of Hunger Strikers," *Journal of Medical Ethics*

The last day of July is Emma's tenth birthday. Kitty's been talking
about it for a week now—not because she's excited to celebrate her
sister's birthday but because she knows there will be cake. She bar-

gains with us: if she doesn't have to eat a piece of cake, she'll eat an ear of corn, an extra slice of bread.

But underneath the drumbeat of Kitty's anxiety, Jamie and I both hear another note, a whisper of longing that surprises me, then horrifies me *because* it surprises me. In just a few months, I've grown used to the idea that Kitty fears and hates food, that she doesn't like to eat. I have, without meaning to, changed the way I think about her and eating. *Of course she doesn't want cake. Of course she doesn't want butter on her bread, or cheese in her sauce, or any food with more than fifty calories.* I'm already thinking about Kitty's fears as if they're perfectly understandable, if not rational—like Emma's picky-eater aversion to chili. Some of my reaction is an instinct to avoid conflict, a strategy I can no longer afford; we've been forced into conflict, like it or not. Some, I see now, is a kind of insidious accommodation. I, too, am a "good girl" personality, given to internalizing rules and playing by them.

Suddenly I can see how the very human propensity to make order out of chaos, to come to terms with change, to adjust, can inadvertently enable an eating disorder. Kitty's been sick for only a few months, but already it's as if I've forgotten who she is without the anorexia. *Of course she doesn't want cake.* Months from now, Dr. Daniel le Grange will tell me, "There's something about anorexia that makes parents and clinicians think in different ways than they would have. I don't know what it is about this illness that gets us to think, *It's not such a bad illness.*"

I wonder if our twenty-first-century ambivalence about food is to blame. I can't think of a single woman friend who has never dieted, never deprived herself of food in the name of something bigger than appetite—health or fashion or sexual attractiveness. And where do we draw the line between anorexic food restriction and other kinds of restricting? We live in a culture where many of us feel shame over eating anything but grilled chicken, lettuce, and fat-free dressing. A friend once told me she wished she could scrape the taste buds off her tongue, so she didn't have to choose between the pleasures of eating and being thin. I'm guessing she's not the only one who feels this way.

When I look at the rich dark chocolate cake, I feel not only Kitty's fear and shame and longing but my own. Kitty wants to eat the cake *and* she's afraid of it. In a fundamental way, I know how she feels. Doctors harangue us about eating too much and being too fat. TV, movies, and magazines present stick-thin women as attractive, and after a while, we begin to buy in to that image. We reinforce it in casual conversations in the grocery store, on the phone, at our children's schools, at restaurants, walking around the neighborhood: *I'm so bad—I ate a piece of cake.* Or *I'm such a pig!* Or *Look at these thighs. It's a wonder I don't break the chair.*

Food as an object of fear and loathing is a strangely seductive idea. Which reminds me of a Yiddish folk tale I heard as a child, about a miser, a miserable old coot who kept a dog to protect the gold coins hidden under his mattress. Being a miser, he was always looking for ways to spend less. One day he had a brilliant idea for how to save money; each week, he would feed his dog a little less than the week before, so the dog would get used to eating less, bit by bit. He did just that. Each week the dog became weaker and hungrier. Eventually the miser stopped feeding the dog altogether, and not too long afterward, the dog keeled over, dead. And the miser lamented: *Just when I'd trained him to live on nothing at all, he had to up and die on me!*

I realize how deeply we as a culture have fallen for the notion that food is a regrettable necessity. As if the ideal, the holy grail we are all working toward, is to do without food altogether—and as if we not only should but could attain this state, were we good enough, determined enough, strong enough. As if that's what we should want.

So I tell Kitty no bargain; she has to eat a piece of cake. We *all* have to eat a piece of cake. Still, I'm shocked when she does, spending half an hour over a small slice of dense chocolate ganache. Afterward she weeps in my arms. "That was scary, Mommy!" she cries.

When Kitty was four, she scrambled onto the back of an enormous quarter horse for a walk around an indoor ring. When the horse reared, she held on without a sign of panic. I asked later if she'd been scared. "Not really," she said. "Can I ride again?"

This is the child who is now terrified by a slice of chocolate cake.

Later that night I prowl the house, unable to sleep. I pad into Kitty's room and lean over her bed, wanting to see her face relaxed even a little, free of the shadow that haunts it when she's awake. She stirs at my approach, rolls her head from side to side, and says clearly, "Make it go away." Her eyes are squeezed tight, her mouth drawn down in a rictus of pain. Physical pain? Emotional pain? I have no way to know.

Make it go away. The shadow is always with her now, even in sleep.

The next day, I decide to run errands before heading to work. For the last month and a half, everyday life in our house has pretty much stopped; the only trips we've taken lately have been to the grocery store and the doctor's office. Emma needs new shoes and a haircut, but she says she doesn't want to go out with me this morning. "I need some time to myself," she says, blowing the bangs out of her eyes. I know what she means: time in the house without Kitty (who's at work with Jamie), or the endless discussions about food that seem to take up every waking moment these days. I kiss the top of her head and lock the door behind me.

At the library, I pay for a stack of long-overdue books, then force myself over to the new books section—not that I have the time or the energy to read. But I always cruise the new books at the library, and right now I'm hanging on to any shred of life as it used to be. As I stand unseeing in front of the New Nonfiction shelf, one title jumps out at me: a book called *Eating with Your Anorexic*, by Laura Collins.

This book is not like those despairing memoirs I couldn't read. It's written by the mother of a fourteen-year-old with anorexia, who was dismayed at the treatment options offered; she found another treatment, one I haven't heard of before. I read the whole book, sitting on the floor in the library, and by the time I'm done I have a glimmer of real hope for the first time.

That night I spend hours online, digging up everything I can find on family-based treatment for anorexia. FBT—or, as it's often known, the Maudsley approach—draws on the work of Salvador Minuchin, who more or less developed family therapy in Philadelphia in the mid-1970s. Minuchin discovered that when he treated anorexic teens with family therapy, about 86 percent recovered—a staggeringly high number, given that typical recovery rates were then (as now) closer to 30 or 40 percent. He reasoned that dysfunctional families must cause eating disorders, and much of his work thereafter focused on "fixing" family problems to help teens with eating disorders recover.

Around the same time that Minuchin was experimenting, three therapists at London's Maudsley Hospital—Gerald Russell, Ivan Eisler, and Christopher Dare—noticed how nurses on the hospital's inpatient unit were able to get anorexic patients to eat by sitting with them, rubbing their backs, talking kindly to them, encouraging them, often for hours. "They made it impossible for someone not to eat," recalls Daniel le Grange, director of the eating-disorders program at the University of Chicago Medical Center. "They were consistent and persistent." I called Le Grange after stumbling across information on an anorexia study at the University of Chicago, three hours away from us; treatment is free if you're enrolled in the study. Maybe Kitty will qualify.

Le Grange trained with Eisler and Dare at the Maudsley Hospital in the mid-1980s, and, along with Dr. James Lock of Stanford University, wrote the clinician's manual on FBT. Now he tells me that the Maudsley therapists also noticed that no matter how kind the nurses and doctors were, being hospitalized was traumatic for both teens and their families. "We were still inevitably giving parents the message, 'You've failed at something that most parents succeed at, which is to feed your kids,'" he says.

Patients at the Maudsley Hospital ate and gained weight. But once they went home, they invariably relapsed, because parents were traditionally told not to sit and eat with them. In fact, eating-disorders specialists often recommended (and many still do) "parentectomies," physical and emotional separation between parents and a child with anorexia. Parents are still advised by therapists like Dr. V. not to pressure their child to eat, not to talk about food, not to be the "food police," to find other subjects to discuss. They're told to butt out, stand down, give their teenager space and autonomy.

They're told, in essence, to watch their child starve to death.

Anorexia, parents are often told, isn't about food; it's about control. Their children need to feel that they're in control of their eating, or, more likely, their noneating. They'll eat when they're ready. They'll eat when the underlying issues that caused the anorexia in the first place have been resolved.

Except a lot of them die before that happens. If it ever does.

Like Salvador Minuchin, both Chris Dare and Ivan Eisler are family therapists. They believed from the start that families played a key role in the recovery process. Unlike Minuchin, they didn't assume that families therefore caused eating disorders. On the contrary. "[Dare and Eisler] always had the whole family present," explains Le Grange. "So there's the kid who has anorexia, but you also see the other two who are perfectly healthy. It's not that the parents don't know how to raise their kids and feed them; something just went awry with this one."

I think I understand what Le Grange is getting at. For the last two months Jamie and I have been trying to get Kitty to eat, mostly without success. The process has felt adversarial—us against the anorexia—rather than supportive, both because we've been told by therapists like Dr. V. that we're not supposed to get involved with Kitty's eating and because we feel like we screwed up in the first place. That sense of self-blame and disempowerment is part of what's preventing us from being effective. But what if we approach Kitty's eating from a different point of view? What if we, like the nurses at the Maudsley Hospital, make it impossible for her not to eat?

That was Dare and Eisler's idea. Patients in the hospital ate with the support and encouragement of nurses; teens at home could eat if their parents supported and encouraged them. Parents love their children, and they have an enormous stake in their child's recovery.

No family's perfect. But maybe they don't *need* to be perfect. Maybe they just need to be able to get the job done.

This perspective marked a paradigm shift in the treatment of eating disorders. Historically, anorexia has been viewed as a biological "solution" to a psychological conflict: a teen starves herself in an attempt to resolve emotional issues, including loss, family conflict, fear of independence, and confusion about sexuality. This case history, cited in 1984 by Pauline S. Powers, M.D., professor of psychiatry and behavioral medicine at the University of South Florida in Tampa, is pretty typical:

> *Ms. E., age 21, could not choose a career, but thought she might become an airline stewardess. Her mother rejected this idea as "not good enough," and described the job as "only a waitress in the sky." This is an isolated example in a woman whose choices had been rejected as poor throughout her life. As a consequence, she felt empty and unable to direct her own life.* [*]

I wonder if there's a mother anywhere in America who has actively supported every single one of her daughter's choices.

Or how about this case history, also cited by Powers:

> *Laura is a 14-year-old girl. . . . Her father was a soft-spoken, highly successful lawyer. Her mother was a guilt-ridden woman with inflexible rules for her daughters and teenage son. She bitterly resented her role as a housewife and mother. . . . The family interaction patterns commonly described in anorexia nervosa were*

---

[*] Pauline S. Powers, "Psychotherapy of Anorexia Nervosa," in *Current Treatment of Anorexia Nervosa and Bulimia*, ed. Pauline S. Powers and Robert C. Fernandez, 18–46 (New York: Karger, 1984), 22.

present. There was an absence of intergenerational boundaries (e.g. the father covertly sided with the patient against the mother) and there were rigid fixed patterns of interaction (e.g. attempts to change Laura's violin practice schedule met with overt resistance from the entire family). Enmeshment was present (e.g. when a cold remedy for Laura's sister was prescribed, the father dosed both daughters "to prevent" Laura from developing a cold) and there was a lack of conflict resolution (i.e. either emotionally charged topics were avoided or occasionally there were prolonged unresolved quarrels). *

More recently, here's what clinical psychologist Richard A. Gordon, author of *Anorexia and Bulimia: Anatomy of a Social Epidemic*, has to say about eating disorders:

Anorexics and bulimics draw upon the common cultural vocabulary of their time, through latching onto the contemporary mania about dieting, thinness, and food control that have become endemic to the advanced industrial societies. They utilize these cultural preoccupations as defenses that enable them to escape from—and achieve some sense of control over—unmanageable personal distress, most of which revolves around issues of identity. [S]imilar to hysteria, anorexia and bulimia are socially patterned, the fashionable style of achieving specialness through deviance. †

---

*   Ibid., 43.

†   Richard A. Gordon, *Anorexia and Bulimia: Anatomy of a Social Epidemic* (Cambridge, MA: Basil Blackwell, Inc., 1990), 11.

It's no wonder the clinical literature reflects this perspective, though, given that Hilde Bruch's book *The Golden Cage* has been considered the definitive text on eating disorders since it was first published in 1978. Bruch, who was a professor of psychiatry at Baylor College of Medicine, described the typical anorexic as a sparrow in a golden cage, a child of privilege who seems to have everything but who deep down feels stifled by her parents' expectations and often unspoken demands, unable to express her feelings directly. The classic anorexia patient, writes Bruch, "was not seen or acknowledged as an individual in her own right, but was valued mainly as someone who would make the life and experiences of the parents more satisfying and complete." Bruch describes families where "clinging attachment" and "a peculiarly intense sharing of ideas and feelings develop," where parents overdirect and overcontrol, pressuring the child to meet their expectations and heal their own emotional neediness.*

The more I read Bruch and Minuchin and others, the worse I feel. Le Grange helps me put things in perspective by pointing out that by the time a family comes in to therapy with an anorexic child, the usual family dynamics no longer apply: parents are anxious, the patient is irrational, the other children are traumatized. So what you see in family therapy for anorexia is not a family's typical modus operandi.

Once upon a time, and not all that long ago, our family ate together, talked and joked and kibitzed at the table. At this point, though, we probably look pretty damn pathological. I think of our last month of family dinners: Jamie and I begging Kitty to eat. Tears and tension. Emma slouching lower and lower in her chair or

---

* Hilde Bruch, *The Golden Cage* (Cambridge, MA: Harvard University Press, 1978), 34.

bolting from the table. I wonder if we'll ever have a normal family dinner again. Or at least one that doesn't leave me shaking and sick to my stomach.

Eisler and his colleagues understood the way family dynamics change when a child has anorexia. In the early 1980s, they developed a set of protocols for weekly family therapy that put parents in charge of their anorexic child's eating, making them, in effect, the food police. Their findings echoed Minuchin's: 90 percent of the adolescents treated with FBT were still doing well five years later, compared with 36 percent of the teens who got individual therapy. (A later Canadian study shows that "involving adolescents' parents in treatment might be necessary, particularly for adolescents who describe the greatest resistance to treatment. . . . Adolescents who perceived their relationship with their parents more positively also reported greater motivation to change their eating disorder.") [*]

That number—90 percent—is the one that catches my eye. It represents the best news I've gotten since Kitty was diagnosed. Why *wouldn't* we try a treatment with such a high recovery rate—especially if the alternative is treatment with only a one in three chance for full recovery?

And there's another reason to try it: chronic anorexia is notoriously tough to treat. Years of malnutrition, restricting, and altered social interactions set up a potent and self-reinforcing pattern that becomes part of an adult's identity and physiology. After five or ten or fifteen years of anorexia, recovery is far less likely.

All the more reason to take this on aggressively and fast. If we can help Kitty recover now, while she's still a teenager,

---

[*] Shannon Zaitsof and Andrew Taylor, "Factors Related to Motivation for Change in Adolescents with Eating Disorders," *European Eating Disorders Review* 17 (2009): 227–33.

while she hasn't been sick for very long, her chances are way better.

We can do this, I know we can—if Jamie gets behind it too. One of the key criteria for the success of FBT is that parents present a united front. Consistency and persistence, as Le Grange told me. That makes sense; all child-rearing efforts, whether they involve potty training or curfew setting or eating disorders, require that parents be on the same page. I know from our experiences so far how hard it is to keep at Kitty to eat another bite, have another sip, finish the milk shake or pasta or cheese. You feel like you're torturing your child by pushing, pressing, insisting. And you are, in the short term. But the long-term stakes are so high. It seems to me a fair trade-off: X number of days, weeks, months of hell, in exchange for a lifetime of recovery. I know what I want to do. What we need to do.

For the next several days, Jamie and I talk and argue and grieve together. "I can't understand it," he says, over and over. "Why won't she just eat?" I can't understand it either. But my gut tells me that we're asking the wrong question. The question isn't *why* but *what:* What do we do now?

What it boils down to is that we have three choices: Send Kitty away. Keep doing what we're doing. Or try some version of FBT, the Maudsley approach.

In the end the decision is easy.

The next morning I call Dr. Beth and Ms. Susan and tell them our plan to begin family-based treatment with Kitty. Ms. Susan has heard of FBT and thinks it could be a good option for Kitty because she's young and hasn't been sick for long. (How long is *long*, I wonder? Because I feel as though Kitty's already been sick a long time. Too long.) Dr. Beth has never heard of it but promises to do some reading and call me.

FBT comprises three phases: Phase 1 is weight restoration, Phase 2 is returning control over eating to the adolescent, and Phase 3 is resuming normal adolescent development. Phase 2 seems a long way off; there's no way we're letting Kitty control her eating anytime soon. I have no idea what "resuming normal adolescent development" means, and frankly, at the moment, I don't care. We are solidly in Phase 1.

Kitty has lost only six or seven pounds since June, but it's painfully clear that she'll need to gain a lot more than that to recover. Dr. Beth graphs Kitty's height and weight from birth, plotting her natural growth curve, and gives us a number to start with: twenty-five pounds. That's how much Kitty needs to gain, at least for now.

In true FBT, I read, a therapist meets weekly with a family, supporting them as they figure out how to get their child to eat. The therapist doesn't *tell* the parents how to do this but rather *empowers* them to find strategies that work. I think back over the last few months of family dinners, remembering one in particular, a week or so before Kitty's official diagnosis, during the time I knew something was wrong but didn't yet understand what. We had company—my mother-in-law was visiting, along with my best friend from college and her young daughter—and we'd gone out to a restaurant, seven of us sitting at a round table. We had to send the waiter away three times because Kitty was negotiating, in a tone of rising hysteria, what she would order. The menu was full of dishes she had once loved: mussels in buttery broth, spaghetti carbonara, salmon in creamy dill sauce. She wanted a salad with grilled chicken, dressing on the side. I looked at my emaciated daughter, the flat hollows under her eyes, the protruding knobs of her shoulder bones. I looked across the table at friends and family who had traveled thousands of miles to see us, whose eyes reflected their concern and bewilderment even as they pretended not to hear our agitated whispers. If we'd been alone, I probably would have let her order the salad, thinking *At least she's eating something*. But in front of the people who knew us best in the world, I felt sudden shame. Kitty was too thin; we knew it, they could see it. We weren't doing our job as parents, Jamie and I. We were failing our daughter.

And so we argued, behind our menus: *You love mussels—order that! Or the carbonara. Remember how much you used to love carbonara?* The more we pushed, the more frantic Kitty became, and the more determined I felt that she would order something reasonable and eat it. Now I was embarrassed about the scene we were making too.

Finally Jamie put his hand on my wrist. He's more private than I; his tolerance for public scenes is low. He shook his head. I knew what he meant. What did it matter, really, what Kitty ordered? We both knew the problem went far beyond one dinner.

And so she ordered the salad, and pushed it around her plate, while the rest of us, as if to compensate, ate heartily, sopping up sauce with slabs of Italian bread, forcing the conversation away from the drama we couldn't talk about. It was as if my daughter's ghost sat at that table, untouchable and alone, watching through an impenetrable scrim. We drove home that night in despairing silence. Another meal—or, rather, another no-meal. Another turn of the screw pulling Kitty's skin tight across her sharpening bones. Another twist of the knife that now sawed away at my heart, night and day.

And now, I think, what next? I'd give anything to avoid another dinner like that. We've been failing with Kitty for weeks. How will things be different? How will we get Kitty to eat? I want someone to tell me exactly what to do.

We have no FBT therapist, because there are none in our small midwestern city. But we do have Ms. Susan and Dr. Beth. And we also have something no one else in the world has: we love Kitty best. No one else in the world can possibly want her to get better as much as we do. No one else loves her as fiercely, as nonjudgmentally, as unconditionally as we do.

And so we make a plan, Jamie and I. We'll take charge of Kitty's eating. We'll serve her breakfast, lunch, snack, dinner, and snack, starting at about fifteen hundred calories a day, and we'll bump up the calories by three hundred every couple of days, until she's getting enough. Until she starts to gain weight. Even though I have no idea how, exactly, we're going to pull this off, how tomorrow will be different from yesterday, I feel an immense relief at the thought of starting over. These weeks of wondering and worrying and feeling helpless, of feeling stalled and in limbo, have taken a toll on all of us—Jamie, Emma, and me. Now, however hard it is, we'll be *doing* something.

The next morning, as Emma sleeps late, Kitty comes downstairs to a bowl of cereal, milk, and some strawberries—a small breakfast by ordinary standards. But when she sees that the cereal is already in the bowl, that she doesn't get to measure it herself, her resistance begins.

"I could have done that," she says in a good-girl, wanting-to-be-helpful tone of voice. "You didn't have to."

I'm ready for this. "I don't mind," I say cheerily. "That's *my* job. All *you* have to do is eat." I pull out the chair, gesturing grandly for her to sit down. I'm inhabiting my role—the happy, helpful mom—to the hilt. There's no such thing as overacting in this play.

Kitty grips the seat back, her knuckles white with effort. "I don't feel like cereal today," she says. "I was really looking forward to some cottage cheese."

"Oh, I'm sorry," I say. "I finished the cottage cheese yesterday." Actually the cottage cheese now resides at the bottom of a large garbage bag by the curb, along with twelve packages of ramen noodles, a frozen loaf of reduced-fat bread, two bottles of nonfat salad dressing, two bottles of low-fat salad dressing, a bag of pretzels, six cartons of yogurt, and a bunch of grapes. Last night, when I couldn't sleep, I purged the kitchen of every nonfat, low-calorie diet food I could find. The grapes I regret, but they had to go; they were one of Kitty's lunchtime standbys.

We move into Act Two: bargaining. "I'll eat some of the cereal and all the strawberries," says Kitty. "I can't eat all that cereal today. I'll eat more tomorrow. I promise."

I muster a sympathetic look. "I know it's hard for you to eat," I say. "But this is your breakfast today. Please sit down."

Kitty's eyes gleam suddenly. The good-girl façade is slipping. I brace myself for Act Three: refusal.

"I don't want cereal," she says mutinously. "I want cottage cheese."

I think back to all the times over the last few months I've rushed to the store to get Kitty cottage cheese or yogurt or grapes—"safe" foods, foods she feels comfortable eating. Of course she expects me to do it again; why wouldn't she?

"This is your breakfast today," I repeat. "Please sit down and start eating."

She sits down, to my surprise, and peers into the bowl. Act Four begins: distraction. "It's all soggy now," she complains. "I can't eat this."

The cereal can't be that soggy; it's only been out for a minute or two. I go to the cupboard, pour another bowl of cereal about the same size, and place it on the table in front of Kitty. I get out the milk, which she tries to take from me. "I'll pour," I say brightly, staying in character.

"You gave me more this time," she says in alarm.

"I gave you exactly the same amount," I lie. I have no idea how the bowls compare. I may be new at the refeeding process, but I've been a parent long enough to have mastered the art of authoritative pronouncements.

Kitty picks up the spoon and dips it into the cereal here and there, inspecting each flake as if she's looking for contamination.

"Please eat before this bowl gets soggy too," I say.

Kitty puts down her spoon and looks up at me. Act Five: pathos. "I'm trying," she says in a pitiful voice. "It's hard, Mommy!" Tears well up in her large brown eyes.

I want more than anything to put my arms around her and say, *Never mind, Kitty. You don't have to do it; I know it's too hard.* But she does have to. And I have to help her do it. Even if it means being tough.

I play my trump card, the one Jamie and Dr. Beth and I agreed on when Kitty came home from the ICU. "OK," I say. "Go on upstairs and pack your bag."

"What?"

"We have to go back to the hospital for a feeding tube if you can't eat," I say matter-of-factly.

I've heard of kids with anorexia who don't mind feeding tubes. Who ask for them. I'm counting on Kitty's fear of the hospital and the feeding tube, but I'm aware that this delicate interaction could go either way.

In the silence that follows I watch a range of feelings pass across her face: Her fear of the tube and the hospital. Her wish to please me. Her true terror of the food that's been set before her. And under it all, the deep and powerful hunger she doesn't recognize but that I can't help seeing in her eyes, in the tremor of her hands, in the birdlike hunch of her bony shoulders.

I remember Sarah, the girl who talked to my neighbor and me, and imagine Kitty's angel and devil, locked in a fierce and vicious fight. They roll on the ground, their claws raking my daughter's skin, their fangs slashing, shrieking and bellowing in my daughter's ear. She can't look away, she can't not hear them, and in my pity and horror and love all I can do is make myself as powerful as I know how and stand beside her, touch her, be present with her suffering.

Kitty picks up the spoon, loads a tiny bite of cereal into its silver bowl, and lifts it toward her mouth. The spoon shakes in her hand, and a flake falls off. She lowers the spoon, carefully scoops up the fallen flake, and lifts it once more. *Go on*, I think. *Keep going*.

And she does.

Breakfast takes a full hour. Afterward, Kitty writhes on the living room couch, crying, berating herself on and on for eating the whole bowl. I'm both encouraged and disturbed by the fact that her inner monologue is now made manifest. I sit with her, stroke her hair, and talk, words spilling out of me without thought or pause: *I love you, you're my girl, you had no choice, I made you eat the cereal.* At this last her head comes up, and I catch a glimpse, the first in weeks, of the child I've known and loved for fourteen years. The real Kitty, whose look of sly but innocent mischief used to make me laugh, whose wide-set, velvety brown eyes popped open at birth as if she couldn't wait to be part of the world. For a while as an infant the only way she could fall asleep was if Jamie held her along his arm, facedown, and whizzed her around. She never wanted to sleep; she never wanted to miss a thing.

I think of everything she's missing now: friends, sports, sleep-overs—the ordinary pleasures of a fourteen-year-old girl. I think of everything she'll miss if she doesn't recover: Love. Friendship. Meaningful work. Her whole life, really. The life she's meant to lead. The life she deserves.

We sit together on the couch until Kitty falls asleep, exhausted, and then I slip away to the kitchen to start making lunch.

We start on a Monday in early August, just over a month after Kitty's diagnosis. For the first three days I call in sick to work—it's not a lie; I do feel sick—and we spend virtually every waking moment taking on anorexia. I cook and Jamie sits with Kitty. I sit with Kitty and Jamie takes Emma to a movie, away from the anxiety (ours and Kitty's) that saturates the air. Breakfast blends into lunch, lunch into afternoon snack, snack into dinner and bedtime snack. Three meals and two snacks, and each one takes at least an hour. In hospitals and residential clinics, patients with anorexia have to finish eating within a set amount of time—half an hour, usually. As long as Kitty's eating, I don't see the point in making an arbitrary limit. That would just put more pressure on her, and there's enough already.

Sometimes we sit there for an hour and Kitty still doesn't finish. If she's eaten at least part of it, we give her a bottle of Ensure Plus to make up the calories.

On Day Three I take Kitty to the pediatrician's office for her weekly appointment. She has eaten everything we've put in front of her—not easily, not happily, not quickly. But she's eaten. Dr. Beth, as usual, greets Kitty warmly, touching her lightly on the shoulder, and Kitty offers a rare smile back, a tight little moue that brings tears to my eyes, for the dissonance between this and her old smile, wide and direct and full of joy. Her eyes full of light. One day, I swear, I'll see that light again.

But not today. When Kitty steps backward onto the scale, wearing a paper gown, I'm horrified to see that she's lost a half pound. How is that possible? I know Kitty's been eating. I've seen it with my own eyes. And I know she's not purging, because either Jamie or I stays with her for an hour after each meal or snack.

As Kitty gets dressed, Dr. Beth motions me out into the hall, where she explains that during starvation, the body's metabolism slows down, trying to conserve energy. It becomes superefficient, wringing every drop of energy out of each calorie that comes its way. When the food intake increases, the metabolism revs up, way up, in response. It becomes less efficient, spending more calories than before for the same activities. That's what's happening to Kitty right now. "It can take a lot of calories to get weight gain going," says Dr. Beth.

Over the next few months we will learn just how many calories it takes—at least twice as much as the average teenage girl eats. Unfortunately, Kitty's psychiatrist, Dr. Newbie, doesn't seem to understand the vicissitudes of metabolism. At our visit to her the next day, she takes me aside to say that if Kitty loses any more weight—even a quarter pound—she'll have to hospitalize her. "Her heart could be in danger," she tells me.

I try to explain what Dr. Beth explained to me. "Kitty's eating now," I tell Dr. Newbie. "If you put her in the hospital, we'll lose momentum."

But Dr. Newbie stands firm. It would be too dangerous, she says; Kitty's heart needs to be monitored if she loses any more weight.

We don't tell Kitty. And that night we bump her daily calories up to eighteen hundred. Kitty complains that her stomach hurts, she's bloated, she can't physically eat this much, her stomach will explode. I'm torn. I know she's eating more than she has in a long while, but she's gotten here slowly, and eighteen hundred calories doesn't seem like that much. Dr. Beth says to keep going, so we do. We try putting a heating pad on Kitty's stomach after each meal, but it doesn't seem to help. Other tactics work better. We watch a lot more TV than we ever have before because Kitty says it's easier to eat while she's watching. And after a meal, TV or movies or books on tape help distract her from the guilt of having eaten.

I expect this influx of calories to produce, if not a miracle, then at least a quick change. And we do see changes. Kitty's eyes don't look quite as sunken; her skin is a little pinker. She gets mad at me one day, and I'm thrilled; until now, she's had neither the confidence nor the energy for anger.

But she's still anxious about eating. *Anxious* doesn't begin to cover it, actually. Kitty's obsessed with food—how many calories it has, how I've prepared it, how it's arranged on the plate. Before each meal she gathers a veritable arsenal of silverware: her baby spoon, its looping silver handle tarnished; an odd hors d'oeuvre fork, half the size of a regular fork; a child-size butter knife. After she eats, especially at night, she berates herself for hours. "I'm so fat, Mommy," she sobs. "I feel so guilty for eating." She often cries herself to sleep, with Jamie or me sitting beside her, rubbing her back the way we did when she was a baby.

And in many ways what we're doing feels like taking care of an infant: We feed her, many times a day. One of us must always be with her. We spend a fair amount of time comforting and entertaining her. She's even dragged her mattress into our room, positioning it on the floor beside our bed because, she says, she sleeps better when we're close. That suits me, too; I need to know that she's not doing a thousand sit-ups in her room in the middle of the night.

In our culture, children are supposed to grow up in as many ways as possible, as early as possible. We expect them to sleep on their own, feed and toilet themselves, tie their own shoes, and make their own peanut butter sandwiches as soon as they're physically able. If they don't, we think there's something wrong with them. We make no allowances for children who need to go slower or stay closer; instead, we pathologize them and accuse their families of unhealthy enmeshment. I'm sure that sometimes too much closeness can be unhealthy. But sometimes a helping hand is just a helping hand, and not a symptom of parental neglect or developmental delay.

Kitty's current regression, for instance, feels appropriate. She is fighting for her life—body and mind and soul. I think it's an excellent sign that she is letting us take care of her, however difficult it may be.

And it is—in fact, it's the hardest thing we've ever faced as a family. As the first official week of refeeding blends into the second, Jamie and I see more and more of the alternate personality I think of as the demon. I'm aware that this sounds strange; I know there's no literal devil inside Kitty, no supernatural force. But giving the illness a face other than hers helps me separate our daughter from the forces that torment her.

Day after day, we live under the tyranny of the scale. I'm almost as anxious as Kitty as her second weigh-in approaches. *Please don't let her have lost weight,* I think. To put her back in the hospital now would be to undo the painful, painstaking work of this last week. When Kitty steps on the scale at Dr. Beth's, I hold my breath. Which will it be—back home or to the hospital?

"A quarter pound up," announces the nurse. "Good girl!" She smiles encouragingly at Kitty, makes a note in her chart, and whisks out of the room. I let out my breath in relief.

That's when all hell breaks loose.

"I gained weight! Oh my God!" cries Kitty. She folds over on herself and begins a kind of moaning chant: *I'm a fat pig, I'm gross and disgusting and lazy. Look what you're doing to me, you're making me fat. I should never have listened to you.*

She lifts her head. Mascara streaks her sunken cheeks. "I'm never eating again," she hisses, and now it's the demon talking. "I won't let you make me fat."

I'm shocked to see the demon out in public. I can't think of what to do. So I don't think. I take Kitty's sharp chin in my hand and look into her dark eyes, which blaze with rage and, yes, fear. "I won't let you die," I say, slowly and loudly. "Do you hear me? I won't let you starve. I will keep you safe."

Tears squirt from Kitty's eyes; her mouth is open in a silent scream. But she's not really fighting me. I have to believe that somewhere inside, she can hear me.

I let go of her chin. She tucks her head down into the bony scaffolding of her arms and begins to cry, softly this time. The demon has receded. For now.

And that's how I come to understand the true nature of my daughter's prison. What we have to do to set her free.

We are walking a delicate line between truth and delusion, between confrontation and collusion, because our daughter is trapped between us and the demon. There are times when we have to face it down, in words and actions, take a public stand against anorexia. There are times when Kitty needs to hear us do that. But there are other times when the pain the demon inflicts on her will be too great to bear. I imagine the terror and agony she lives with and I want to scream. So sometimes we'll have to appease the demon with words, to spare Kitty.

Weighing in, for example. Kitty gets weighed in a hospital gown, standing backward on the scale, so she doesn't know the number. Now I ask the nurses who weigh her to refrain from any comment at all, explaining that if they tell her she's done a good job, she feels so guilty that it's hard for her to keep going. Best not to say anything at all, or show any emotion. We'll all try to be matter-of-fact, downplay the number on the scale, at least outwardly.

Yeah, right. I'm the least matter-of-fact person I know. Which is why it's all the more important to create a bland, superficial persona—The Mother—and stick with it. The Mother, I hope, will block the empathetic connection Kitty and I share. Kitty has to believe that I am calm and in control. She has to believe I can keep her safe. The Mother will speak in platitudes and generalizations, telling Kitty, for instance, "Everything will be all right. I promise." That's not a promise I would normally make, even before anorexia; and even if I did, Kitty would never buy it. But she has to buy it now. She has to trust me and Jamie to override the demon in her head. She has to trust us to be stronger than the demon, which hates every quarter pound she gains because it's one tiny step toward freedom. And somewhere inside, Kitty wants to be free. She's relying on Jamie and me to let her out of the prison she inhabits. I believe this, deeply, passionately, truly.

We will make many mistakes. The trick will be to keep going.

On our last eighteen-hundred-calorie day, I get a call from an acquaintance, Mary, who has a daughter Kitty's age; they took dance classes together for a couple of years. She's calling to say that she spotted us the week before in a store and was shocked at Kitty's appearance. "I didn't recognize her," she says. She didn't want to approach us, so she called one of our neighbors, Delia, whom she also knows, and Delia told her that Kitty has anorexia.

And what am I supposed to say? "Yes, I know my daughter looks like a walking skeleton"? I haven't even talked to Delia about it. Anything she knows comes secondhand at best. How dare she spread this kind of news?

I hang up as soon as I can and go out on the porch to glare at Delia's house. I'm ready to storm across the street and tell her off, but Jamie stops me. "She cares about Kitty," he says.

"Well, it doesn't feel that way to me," I snap. "It's none of her business."

Jamie gives me the look, the one he's been giving me for the eighteen years we've been married: kind, steady, reassuring. Usually it calms me down. But not today.

We've told a few close friends what's going on, but we haven't broadcast the news of Kitty's anorexia. For one thing, it's her life, her illness, and she's made it clear that she wants as few people to know as possible. For another thing, both Jamie and I also feel a sense of stigma and shame. People judge you when your child has an eating disorder, rightly or wrongly. Which is why I react so strongly to this bit of gossip.

I know I'm being defensive. But I can't let myself feel anger toward the demon, because right now the demon inhabits Kitty, and that would mean getting mad at her. And I'm not mad at her, not really. Sometimes I *feel* angry—when she's been sitting in front of a plate of chicken stir-fry for forty-five minutes, for example, picking out all the cashews. But it's not her flinging the nuts off her plate in disgust. I have to remember: that's not Kitty.

That night, we eat a late dinner; the temperature has been in the nineties for days now, but eat we must. Kitty uses a baby spoon to scoop up tiny bites of mashed squash (into which I've mixed butter and honey). One minute she's fine, or what passes for fine these days: she's not crying and she's eating. Then she looks up from her plate and I can literally see her flip from Kitty to Not-Kitty. I feel a jolt of adrenaline. And sure enough, when she opens her mouth, the demon's voice emerges, spewing its usual litany of self-loathing and rage.

"Why don't you take your plate onto the porch?" Jamie asks Emma. We've been trying to protect her from the worst of the poison. Emma gets up from the table, but before she can make it out the door, Not-Kitty says, "I just want to go to sleep and never wake up."

Emma freezes. Jamie and I look at each other. My heart turns over in my chest—literally, that's what it feels like, a heaviness revolving under my breastbone.

Not-Kitty says it again, louder this time: "I want to go to sleep and never wake up! I don't want to be alive anymore!"

Emma drops her plate and bolts from the kitchen as Not-Kitty begins to shout. I grab a bottle of Propel from the refrigerator, put a straw in it, and plunk it in front of my daughter. "Drink," I hiss, and run after Emma.

I find her downstairs, crying hysterically at the bottom of the laundry chute. When the tornado sirens sound and we head for the basement, this is where Emma goes to feel safe. I put my hand on her back and she rears up out of the pile of dirty clothes, furious. "Don't touch me!" she shouts. "I hate you! It's *your* fault Kitty is sick!"

Her words smack the breath out of me. I try to suck in a lungful of air, but something inside me is paralyzed. Maybe I'm having a heart attack. Maybe the stress is killing me, right here in a pile of rumpled underwear. *Don't air your dirty laundry,* my mother used to say. *Don't be so quick to tell everyone your business.* This, then, will be my punishment for failing both my daughters.

Emma cries, her face contorted in grief and pain, and then I'm crying too, because I don't know what else to do. We kneel side by side and howl ourselves hoarse.

Eventually Emma blows her nose and says, "I don't want to go to my sister's funeral."

I put my arms around her, and this time she doesn't pull away. "I don't either," I tell her, and hope my intention can magically keep the worst from happening.

chapter four

The Country of Mental Illness

If you're going through hell, keep going.

—WINSTON CHURCHILL

Anorexia is possibly the most misunderstood illness in America today. It's the punch line of a mean joke, a throwaway plot device in TV shows and movies about spoiled rich girls. Or else it's a fantasy weight-loss strategy; how many times have you heard (or said yourself) "Gee, I wouldn't mind a little anorexia"?

The symptoms of anorexia nervosa are detailed in the *Diagnostic and Statistical Manual of Mental Disorders,* known familiarly as *DSM-IV,* the so-called bible of psychiatric illnesses. And the first item on the list of diagnostic symptoms is "a refusal to maintain body weight at or above a minimally normal weight for age and height." Notice the word *refusal* rather than *inability*. No wonder anorexia is so widely perceived as an illness of choice or lifestyle; the psychiatric profession defines it that way. [*]

In fact, the very name *anorexia nervosa* is ironic. The literal Latin translation is "nervous loss of appetite." But people with anorexia don't truly lose their appetites. They may be disconnected from the physiological sensation of hunger, but they are deeply, profoundly hungry. That's why they draw out their meager meals for hours, savoring every scrap they allow themselves. It's why they douse their food with mustard and salt and other condiments to sharpen the taste of what they're eating. It's why they read cookbooks like other people read pornography, why they plan elaborate menus they know they will not eat, why they stand longingly in front of bakery windows but never go inside.

Hunger is hardwired into us, physically and psychologically, and for good reasons. The drive for food must be insistent enough to propel us to seek it out three times a day. In twenty-first-century America, many of us have only to go to the kitchen, the grocery store, a restaurant to fill our bellies. But for most of the long story of human evolution, satisfying hunger has been a drawn-out and often perilous process.

Accounts of people with little or no appetites, who do not eat or have strong aversions to food, go back to at least the first century A.D., when the Roman physician Galen described people "who refuse food and do not take anything" and who "are called by the Greeks *anorektous* or *asitous*." The Greek physician Alexander of Tralles, who practiced medicine in the sixth century, believed that

---

[*] One of the proposed changes for the next edition, *DSM-V*, removes the word *refusal*.

anorexia developed from an imbalance of what classical philoso-
phers called "humors"; people with anorexia, in this view, had too
many "cold humors" and needed herbs like cinnamon, pepper, and
vinegar to restore balance and bring back appetite.

This perspective on anorexia persisted into the seventeenth century, when an English dictionary described it as "a queesinesse of
stomack." Lack of appetite, it was thought, must stem from physical
disturbances—stomach problems, "humors," and other bodily ailments. And in fact, a loss of appetite alone can be a symptom of all
sorts of physical illnesses, from cancer to gallbladder problems.

In the Middle Ages, the culture around not eating shifted from
physiology to spirituality. Religious women like Catherine of Siena,
Beatrice of Nazareth, and Margaret of Cortona became known for
fasting or eating almost nothing for years; some undoubtedly died
from malnutrition. Their behavior was seen as a holy endeavor, a
kind of reaching toward a state that transcended the body. Many of
these women were later beatified by the church, and their starvation acquired a new name: *anorexia mirabilis,* a loss of appetite that
was miraculously inspired. If they were good enough, holy enough,
they were set free from the physical necessity of eating, lifted into
an idealized state where food was irrelevant—or so the notion
went.

Historians adamantly distinguish the self-starvation of these
medieval women from later forms of anorexia. They argue that we
don't know enough about what inspired women in the Middle Ages
to starve themselves and what kept them on that path. They say
it would be naive to think that shared physical symptoms like an
aversion to food, extreme thinness, and loss of menstruation derive
from the same illness. They say that anorexia mirabilis and an-

orexia nervosa are two completely different disorders that originate in completely different ways.

To support this notion, medieval scholar Caroline Walker Bynum argues that fasting saints did much more than fast; they castigated themselves in all sorts of ways. Catherine of Siena, for instance, whipped and scalded herself and regularly slept on a bed of thorns.

I don't buy it. The roads to anorexia mirabilis and anorexia nervosa may indeed start in different spots, and those spots may be defined in terms of the culture: in medieval times, young girls aspired to saintliness the way girls today aspire to thinness. But those roads quickly converge on the same highway to hell. Catherine of Siena, for instance, died at age thirty-three after years of subsisting on a daily handful of herbs; when forced to eat other food, she reportedly put twigs down her throat to make herself vomit it up.

Sounds like anorexia with a side of bulimia to me.

The difference in terminology underscores the idea of anorexia as a relatively new disease, an affliction of modern times. The first two medical descriptions of anorexia nervosa were published nearly simultaneously in 1873, one by a highly respected British doctor and one by a French neurologist. Sir William Withey Gull practiced medicine in London and was on close terms with Queen Victoria and the royal family. He spoke and wrote about an illness that affected mainly upper-class adolescent girls who suffered from diseased mental states and, as he put it, "perversion of the will." Charles Lasègue was a neurologist in Paris when he described what he called *l'anorexie hysterique* as a "hysteria of the gastric center."

Interestingly, their characterizations of the illness diverged from their recommended treatments. Gull believed that medicines were useless and that only food could cure the illness. He prescribed high-fat, high-protein meals, administered every two hours by a trained nurse, along with bed rest and a hot water bottle along the spine; he believed that the person who was ill needed someone outside herself to compel her to accept food. "The inclination of the patient must be in no way consulted," he wrote. He thought a trained nurse was best because friends and family lacked the "moral authority" to insist that a young patient eat.

Lasègue's treatment veered more toward the psychological. He was the first to suggest that anorexia stemmed from family conflicts over an adolescent girl's transition to adulthood—a view that remains stubbornly entrenched today.

I think Gull had it right. When it comes to anorexia, food is medicine, and it's a given that someone with anorexia will not willingly come to the table.

In her book *Fasting Girls: The History of Anorexia Nervosa*, Joan Jacobs Brumberg writes that Lasègue's research "captured the unhappy rhythm of repeated offerings and refusals that signaled the breakdown of reciprocity between parents and their anorexic daughter. In this context anorexia nervosa can be seen for what it is: a striking dysfunction in the bourgeois family system."

Like Hilde Bruch and so many other "experts" on anorexia, Brumberg mistakes effect for cause. Typically, by the time parents consult a doctor or therapist about a teen with anorexia, the family has become dysfunctional, no matter how competent it was to begin with. The pattern of insistence and resistance Brumberg describes is absolutely normal in the context of a child who is starving herself. *Of course* parents become edgy and upset, frantic to get their child to eat. And *of course* the child becomes terrified, hostile, and manipulative—anything to avoid eating.

But eating-disorders therapists don't see a family before anorexia strikes. So they don't know, they *can't* know, the true rhythm and flow of a family's previous life. Which means that they can't establish cause and effect between family dynamics and eating disorders. There's no way to predict who will develop an eating disorder, based on family dynamics or on any other criteria.

Somehow the medical and psychiatric professions have confused hindsight with understanding. There's a saying in the scientific world: "Correlation does not equal causation." Just because two things happen at the same time doesn't mean that one causes the other. Maybe an unknown third variable causes them both. Maybe they coexist coincidentally. We know that anorexia changes family dynamics. But we don't know whether those dynamics caused the anorexia in the first place.

Most years we take a vacation in August, but not this year. Just as well, because we're not a beach family. Our vacations usually revolve around activities: kayaking in Lake Superior, skiing in the Porcupine Mountains, hiking in the Catskills. All of these would cost Kitty too many calories. Instead, we spend most of the month, when we're not at work, watching movies and playing board games, which Kitty hates but Emma loves. Poor Emma, whose summer has been one big nonvacation. She'll be glad to get back to school, I think.

In the second week of August, Jamie and I bump Kitty up to twenty-one hundred calories a day. For two days beforehand she frets and worries over the coming change, so much so that Dr. Newbie prescribes a mild antianxiety medication—just in case, she tells us. *Just in case of what?* I think as I pay for it at the pharmacy. *In case things get any worse?* I allow myself a small sardonic laugh.

But even as I walk out, bag in hand, I know there's nothing to laugh about. Things can always get worse.

With the increase in calories, meal planning becomes more of a challenge. Eating large volumes of food is stressful for Kitty physically as well as emotionally. We add in a midmorning snack, to spread out the calories, but still she complains of bloating and stomachaches—common side effects of refeeding. Starvation affects the entire body in ways both profound and minute, and it will take a while for her metabolism and digestion to normalize. I'm hoping to minimize the unpleasant gastric consequences by cutting back on fruits and veggies, which are hard to digest and which in any case don't contain enough calories, and feeding her smaller amounts of calorie-dense foods.

I turn to my collection of cookbooks; leafing through them is an exercise in cognitive dissonance. Nearly every recipe seems to emphasize how low-fat and/or low-cal it is. Like Alice in *Through the Looking-Glass*, I have the curious sensation of looking through a mirror into an alternate universe. While the rest of America hunts for ways to cut down on calories, I'm searching desperately for ways to pack them in.

Frustrated, I go online and wind up on Web sites aimed at families of cancer and cystic fibrosis patients. I print out recipes for macaroni and cheese, chicken and peanut stew, lasagna made with ricotta and béchamel sauce, guacamole. Kitty's still terrified of foods like these—creamy foods, sauces, and pasta. Foods with fat in them. Even if we wanted to, we couldn't get enough calories into her by serving only "safe" foods—grilled chicken breast, steamed vegetables, plain whole wheat bread. And we don't want to. On my single trip to a nutritionist, I learned that the brain is made up largely of fat. That both the brain and the body *need* fat—not just any old calories but the right kinds of calories—to begin the slow process of healing from starvation.

And it's more than a physical thing. Instinct tells me that if we are ever to rout the demon completely, we'll have to break all its rules, flout its proscriptions. We'll have to tar and feather it and run it out of town. We can't appear to collude or appease it in any way; we need to win this war visibly as well as tactically. We're engaging in a kind of exposure therapy, slowly desensitizing Kitty to the things she fears. And there's nothing she fears more right now than fat, whether it's on her body or in her food.

One night, poking around online, I find a glimmer of evidence that we're on the right track. I come across a 1967 study done by a grad student at Northwestern named Aryeh Routtenberg, who discovered, more or less by accident, that rats given access to food for only an hour a day became more physically active, running on their wheels for hours. After a few days the rats ate less and less and ran more and more. Most of them died within ten days, starving and running themselves to death.

I sit back in my desk chair. So many of Kitty's behaviors are analogous to the rats'. If we didn't stop her, she, too, would exercise more and more. She, too, would starve herself to death. This study doesn't shed light on what triggers someone like Kitty into restricting her food in the first place. But it does lay out a pattern of effects that looks all too familiar. The rats' refusal (or inability) to eat, their compulsive overexercising—even unto death—reflect a biological imperative. Their self-destructive behavior didn't derive from psychological "issues" or screwed-up family dynamics; it was, as Routtenberg later discovered, a function of neuroanatomy.

The brain works on three main systems of neurotransmitters: serotonin, dopamine, and norepinephrine. These chemicals leap the synapses among the brain's millions of neurons, creating and regulating processes that affect everything from movement to behavior to mood. Like the rest of the body, the brain exists in a complex and delicate balance; one little misfire can bring down a big chunk of the system. In this case, Routtenberg theorized, the rats' limited access to food and unlimited access to the running wheel interfered with the brain's dopamine system. Which makes sense, because among other things dopamine helps regulate physical movement (it's connected with the basal ganglia, a cluster of nuclei involved with motor functions), motivation, and reward.

Just as interesting was a 1971 follow-up study done at the Medical College of Wisconsin by Joseph Barboriak and Arthur Wilson. They duplicated Routtenberg's conditions, but divided rats into two groups. One group got the usual low-fat, high-carbohydrate laboratory chow; the other got a special high-fat mix with no carbohydrates. Both groups were fed the same total number of calories and, as in the earlier experiment, had access to the food for only an hour a day. The lab chow rats behaved just like the rats in the original study; they amped up their activity levels until they were running nearly all the time. Each rat lost about 20 percent of its body weight. At the end of the experiment, twelve out of fifteen had died.

The rats on the high-fat diet, by contrast, didn't go into exercise overdrive. Their activity levels rose, but only a little, and they didn't lose weight. Only one of the fifteen rats in the high-fat group died, and that one had increased its running more than most of the others.

So something about the higher-fat diet protected the rats from running and from starving themselves to death. Barboriak and Wilson didn't speculate on cause and effect; they simply reported what happened. I want to know why, so I can keep Kitty safe from the same deadly cycle.

For now, I suppose, it's enough to know that fat is an important part of the equation. Knowing will help me resist both the demon's imprecations and Kitty's fear of eating fat.* It's so tempting to want to spare her suffering, to avoid some of the trauma. To feed her the foods she feels safest eating and hold off on the others until later. But I'm beginning to understand that there won't *be* a later if we give in to Kitty's terror, if we enable the demon in any way. There is no compromise possible. The stakes are too high and the process is too painful.

For instance: the next day I make one of our favorite meals, homemade pizza, which Kitty used to love. We've been keeping Kitty out of the kitchen during meal prep, but she sees the dough rising on the stove and falls apart instantly. "Oh my God, not pizza," she cries. "I already feel so fat, Mommy. My thighs are jiggling. Please don't make me eat it." She is keening now, there's no other word for it, crouching on the floor, rocking back and forth, arms wrapped around herself.

I feel like the worst parent in the universe. I am causing my child so much grief and fear and pain. My job is to protect her, not hurt her. I want to give up. I want to go back to the way things used to be, I think, before anorexia. B.A. Ha. We're all getting an education in eating disorders. An education we don't want and could live quite well without.

Then I think, If I feel this way, how must Kitty feel? I can take a walk, read a book, shut out the anorexia for a little while. But it's

---

* In 2007, Laurel E. S. Mayer and other researchers at St. Luke's–Roosevelt Hospital Center in New York City published a study showing that recovered anorexics with lower levels of body fat do worse, in the long term, than those with higher levels of body fat.

inside her. She can't get away, not for a second. And every minute she spends trapped with the demon must be hell. Pure hell. My child is going through hell. I could sink down right now onto the floor beside her. I could howl and cry and tear out handfuls of my hair. That's what I feel like doing. But that would be self-indulgent. That would be abandoning my daughter.

In our family, as in all families, my husband and I have taken on certain roles. Jamie is the one who fixes things: the vacuum cleaner, the car, the computer, the broken chair. When someone gets a splinter, he's the one who pulls out the hydrogen peroxide and tweezers. My role is to figure things out. I'm the one who makes the plans, who asks the questions (sometimes obsessively) about what it all means and what we should do. I'm the one who calls people and goes online and tears through the library looking for answers to whatever the problem.

The point is, Kitty needs both of us now. Jamie's strengths and mine are complementary, and she needs every shred of power and steadiness and stubbornness we possess. No matter how much I feel like giving up, I can't. Jamie can't. There is no way we're abandoning her. No way in hell is the demon going to win.

I slide down onto the floor beside her and put one hand on her back, to let her know I'm here. I sit beside her and I stay with her until she's all cried out. Until Not-Kitty is gone, and Kitty is, for the moment, wholly herself.

Impulsively, I say, "This is really hard on you, isn't it?"

Kitty hates the idea of anyone feeling sorry for her. Some of her biggest outbursts in these last few weeks have come in response to someone's expression of sympathy, or empathy. I brace myself for her reaction.

But instead of stiffening in anger, Kitty simply turns her face toward mine. She's always had beautiful eyes, my daughter, and they are still lovely, large and complex, the dark irises flecked with light. Now they look too big, out of proportion, like the oversized, pathos-filled eyes of puppies in flea-market paintings. I was raised to think thin is beautiful, that there's no such thing as too thin. I will never again believe it.

Kitty leans her cheek into my hand, a rare moment of connection in our newly adversarial relationship. Once upon a time she trusted me. Once upon a time Jamie and I were not the enemies. Now the feel of her skin against my palm tells me what we have to do next. Each time we've raised her calorie intake, Kitty has suffered, her anxiety and terror flaring out of control. It's as if we're peeling away a Band-Aid, inch by agonizing inch. Wouldn't it be kinder to rip it off in one go?

"What if we raised your calories to three thousand now, in one fell swoop?" I ask Kitty, bracing myself for panic, rage, the demon's hissing.

But instead, she says slowly, "In some ways that would be easier." As soon as she says this her eyes cloud, she claps one hand over her mouth, and she begins to cry.

"What is it?" I ask, but I already know. She'll pay dearly for saying this, my brave and honest daughter. She'll suffer guilt and terror at the hands of the demon inside her for even this small defiance. I'm her mother; I'm supposed to be able to protect her. Instead, I have to make it all worse, at least for now.

I remember a picture book we used to read when Kitty was small that described a family who ran into obstacle after obstacle— a swamp, a bear, a mountain—on their way to a picnic. Each time, they tried silly tactics to avoid the obstacles, and each time they succeeded by confronting rather than evading them. Kitty and I used to chant the refrain together each time: "We can't go over it. We can't go under it. Oh, no, we have to go through it!"

It's the same with anorexia. We can't go under it, we can't go over it. Oh, no. We have to go through it.

The week after we start our higher-calorie regime, Kitty gains three pounds. I feel like dancing around the doctor's office, but I keep my face neutral. I stay in character as The Mother.

"I did good, right?" asks Kitty anxiously. "Did I do good?"

What do I say? It depends who's asking, Kitty or Not-Kitty. My daughter or the disease. Either way, my answer could provoke a meltdown. My instinct is to speak to my daughter, and deal with the demon if it shows up.

"Good," I say calmly. "You did really good."

I see the conflict in Kitty's eyes, guilt and relief and fear swirling together, and wait for one of them to win out. "OK," she says eventually. We move on.

For weeks now we've lived in a kind of bubble. We've seen few friends, kept no social engagements. I've barely gone to the office; I've done the essentials of my job at home, late at night, after Kitty and Emma are asleep. I'm usually too anxious to sleep, anyway. Our lives have narrowed to a few basic activities: shop, cook, eat, clean up, watch movies, do it all again. We're lucky, if you can call it that, that it's summer, when schedules are more forgiving. But school will be starting in two weeks. Fifth grade for Emma, and ninth for Kitty. If she goes.

That's the question: Should she start high school? Some of the answer depends on what happens in the next few weeks. Right now, Kitty stays close to home, literally and metaphorically. Can she handle the emotional demands of high school, or would it be cruel to send her? Would it be crueler to keep her home, setting her back in a way that will feel humiliating? Then there are the practical considerations, like the logistics of lunch and snack, which have to be eaten with one of us.

From the time Kitty was a toddler, she's been an intensely social person, always wanting playdates, always up for going places and seeing people. She's the kind of person who's reenergized by hanging out with friends. This year, though, she doesn't want to see her friends and she doesn't want to go to school. I know a lot of her anxiety is a by-product of both the anorexia and the refeeding process. But I can't help wonder if on some level she's always felt anxious about school, and just never told us. Does the illness give voice to feelings that have been hidden to her, or does everything get mixed up in its chop and churn?

Ms. Susan says it's not helpful to get tangled up in this kind of thinking. She says people in recovery from an eating disorder do best when they limit the stress they're under, and I believe her. On the other hand, to keep Kitty out of school entirely would create a different level of stress for her. She'd feel like a failure, a freak, a weirdo. And, to be honest, it would be good for all of us—including my relationship with my staff and my boss, who have been immensely patient—to have her out of the house for a few hours a day.

One late August afternoon Kitty sits in front of a milk shake and weeps with anxiety. This is her talking, the real her in her own voice, not the creepy distorted voice of the demon. And yet—and yet she's irrational. She stares at me, her face full of worry, and says, "I don't want to go to high school and have everyone look at me and say, 'Look at Kitty, she got so fat over the summer!'"

"You're not fat!" I say, but I might as well be speaking in tongues, because she can't hear or understand.

"I'm so fat, everyone will be talking about me," she insists.

I don't want to tell her the truth: that kids *will* talk, but not about how fat she is. God. They'll be gossiping and speculating about the fact that she has an eating disorder. They will comment on how she looks, but it will be about how thin she is. And yes, some of them will say and do stupid, insensitive things. Not that teenagers have a corner on the insensitivity market—some of our acquaintances have made some appallingly hurtful comments.

Like the acquaintance I run into at the food co-op, who had us to dinner early last spring, before we realized Kitty was sick. Now she leans across the sweet corn and says, in a voice dripping with concern, "How *is* Kitty?"

I don't know why it rubs me the wrong way. She means well, I tell myself. "She's doing all right," I say, and then, to shut down the conversation, "Thanks for asking."

She leans in closer. "You know, I could have told you she had anorexia," she confides.

What I want to say is "Then why didn't you?" Instead I grit my teeth and say, "How so?"

She smooths her glossy hair. "I noticed the way she cut all her food into tiny pieces and pushed it around her plate," she says, her voice low and intimate. She gives me a look of concern and adds, "She didn't eat a thing. Didn't *you* notice?"

Now I feel like slapping her. No, punching her in the mouth. No, garroting her. Anything to make her stop talking. "I have to go," I say, leaving my basket on the floor. I manage to get out the door and into my car, where my rage quickly evaporates, leaving an acid bath of shame. Of course people know exactly what's going on. And of course they blame us. Hell, *I* blame us. We're Kitty's parents; we're supposed to be in charge. We're supposed to protect her.

What I didn't realize was that they would blame Kitty, too. That they would see her behavior as willful and manipulative. That they would ascribe to her a kind of devious intention, not just now but always. That they would recast her whole life in the light of anorexia, and judge her harshly for it. So while Kitty's completely deluded on one level, her emotional radar is working. She's right to be self-conscious; she's right to feel judged. Just not for being fat.

Later that night, for the first time in weeks, Kitty will not eat her bedtime snack. Jamie's reading to Emma downstairs while I sit with Kitty in her room. Her snack tonight is four pieces of toast, with butter and cinnamon sugar on them—a nursery meal, one that both my daughters have loved since they were small. Kitty takes one tiny bite and spits it out, and the demon is back, with its infantile, sing-song voice and vicious words.

I've learned by now that there's no point in arguing. Words seem irrelevant, so much more fuel for the self-loathing and despair. Usually the demon runs down eventually, but not tonight. Not-Kitty rants on and on, possessed by a manic energy, pacing, practically leaping around her room. I take hold of her shoulders, both to comfort her and to stop her frantic motion. The toast lands on the floor, and I don't want to leave her to make another batch.

"Come on, Kitty, you can do this," I encourage, but she gives no sign of hearing me. Jamie opens the bedroom door, holding a bottle of Ensure, bless him. "OK, you don't have to eat tonight," I tell her. "Just drink this."

She knocks the bottle out of my hand, spraying its sticky contents all over herself, me, and the floor, and begins hitting herself in the head with her closed fist.

Jamie grabs for her wrists. "Kitty! Stop it!" I shout. My words are tiny feathers in a blizzard of hail. I plead. I threaten. I tell her if she doesn't eat or drink the Ensure we'll take her back to the hospital for the feeding tube. She flails and shrieks, and even though I'm right up in her face I don't think she can hear me.

Jamie wraps his arms around her and pulls her down to the bed, trying to keep her from hurting herself. I phone Dr. Beth and Ms. Susan. Neither of them is on call. I call Dr. Newbie and leave a message with her service. She's not on call either, but another psychiatrist calls back and suggests, just for tonight, letting the snack go and giving her one of the sedatives Dr. Newbie prescribed. I'm afraid Kitty won't take it, but she does, and we sit with her as her sobs subside and the demon's voice falters and trails away. She falls asleep in Jamie's arms. Together we pull down the sheets and lift her into bed, clothes and all, turn out the light and tiptoe out of the room.

Now I know what "just in case" meant.

Emma is standing in the hall, her face blank and unreadable. I put my arm around her shoulders and take her to her room, sit with her while she undresses, brushes her teeth, gets ready for bed—all the ordinary moments in a ten-year-old's evening ritual. Yet this night is anything but ordinary. The demon has upped the ante, or so it feels to me. We're in a different place now, the country of mental illness, and it scares the hell out of me. I don't know how we got here and I don't know how to get home and I don't want to be here. I don't want any of us to be here. What if this refeeding process doesn't work? What if Kitty wakes up tomorrow and it's more of the same, if she won't eat and won't eat? I've heard of girls tethered to feeding tubes for months and girls who rip out feeding tubes. I've heard of girls dying, their hearts giving out in their sleep, just like that, and I can't help imagining Kitty dead in her bed, the sharp point of her chin, her sunken eyes closed, the demon getting the last word.

I don't know if we can save her. Tonight I don't know anything.

Emma takes off her glasses, turns out the light, and climbs into bed, snuggling into her blue-and-green quilt as she does every night, until only her thick dark hair is visible. I lie down beside her, ducking to avoid the top bunk. "I hate the anorexia," she says. I expect tears, but instead there's an edge to her voice.

"Me too," I say. "How much do you hate it?"

Part of our bedtime ritual has been a kind of call-and-response: *How much do you love me? More than bread loves salt.* This inversion of the usual question makes Emma giggle. "Come on, how much do you hate it?" I ask.

"I'd like to poison it," she answers. "No, wait. Stab it in the heart!"

"That sounds sufficiently evil," I say. "Maybe we could put a noose around its neck and hang it."

"I've got it," she says. "Burn it to death!"

She starts to laugh, and I smile too. Then she says, "I want to put anorexia in the blender, grind it up, and feed it to the cats!" And suddenly we're both roaring with laughter, rolling around on the bed, breathing in great gulps. "The blender!" she says hysterically, and we're both off again.

"But the poor cats," I say at last. "They don't deserve it either."

"They can't catch it!" Emma announces triumphantly.

"So it's just like cat food for them?" I ask. "Crunch crunch, yum yum?"

We're off again, laughing in the face of the worst thing that's ever happened to our family.

I hate the fact that Emma, too, has to deal with this illness. Mealtimes have gotten a little easier, but they're still tense and often explosive. Jamie and I are preoccupied with taking care of Kitty. I wish there was somewhere I could send Emma for a week or two, just to get out of the house. I feel guilty for putting her through this.

Not long ago, another mother told me about a conversation with her younger son, when she told him she was sorry he had to go through his sister's anorexia too, sorry that mealtimes had become so painful for the whole family.

"And you know what he said?" she told me. "He said, 'Mom, the worst part was before.' I said, 'Before what?' And he said, 'Before you started helping her eat, when we were all pretending.'"

That story comforts me now. Maybe Emma will benefit by seeing Jamie and me tackle Kitty's illness. Maybe in the long run she'll feel safer because she'll know that no matter what happens, we'll take it on. That we'd do our best to protect her, too.

I shuffle downstairs to turn out the lights and find Jamie lying on the living room couch. For the first time in months, we're awake and both of our children are asleep. I nudge him over and lie down beside him, and we don't say a word. We don't confer about logistics: who's shopping where, what's for snack or dinner, who's taking Kitty to the doctor or psychiatrist. We don't go over how this happened, when it happened, why we didn't see it coming and stop it. We don't talk about hard it is to walk around feeling so raw, to take in Kitty's terror and rage, to stay present for Emma.

We've done all that, and no doubt will do a lot more of it, though it's usually me who needs to talk things out, perseverate, go over and over events and feelings and worries about the future. But not tonight. Tonight I lie beside my husband, feel the warmth of him through his clothes and my own. Kitty is built like him, long and angular, muscled but not obviously so—more Clark Kent than Superman.

I look into my husband's face. His eyes are tired; his face is lined. He needs a haircut. But he is still handsome to me. Eighteen years ago I had the great good fortune to marry a man who believes in showing up. He might not always know what to do. He might not always have the words to describe how he feels. But no matter how awkward or terrible the situation, no matter how bad things get with Kitty, he will be there. I don't have to do this alone.

At the moment, I can't imagine anything more romantic.

By the end of the week, we have worked out a plan, along with Ms. Susan: Kitty will start high school, going part-time, at least for the fall semester. I worry that the school will give us a hard time about asking for accommodations—this school district, like many others, makes a practice of saying no to parents—but Ms. Susan suggests we use the words *medical necessity* in talking about what Kitty needs. Sure enough, when I put it that way, Kitty's guidance counselor, Mr. C., becomes extremely helpful. He arranges for Kitty to attend the first and last two periods of the day. In between she'll come home to eat lunch with one of us; we live three blocks from school, which makes this schedule workable. In theory, anyway.

I hope classes and friends will distract Kitty from the misery of recovery. I hope the stress of performing academically—a stress she puts on herself; we've told her many times the world won't come to an end if she gets a B—won't prove too much for her. Kitty wants to go to school because she wants desperately to be "normal." She hates being sick, hates us thinking of her as sick. Most of all, she can't stand the idea that people will pity her, because she can't bear the idea that she messed up, that she made mistakes or is in any way less than perfect.

"Everyone makes mistakes," I tell her. "We're *supposed* to mess up. We learn and grow by trial and error. That's part of what makes us human."

Kitty shakes her head. "I'm supposed to be smarter than this," she says. "I'm supposed to be able to figure things out without screwing up."

I try another tactic. "You've seen me make mistakes, right?" She shakes her head. "Come on," I say. "I screw up all the time. Remember the bread I made without salt? Disgusting. Remember how I used to get lost in the car when we first moved here? I told you we were having 'adventures,' but really I was trying to find our way home."

I'm hoping for at least the hint of a smile; instead, Kitty frowns. "That's different," she says.

"Why?" I ask. "Because it's me and not you?"

She nods, slowly.

"So you think you're supposed to be better than everyone else in the world?" I ask, smiling so she knows I'm making a joke. Clearly I am no comedian, because she hears my words as criticism and stalks off.

The answer is yes, she really does believe she's supposed to be perfect in a superhuman way. I wonder if somehow we've given her the impression that we expect perfection. I don't *think* so. But what if I'm wrong?

I'm not usually defensive about my parenting. I know I make plenty of mistakes. Like missing the early signs of anorexia—that was a mistake I wish like hell I'd avoided. And I know other people, including my children, make mistakes. It's part of being human. I *think* Jamie and I have given them the message that we love them the way they are.

So why does Kitty hold herself to such an unrealistic, inhuman standard—yet not expect that from other people too? This emotional blind spot feels analogous to her perceptual blind spot about her body: when she looks in the mirror, she sees rolls of fat rather than ribs and hollows. Yet she sees other people's bodies accurately.

Neurologists talk about interoceptive information, data that flows from the body into a part of the brain called the insula—things like taste, touch, temperature, and other visceral sensations. The insula helps transform this physiological input into both self-awareness and emotions. For instance, if you eat something that tastes bitter, you might feel disgust or aversion; the chemical stimulus of *bitterness* becomes the emotional and physical response of *disgust* in the insula. According to Walter Kaye, anorexia symptoms like distorted body image might be related to glitches in the body's interoceptive system.

Maybe someday information like that will lead to better treatments for anorexia. In the meantime, we're stuck with slogging through this, one meal—sometimes one spoonful—at a time.

On the first day of ninth grade, I plan to meet Kitty in Mr. C.'s office and eat lunch with her there, because it's a short day and there's not enough time for her to walk home and eat. When I wake her that morning, the first thing she says is, "I don't want to go! I want to stay home with you!" But she gets dressed in the new clothes we bought last week—a silver T-shirt and plain dark jeans—which I insisted on buying a size larger than necessary; even so, the jeans, which came from a children's store, look painfully tiny. She spends ten long minutes straightening her hair, so now it hangs to her shoulders in a clean blond sheet. Most important, she eats breakfast with Jamie while I walk Emma to her school. By the time I get back, Kitty is losing her nerve; she takes one look at me and her face starts to crumple. I'm afraid she's going to fall apart in a big way. But miracle of miracles, the phone rings; it's a friend asking if she'd like a ride to school.

"Oh, why not," says Kitty with some of her old spirit, and two minutes later she's out the door without time to worry or fret. It's a miraculous exit for us, too, as we try to walk the line between acknowledging her anxiety and neediness on one hand and encouraging her glimmers of independence on the other.

Lunch goes all right, considering Kitty has only about twenty-five minutes in Mr. C.'s office to eat. And—another miracle—she tumbles in the door at the end of the day with three friends in tow, girls she's known for years. She's animated and laughing, as relaxed as I've seen her in months. It's so good to see her like this, like her old self, I think as I make milk shakes for all of them.

Kitty even cracks a joke. "At our house, we know which ice creams have the most calories," she says, catching my eye and grinning. It's true; I've made a science out of packing as many calories as possible into everything Kitty eats, both to make it easier for her to get it all down and to speed up the very slow process of gaining weight.

The fact that she's made a joke about food—about how much food she has to eat—makes me giddy with happiness. That's my Kitty—funny, observant, alive to nuance and language.

Of course, the joke's for me. Her friends prove sadly unable to understand it.

"We want to know which ice creams have the *least* calories!" says one.

"Yeah, because we have a problem over here!" says another, patting her flat stomach.

The third chimes in. "My thighs are *enormous,*" she says, glancing down at her legs, encased in narrow boot-cut jeans and looking absolutely ordinary.

Kitty, I notice, has gone silent.

I dither for a minute: stay out of the conversation, or jump in? I can't keep quiet. "Wait a minute," I say. "There's nothing wrong with any of your thighs or butts. You're all beautiful and healthy and strong. Thinking there's something wrong with you—*that's* the problem."

I might as well be talking to myself. I've heard girls this age refer to fat-bashing as a bonding experience, and I can see that as a kind of process of establishing social hierarchy—like the submissive behaviors dogs engage in to find their place in the pack. Saying "I'm so fat!" can be a coded way of expressing social submission, or at least the urge to be accepted, to conform.

But I can't believe these girls are joking about being too fat in front of someone who's struggling with anorexia. Of course, they're only fourteen years old, an age not exactly known for sensitivity to other people's feelings. And, I remind myself, they have no idea of the hell Kitty's going through. They know only that she's been "sick" and is doing better now; a few know it's anorexia, but some likely don't. They probably envy her slenderness, though no one says that out loud.

I wonder what would happen if one of them said, "I like the way I look." In today's girl culture, would she lose status, become an outsider? Or might she start something positive? Teenagers are herd creatures; at this age, and in this society, it will take more than one voice of reason to start to turn things around.

At least they drink their milk shakes. Kitty, too.

chapter five

The Trouble Is Now

*If the case for somatogenesis [an organic, physical cause]
were conclusive, our view of the patient would have to change:
anorexia nervosa would then be an involuntary disease,
perhaps even inheritable, and best treated by purely medical
rather than psychotherapeutic techniques.*

—JOAN JACOBS BRUMBERG,
Fasting Girls: The History of Anorexia Nervosa

*Eating disorders are familial and highly heritable
in twin studies—50 to 80 percent.*

—WALTER KAYE, M.D., professor of psychiatry at
University of California San Diego and director of its Eating
Disorders Treatment and Research Program

Anorexia nervosa is one of medicine's biggest mysteries. Doctors have been trying to make sense of it for hundreds of years. From the outside, anorexia seems inexplicable. More than that—it's a perversion and a denial of the force that animates every living creature. We've come to understand suicide as the urge of a moment, with permanent consequences. But anorexia plays out over weeks, months, years. It's not a single moment of despair, an impulsive turn of the wheel that sends you headfirst into traffic. You need to be determined and stoic to suffer the slow whittling of flesh into bone, the painful alchemies of the starving body. Anorexia makes no sense as suicide; it's too indirect. Its bizarre and ritualistic elements seem like they must have some purpose beyond death.

There's no shortage of theories about anorexia's essential nature, what causes it, what its symptoms mean, whether and how it can be cured. And there's no shortage of doctors and therapists who will say with great certainty that they know what anorexia is (and isn't) "about." Such definitive pronouncements astound me, in part because they can't all be right: anorexia can't be "about" lack of boundaries in the family *and* "negative family food-related experiences" *and* "problems with communication." * More important, none of these pronouncements takes into account what we've learned in the last decade or so about eating disorders—most of which contradicts these closely held beliefs.

We now know, for instance, that many of the cognitive and emotional symptoms associated with anorexia are actually physical by-products of starvation. In the mid-1940s, at the tail end of World War II, Ancel Keys, a physiologist at the University of Minnesota, became interested in the experiences of the millions

---

* Theories put forth by, respectively, Joanna Poppink and Annette Kluck.

of malnourished people in Europe, including concentration camp victims. Keys devised a yearlong study, known as the Minnesota Experiment, to explore the effects of both starvation and refeeding. He recruited thirty-six healthy young conscientious objectors and, starting in November 1944, fed them normally for three months, observing and recording the most minute details of their personalities, eating patterns, vitals, and behavior (the full study results run well over a thousand pages). For the next six months, Keys and his researchers cut the men's rations in half; most volunteers lost about a quarter of their weight, putting them well under the physical cutoff point for anorexia. For the last three months of the experiment, the men's rations were gradually increased until they were eating at or above prestudy levels.

During the months of starvation, the volunteers showed all the physical signs of malnutrition. Their heart rates and metabolisms slowed; they felt cold even in hot weather. They lost so much fat and muscle that sitting, and sometimes walking, became painful. Their feet shrank; their knees, ankles, and faces swelled. Their hair fell out and their muscles cramped. Cuts and wounds bled less and took longer to heal. Hands and feet often went to sleep. The volunteers suffered vertigo and had trouble focusing their eyes, but, interestingly, their hearing improved. Toward the end of the six months, the men had trouble with certain physical actions, including laughing, sneezing, and blushing.

Despite feeling weak, tired, and uncoordinated, some of the men exercised compulsively. They lost interest in sex. They became irritable and depressed. Some of them reported no hunger after a while; others remained ravenous. All of them developed obsessive thoughts and behaviors around eating. They became possessive about their rations, putting their arms around meal trays at the table. They toyed with food to make meals last longer and used large quantities of salt and other spices. They licked their plates to get every crumb and ate everything with enthusiasm, even foods they'd disliked before the experiment began.

Food became, as Keys later wrote, "the principal topic of conversation, reading, and daydreams." [*] The volunteers pored over cookbooks and collected coffeepots, hot plates, and other cooking utensils. They took vicarious pleasure in watching other people eat. They fantasized about restaurant careers; three of them actually went on to become cooks, though they'd had no interest in cooking before the experiment.

Keys and his colleagues evaluated psychological and personality changes by giving the volunteers the Minnesota Multiphasic Personality Inventory (MMPI) before, during, and after the experiment. During the six months of starvation, the men's levels of hypochondria, depression, phobias, obsessions and compulsions, and schizophrenia went up. After three months of refeeding, their scores on those scales were still higher than they'd been at the start of the study; it took eight months of refeeding for their profiles to return to normal.

Some of the most interesting data was collected during those first three months of refeeding. Some volunteers lost weight, especially at the beginning; the rest gained weight slowly. Some didn't gain for weeks, despite the increased calories. Some became more depressed, anxious, impatient, and aggressive toward themselves and others; one man deliberately cut off three of his own fingers.

As the men's calories increased, so did their appetites. A dozen

---

[*]   Ancel Keys et al. *The Biology of Human Starvation* (Minneapolis: University of Minnesota Press), 833.

of the volunteers agreed to stay on after the twelve-week refeeding period, so Keys's team could observe them. They ate prodigious amounts of food and found it hard to stop eating, saying they still felt hungry even when they couldn't physically eat another bite.

Most of the men gradually returned to their prestudy weights and eating habits. A few continued to deliberately limit their food intake. One volunteer restricted his eating to keep himself at 160 pounds, 18 pounds lighter than he'd been at the start of the experiment.

The findings of the Minnesota Experiment were published in 1950 as a two-volume treatise called *The Biology of Starvation,* which was more or less ignored by eating-disorders specialists until about twenty years ago. But these results are crucial for several reasons. First, they establish the fact that the *physical* process of starvation also causes *psychological* symptoms, which can include depression, anxiety, and obsessiveness around food and eating— all of which are hallmarks of anorexia. Psychiatrists commonly diagnose depression or anxiety rather than anorexia; Dr. Newbie diagnosed Kitty with a primary depression, and an eating disorder second. But Keys's study demonstrates that when these psycho-logical changes start during starvation—that is, when there are no signs of them beforehand—they're typically caused by malnutrition and resolve along with the physical symptoms. And although some people with anorexia also suffer from other psychiatric disorders (a concept called *comorbidity*), it's impossible to diagnose depression or anxiety or OCD while a patient is starving. A better approach might be to feed the patient first, and then see which psychological symptoms persist after physical recovery.

Second, as Keys wrote in his two-volume study results, "Star-vation affects the whole organism and its results may be described in the anatomical, biochemical, physiological, and psychological frames of reference." This rather clinical sentence has profound implications for the way we think about anorexia—and, more important, for how it's treated. It puts starvation at the heart of the illness rather than considering it an almost secondary symptom. Rather than getting caught up in theories about family dynamics and psychological dysfunction, those who treat anorexia should aim to reverse starvation first—by any means necessary. The idea that a person with anorexia has to "choose" to eat is both irrelevant and dangerous, especially early in treatment, when nearly all sufferers are anosognosic—literally unable to perceive or understand that they're ill. They can't "choose" to eat; expecting them to, as we saw with Kitty, is both cruel and counterproductive.

If all treatment for anorexia started with nutritional rehabilitation, I have no doubt that patients would recover faster and suffer less.

Keys's study doesn't answer the question of what causes anorexia in the first place. But its findings go a long way toward explaining how malnutrition and starvation affect the human body, and how difficult it can be to reverse those effects.

The men in the study starved for six months and were refed for three. They weren't anorexic; they didn't exhibit the same fear of fat or distorted body image that's common (though not universal) among people with anorexia nervosa. They shared none of the risk factors of anorexia: they were men in their late teens and twenties, not adolescent females. Nor did they set out to diet; their starvation was imposed on them, though they volunteered for the experience.

By contrast, anorexia nearly always starts with a diet or an inadvertent weight loss from illness or exercise. At some point, probably early in the process of restricting, anorexics are overwhelmed by the effects of malnutrition. Their brains as well as their bodies stop working well. They fall down the rabbit hole. And they can't climb back out until they eat. Not just a little, but a lot. And not just for a week or two but for months and months.

Keys's findings contributed to what Walter Kaye describes as the neurobiology of eating disorders. Kaye's current research focuses on using brain imaging to connect physiology and pathology, looking at how brain structures and pathways vary in people with anorexia nervosa. His theory about causation begins with a strand of DNA—specifically, with chromosome 1p, which has been associated with anorexia. "People with anorexia have a relatively large section of a chromosome in common," says Kaye. "However, there are hundreds of genes in this region, and we don't know which ones are involved."

Kaye started studying the genetics of eating disorders in the 1990s. In 2001, the National Institutes of Health gave him funding to create the Genetics of Anorexia Nervosa Collaborative Study, a multisite international study looking at whether and how genetic variations make some people more vulnerable to anorexia. "We don't expect anorexia to be caused by a single gene," he explains. "Rather, it's a complex combination of many genes that, in turn, cause alterations in neural pathways." Kaye and other researchers from around the world will have to study thousands of people and sequence many genes before they can hope to understand exactly how genetics come into play.

The debate about what causes eating disorders is often framed as "state versus trait": states refer to a psychological condition—a state of confusion or excitement, for instance. Traits are biological, passed down genetically from parents to children. Certain personality traits are strongly associated with anorexia: perfectionism, obsessionality, negative emotionality, neuroticism, and harm avoidance. These traits often manifest in childhood, long before the eating disorder; run in families (just as eating disorders do; my mother's sister and several of my cousins struggled with bulimia), turning up in family members who don't have eating disorders; and persist after recovery. In other words, a tendency toward perfectionism doesn't disappear when normal weight is restored.

Kaye's working theory about what causes anorexia goes something like this: Some people are born with a biological predisposition, a genotype that produces personality traits like perfectionism and obsessionality, which typically show up early in childhood, long before any symptoms of an eating disorder. This underlying biology may include irregularities in the neurotransmitter systems, which can lead to a certain rigidity of thinking and personality; people with eating disorders, for instance, often have trouble with what psychologists call *set shifting*, meaning the ability to change what you're doing in response to a changing environment. They have trouble being flexible in certain ways.

People with anorexia often believe they should be able to do things perfectly, and they don't understand that mistakes are part of the normal learning process. They may also have abnormalities of the central nervous system, which controls how much cortisol, a stress hormone, and other hormones are released into the bloodstream. The central nervous system also regulates neuropeptides, molecules that help neurons communicate with one another. Leptin, a substance that modulates appetite and behaviors around eating, is a neuropeptide; so is galanin, which affects waking and sleep as well as eating.

These biological vulnerabilities may be activated by environmental factors; maybe the flood of female hormones around puberty pushes the brain chemistry further out of sync. Stress (or perceived and/or self-induced stress, like the internal pressure to achieve) can exacerbate an already anxious and obsessive temperament.

Starvation may actually represent a kind of self-medicating. People with anorexia have disturbances in the 5-HT system, a network that revolves around the neurotransmitter serotonin. Too much 5-HT action causes anxiety and a loss of appetite. In the long run, starvation leads to malnutrition, which triggers anxiety and depression. But in the short term, for some people, not eating lowers the brain's levels of carbohydrates, which in turn reduces anxiety. When people with anorexia eat after a period of starvation, the 5-HT system revs up, raising anxiety even more and creating negative reinforcement for eating. So people become trapped in a vicious downward spiral of starving and suffering.

Walt Kaye is quick to point out that no one really understands the mechanisms involved in anorexia and other eating disorders. Some of the differences in brain chemistry may be the result of anorexia rather than the cause; since it's impossible to know who will eventually develop anorexia, how can we distinguish cause from effect?

"Is it physiology that causes you to think in [anorexic] ways, or is it your thinking in these ways that gets you to starve and causes physiological consequences?" asks Daniel le Grange of the University of Chicago. "I would get a handsome award if I could figure out what comes first." What we know for sure, he says, is that the causes of eating disorders are complex, multifaceted, and hard to tease apart.

But neurobiology clearly plays a role, which is one reason why Kaye's research uses new technologies like functional MRI and CT scans to literally look into the human brain as it's working. In one recent study, women who had recovered from anorexia showed different neurological responses to the taste of both sugar and water. Areas of the brain connected with both pleasurable tastes and with rewards lit up far less in recovered anorexics than in a control group. The fact that both of these responses are lower than usual might help explain why people with anorexia tend to avoid high-calorie food that tastes good; they experience it as less rewarding on a physiological level. Or their ability to experience a sense of reward may be impaired. Other recent research suggests that for people with anorexia, the part of the brain that signals punishment lights up along with the rewards center, indicating that reward comes with a sense of guilt or anxiety. Or, says Kaye, the neural shifts might reflect a kind of scarring in the brain, the consequences of past malnutrition and weight loss.

Another study compared brain activity in women who were recovering from anorexia with brain activity in healthy women. The participants played a computer game where they won money for guessing correct answers. In healthy women, areas of the brain tied to emotional responses lit up differently when they won money than when they lost. In women with a history of anorexia, there were fewer differences; winning and losing felt very much the same. Kaye suspects this neurological effect applies to eating, too. "For anorexics, perhaps it is difficult to appreciate immediate pleasure if it does not feel much different from a negative experience," he told a BBC interviewer. By contrast, the part of the brain that links actions to outcomes and planning lit up far more in the recovering anorexics than in the healthy women, reflecting high levels of anxiety about making mistakes and worries about negative consequences.

"There are positive aspects to this kind of temperament," Kaye points out. "Paying attention to detail and making sure things are done as correctly as possible are constructive traits in careers like medicine or engineering." Taken too far, though, such traits can hurt more than they can help.

The language of neurobiology describes the nexus between brain chemistry and behavior. It's observational and nonjudgmental, a far cry from the pronouncements of Minuchin, Bruch, and so many others. What it boils down to, in Kaye's words, is that "circuit-based abnormalities" lead to changes "related to appetite, emotionality, and cognitive control." Cause and effect (though it's hardly that simple), seen as a series of system malfunctions, glitches in the hardware that affect the software. There's no blame or shame attached, just descriptions of where the system gets wonky or goes astray.

On the other end of the spectrum from Walt Kaye, some researchers are investigating parallels between anorexia and autism. Nancy Zucker, a psychologist at Duke University Medical Center in Chapel Hill, North Carolina, believes that both people with anorexia and people with autism show impairments in what scientists call *social cognition*—attachment, anxieties, and interpersonal relationships. She published a paper in 2007 suggesting that looking at the social deficits of people with anorexia might help researchers devise better treatments for the illness. But since so many of the "social impairments" seen in anorexia are a function of long-term malnutrition (think of the volunteers in Ancel Keys's study, who became depressed, anxious, withdrawn, and aggressive), I'm not sure how useful this line of research can be. And I don't see how comparing anorexia to autism helps people with either disease. The last thing people with anorexia need is another stigmatizing label slapped on them.

One of the most intriguing theories about what causes anorexia comes from Shan Guisinger, a psychologist in Missoula, Montana. Guisinger wondered why anorexia nervosa developed in the first place, what biological function it fulfilled, and why it's persisted, given its high mortality rate. She came up with what she calls the *adapted-to-flee-famine hypothesis,* which explains the illness in terms of evolutionary biology.

According to Guisinger, the symptoms of anorexia—the inability to see one's own extreme thinness, the hyperactivity and restlessness, the aversion to eating, the ability to function on very little food—make sense if you think of them as strategies for surviving famine. Thousands of years ago, she suggests, before humans started farming, they were nomadic, often traveling great distances to find food. In times of famine, malnourishment made people lethargic, weak, and depressed—unable to forage successfully. Guisinger theorizes that the whole group benefited from having a few members who reacted paradoxically to starvation. These evolutionary outliers stayed energetic, becoming restless rather than lethargic during times of scarcity. They didn't see themselves as dangerously thin and, therefore, stayed optimistic and motivated to survive. All of these qualities made them natural leaders in times of food shortage, leading the drive to find greener pastures. In this context, says Guisinger, the characteristic abilities of anorexics to work hard, delay gratification, and ignore suffering to achieve a goal would have been essential to the group.

To support her theory, Guisinger points to a number of factors: The fact that anorexia nervosa appears across cultural, ethnic, and socioeconomic lines, which suggests that it is biological rather than cultural. The fact that anorexia seems most common in peoples who were more recently nomadic—Hispanics, Caucasians, and

Native Americans—and least common among Asians and African Americans; in Africa over the last hundred thousand years, Guisinger argues, "it was probably better for starving people to stay put, conserve energy, and keep searching locally for food, as traveling could result in encounters with hostile neighbors." Finally, the fact that anorexia affects primarily women. In other primate species, says Guisinger, males who wander from their own territory are typically killed, but females are often accepted and integrated into a new group. So females make the best migrators, in a way.

If the adapted-to-flee-famine theory is true, says Guisinger, maybe one reason anorexia recovery rates are so low in our culture is that the illness was designed to be "switched off," so to speak, in a social context that no longer exists. "In the radically individualistic western culture, it may be hard to imagine the social pressure that is brought to bear on deviant individuals in tribal cultures," she writes. Once the tribe settled into a new area where food was more abundant, ritual prayers, thanksgiving celebrations, and food sharing might have pushed anorexics to begin eating again. She points to the fact that recovered anorexics in our culture often say that support from friends and family helped them beat the illness.

By contrast, many therapists and eating-disorders specialists still believe that psychodynamics cause eating disorders. Much of the literature emphasizes the way starvation unsexes a teenage girl, shrinks the budding breasts, damps down new sexual feelings. Therapists like Hilde Bruch wrote about girls (and boys) with anorexia who are afraid of the complexities of adult sexual relationships and so choose to starve themselves back into childhood to avoid them.

To me this feels awfully contrived. Primitive people observed lightning and thunder and came up with a story to explain them:

the gods were angry. They looked for intention and meaning in the world around them because that's what humans do; our brains seek to make order out of chaos, narrative out of random occurrences. Theories like Bruch's are equally unscientific; they conflate correlation—things that happen at the same time—with causation. It's true that eating disorders often start at adolescence, but we could come up with a dozen theories that "explain" that correlation—say, eating disorders are physiologically triggered by hormones. It's just as likely as the ambivalent-about-growing-up theory, to my mind.

Guisinger's theory seeks meaning in the illness too, but her conclusions seem more genuinely aligned with reality—though it's a reality that no longer literally applies.

At the end of the day, of course, no one knows what causes anorexia, and no one is likely to know for a long time, if ever, which is yet another reason why family-based treatment appeals to me: in the clamor of competing theories and hypotheses, the Maudsley approach says simply, "We don't need to know in order to treat the illness." FBT emphasizes recovery over etiology, results over theories. Human lives over intellectual jousting.

As a journalist, I want to know what's behind this deadly disease, what makes young women and men starve themselves, what are the causes and risk factors. I follow the research, collecting scientific articles the way some people collect baseball cards. I go to conferences, look up medical terminology, try to teach myself the essentials of anatomy so I can understand what the insula does, why tryptophan is important, how ketosis works. I read and reread descriptions of metabolism and appetite, hunger and satiety. My curiosity is piqued by the mystery that is anorexia.

As a mother, I care about only one thing: my daughter. The dead look in her eyes makes me feel dead inside. What drives me is the terror that she will never come back. That her life will be a wasteland without landmarks or topography. That Kitty's face, more known to me than my own, will harden and set into the mask of Not-Kitty, and that when I look into her eyes years from now I'll see the demon looking back.

Or worse: I'll see nothing, because she'll be gone.

One night I sit at the computer and explore a Web site called somethingfishy, which is dedicated to people with eating disorders. I read some of the threads in the chat room for families and feel ill at the despair and hopelessness expressed there. But the most disturbing part of the site is a page of memorials to people who have died from eating disorders. I scroll through screen after screen of candles, each marked with a name, a date, a fragment of a story:

Christy Henrich, died July 26, 1994, from anorexia. Number 2 gymnast in the USA in 1989.

Jane, died December 26, 1995, from anorexia and bulimia; she is survived by her husband, Andy, and their 14-month-old son.

This is in prayer to light a candle for Baby Angella Hope, born September 17, died December 2, 1996. She is the result of a practicing bulimic.

Heidi Guenther, age 22. Died of a sudden fatal heart attack on June 30, 1997, in California on her way to Disneyland.

Deborah Simone Fradin. Debbie died from anorexia nervosa after battling this disease with every fiber in her being for 18 years. The disease ravaged her body, but not her gentle soul.

Candle after candle. Name after name. Story after story. She struggled with this disease for a year, for five years, for twenty-five years. Bright shining girls who should be giggling with friends in the halls of high schools and colleges, studying Latin and microbiology and dance. Girls who should have been walking through fields of light and dark, who instead fell into shadow. They died of heart attacks in bathrooms, in beds, in hospital rooms. They died at home, at school, alone. They died with their parents crying over them, their friends confused. They died before they had a chance to live, because once the demon moves in they're not really living. I know. Believe me, I know.

Tears stream down my face, tears I haven't been able to shed for my own bright shining daughter because I haven't been able to face the fact that she might have died this summer. She still might die. I hope she's on the road to recovery, that she'll have to walk this particular stretch only once. But the numbers are against her. The statistics say she'll come back this way again and again, her body getting weaker and more adapted to starvation until it comes to feel natural and right to her, until her very cells learn the pattern and shape and feeling of constant gnawing hunger. Until that skull face in the mirror looks like her face. Until it *is* her face. Until it has obliterated her real face not only in her own eyes but in ours.

And that's when my fury rises. Between our reality—where Kitty's life hangs in the balance—and the theories about *why* she is sick and *how* to help her lies an enormous chasm. I have no idea how to get across it. I don't even know if it's possible. And all the research is no help. It exists only on paper, tidy and two-dimensional, disconnected from the messy, dangerous, three-dimensional world we're trapped in.

Every paper I read, every doctor I talk to, seems to have a different explanation for and approach to anorexia. No wonder the field has such a lousy track record. A higher percentage of people with anorexia die than people with schizophrenia or bipolar disorder or depression or any other mental illness. Of those who survive, only half truly recover.

You'd think numbers like these would inspire a little more soul-searching among the professionals. You'd be wrong.

A heart surgeon who used outmoded techniques would be barred from the operating room. Yet eating-disorders therapists cleave to theories from sixty years ago as if they represented the most up-to-date thinking, and they defend their beliefs with the self-righteous vigor of zealots. Maybe this is because so many of the people who treat eating disorders had (or still have) the illness themselves. On one hand, this gives them great empathy. On the other, it weds them to a particular narrative—their own personal story line. For instance, if they recovered by finding God—which isn't that unusual; one of the biggest residential treatment chains, Remuda Ranch, offers a twelve-step, Bible-based approach—they'll push their patients in that direction. If, as is all too common, they themselves still struggle with disordered eating, they're likely to believe, and to communicate to their patients, that full recovery is impossible, that anorexia is an illness you have to manage for the rest of your life. They will, however inadvertently, convey a sense of hopelessness and resignation based on nothing but their own experience.

What I want is what's commonplace in every other area of medicine: best practice. Evidence-based treatment, based on the most up-to-date research and clinical practice. It doesn't seem a lot to ask, to advise patients out of knowledge rather than belief. That's what doctors do, isn't it?

Not in the world of eating disorders. Not yet.

When Kitty was four or five, she went through a fairy-tale phase. Every night Jamie and I read her parables about good and evil, usually featuring a young girl in mortal danger who, in the end, lives happily ever after. So I know how fairy tales work. Events unfold according to a formula known or intuited in advance. They have a predictable story line, complete with warnings and foretellings, symbols and metaphors that make them both universal and compelling. Which, now that I think about it, might be why Kitty loved them so much. She's always been the kind of child who likes rules, who needs to know not just what to do and how to do it but what not to do and how to stay out of trouble.

If our story were a fairy tale, there would be a magic needle, a bridge rising out of the mist, a talking fish that would whisper instructions in my ear about how to trick our way across that chasm. And we *would* cross that chasm. We would overcome all obstacles, real and supernatural, and make our way to safety.

One of Kitty's favorite childhood books was a gorgeously illustrated retelling of the Russian firebird myth. The main characters are a dim but handsome young prince named Dmitri and his wise talking horse. Together they face dangers, pass through trials by fire and water, and pit their wits against the machinations of an evil king. Each time they face a seemingly insurmountable obstacle, Dmitri runs crying to the horse, wringing his hands, sure that he'll fail. And each time the horse says, "The trouble is not now. The trouble is still to come," and then tells Dmitri what to do. Those phrases—*The trouble is not now. The trouble is still to come*—become a refrain in the book, and over time they've become a kind of family motto for us, a joke we tell each other to remind ourselves that we can handle it, whatever *it* is.

Toward the end of the book, Dmitri must leap three times into a cauldron of boiling water without getting scalded or drowned. When he runs to the horse, anxious about this final test, the horse replies, "The trouble is now." It comes as a shock because you've been lulled by the reassuring leitmotif: *The trouble is not now. The trouble is still to come*. Of course, thanks to the horse's quick thinking, Dmitri passes unscathed through the boiling water, vanquishing the evil king and winning the hand of the woman he loves. Happily ever after for everyone, including the horse.

I want someone to tell us not only what to do and how to do it but that we *can* do it. I want to live inside a fairy tale, where good triumphs over evil and love overpowers greed, envy, resentment, and fear. Because the one thing I know for sure is that the trouble is now. The water is boiling, the demon is laughing, the young woman's life is in mortal danger.

If I can't have a talking horse, I at least want a guide, someone who's traveled this road and knows how to make it across the chasm. Who will talk us through the scary parts. The trouble is now and the trouble is still to come. And I don't know if we'll be all right.

{ chapter six }

September

Through all my growing up, and through all my marriage and
through all the tough times, I was always trying to measure up,
or trying to be somebody else. And all of a sudden you said,
"I just love you. I don't need you to be well. It doesn't matter."

—BETSY HALL, who has struggled with anorexia and bulimia for
much of her life, quoted in a film made by her daughter, Hope Hall

To mark the end of the first week of school—a week that's gone
pretty well for both Kitty and Emma—Jamie and I make plans
for Sunday afternoon. We'll take our kayaks to a nearby lake and
paddle around, then hang out in the park onshore. Our last family
outing was the opera in the park concert back in July. The night
Kitty ended up in the hospital.

We've avoided going out since then because Kitty has needed to stay close to home. Eating is beginning to seem easier, but the prospect of eating a meal in front of other people still sends her into a panic. And I've come to realize just how much socializing is based around eating. Every party and backyard get-together includes food, and even when the focus isn't a meal—say, a graduation party, even a neighborhood meeting—food is almost always on the table, literally and metaphorically. I think of Shan Guisinger's comment about how social pressure facilitated eating in primitive societies and wonder if the urge to share food is an instinct coded into human DNA because it helps us build community.

Community, in any case, is the last thing on Kitty's mind. Truly, I think she's grateful to have homework, glad to have something else to think about, even if it is algebra. Maybe *because* it's algebra, which is completely unconnected with anorexia. What makes school hard for her is what she used to love most about it: the friendships. She obsesses over what people think of her and is convinced they're judging her because she has anorexia. I tell her no one blames her, that people understand she's ill, that they feel empathy and compassion. I wish I believed that. I'm sure her closest friends do feel for her. But I'm also sure she is being judged, and harshly, by plenty of others. I know we're all being judged, and found wanting, by some of the people who smile and cluck sympathetically in the grocery store, in the neighborhood, at the office or school. I know it hurts Kitty, because I know how much it hurts me, and Jamie, and even Emma.

We all have our reasons for staying close to home.

Kitty objects strenuously to the Sunday plan, and I nearly say never mind. But I feel as though that would be giving in to the anorexia, validating on some level her worries about—about what?

I'm not really sure. So we load up our picnic, tie the kayaks onto the roof of the car, and go.

Lunch at the park takes more than an hour; Kitty dawdles and picks at her sandwich, insists she can't eat the chips, tries to refuse the chocolate milk. I wonder again if this is a mistake. But we're only five minutes from home; we can always leave if we have to.

Once we actually get into the kayaks, though—Jamie and Emma in a rented double, Kitty and I each in our own—it's as if some switch gets flipped and Kitty is her old self, smiling, enthusiastic, even cracking a joke about my less-than-stellar steering skills. We paddle in loose formation under a watercolor-blue sky, waving at other boats, watching a muskrat swim away from our wake. Emma, too, seems more relaxed than usual. For the first time in months I remember the ways we all fit together. We share a sense of humor. We are a family.

Which is why it's such a shock to see the demon emerge the very second Kitty steps out of the kayak. "I'm so fat," she starts. "I'm horrible and no one loves me. Why doesn't anyone love me?" When I try to calm her down, she accuses me of speaking harshly. She tells me I'm not listening to her feelings. The monotonous ranting of the demon goes on and on. Emma puts her hands over her ears, and Jamie walks her toward the car, dragging two of the kayaks with them. I give up talking to Kitty and just stay with her, on an isolated bench, until she winds down.

We walk up to the playground, and I give Kitty and Emma each a protein bar. We've learned the hard way that she has to eat something, even a small snack, every two hours or so; she's gained eight or nine pounds, but her body still has no reserves. We feed her as often as you'd feed an infant.

I'm expecting resistance, but Kitty opens the wrapper and begins to eat. She takes tiny bites and chews each one with infinite care, the way she eats everything now. But at least she's eating.

Jamie looks at me quizzically—*What happened?*—and I shake my head: *Tell you later.* Emma finishes her snack and runs over to the swings. Kitty stands up abruptly and starts toward the garbage can.

"What are you doing?" I call.

"I'm done!" she answers, not turning around. "I'm throwing away the wrapper."

"Please come here," I say, raising my voice so she'll hear me. I don't know why I want her to come back. I just do.

She turns, reluctantly, and walks toward me, one hand closed behind her back. "Show me," I say, and even so, I'm shocked when she uncurls her fist and reveals half the protein bar, uneaten.

My daughter is fourteen years old and this is the first time I know of that she's tried to deceive me. I feel like I'm watching the scene from a great distance as it happens to someone else. Kitty's always been the good-girl type, afraid to break the rules or get into trouble. I know she's lied before; every kid does. But this feels different. This isn't Kitty.

She sits down beside me on the bench, folds back the paper, and begins to eat again. She keeps her eyes cast down and her face empty. What is she feeling? Is she angry or embarrassed, frustrated or defiant? She looks like a sleepwalker—blank, quiet, driven by some force deep within her.

For the first time it occurs to me that my daughter will be permanently changed by this—this thing inside her, this twisted creature that shrieks and writhes and spits poison into her blood and bone and mind. And that, in fact, each one of us will be changed, Jamie and Emma and I. Our family will never be the same. Even if Kitty gets well—and at this moment that seems a distant possibility—things will never go back to the way they were.

Of course this is always true, in every family, all the time. Children are walking palimpsests, continuously evolving, and as parents we change along with them, accommodating and responding to who they are in the process of becoming. Part of the pleasure and reward of parenting is watching the alchemy of childhood, seeing our offspring transform themselves from generic infancy into gloriously individual adulthood. And part of our necessary sorrow as parents is having to accept the kinds of change we fear for our children.

That night in bed, I say to Jamie, "Maybe we've hit the bottom now, and there's nowhere to go but up?"

"Maybe," he says.

We are, of course, wrong again.

The next morning Kitty comes down to breakfast with her hair in pigtails, a style I haven't seen her wear in years. She dawdles at breakfast, stirring her bowl of granola and yogurt for twenty minutes, until I say, "You're going to be late for school."

"I'm not going," she says.

"Why not?"

"Everyone there thinks I'm a freak who got fat over the summer. They won't stop looking at me."

"Who's looking at you?" I ask.

"*Everyone*," she says impatiently, and I wonder if this is normal teenage impatience or eating-disordered impatience. I hate the fact that I wonder about this. This is another legacy of anorexia: the need to question, analyze, worry every interaction like a dog with a bone. When all I want is to be like we used to be, Kitty and I, easy with and on each other.

I tell her I think she should go and at least try to stick it out. I tell her it's only two morning subjects, and if she starts missing classes this early in the year, it will be hard to catch up, and that will feel even more stressful. I tell her (though I doubt she can take this in) that it's important for her to stay involved with the world as much as she can. I know that if we let her stay home today, she'll want to do it again tomorrow and the next day.

My words seem to have no effect. So I coax her up from the table after she's eaten. "Come on, I'll walk you," I say.

I have to practically drag her out the door, into the steamy late summer air. I figure once we're outside, her aversion to public scenes will make things easier. But this morning Kitty doesn't seem to mind making a scene. She wrenches her arm out of my grasp and balks like a horse who's come up against a jump too high. "Why are you torturing me?" she shouts, standing in front of our next-door neighbor's house. "Why don't you understand that I can't go to school this morning?"

I speak in a low, soothing tone. "Come on, Kitty, you know you have to go," I say and try to somehow urge her down the street without actually touching her.

She glares. "Why are you doing this to me?" she shouts, her voice rising to an actual scream on the last word. I consider taking her back inside—how can she possibly go to school like this? But my gut tells me that to back down now would be to let the demon win. I'm not letting this illness take one more thing from Kitty if I can help it. She's suffering now, I know, but her whole life is at stake. We can't go backward, even for a second.

And so I take hold of her arm again, firmly, and try to move her down the block, one step at a time. Two doors down from our house she sits down abruptly on the sidewalk, her short black skirt flipping up for a moment around her waist. I'm sure the neighbors are watching, not that I care; I'm not easily embarrassed. But Kitty is, and she would care, if she could process anything but the anxiety and terror overwhelming her.

By the time we get to the school she's fifteen minutes late, which normally would freak her out; today I'm not sure she even notices. Clearly she can't go to her first class. Last week, we met with the school psychologist, Mr. R., an earnest young man who told Kitty she was welcome in his office anytime, even in the middle of a class. Now I tell her I think she should go to Mr. R.'s office.

She whirls toward me with a look of pure rage, her pigtails bouncing incongruously. "The minute you leave I'm going to the bathroom to make myself throw up!" she yells.

Inside my head a voice is shouting *No! No! No!* I've read enough to know that up to 30 percent of people with anorexia cross over into bulimia, and that purging complicates recovery even more. It's the last thing Kitty needs.

What should I do? Take her home? Follow her to class and keep her out of the bathroom all morning? I'm paralyzed. Kitty makes the decision for me. Standing in the empty hallway, she says, "Fine, I'll go to Mr. R.'s office!" Then she's running down the hall away from me, her backpack slapping against her shoulders. She rounds the corner and disappears. I have no idea which way Mr. R.'s office is, so I don't know if she's heading there or not. I stand there, irresolute. Eventually I walk home.

I spend the rest of the morning cleaning, unable to concentrate on anything else, picturing Kitty in the girls' bathroom at school, a finger down her throat, or running out the door, away from school. Running away from us. In a school of several thousand, no one would notice she was gone.

I finally unclench my jaw when I hear the front door open at the usual time. Kitty seems calmer than when I left her at school. But within minutes the demon is raging again. My heart aches for her, but I have to know.

"Did you throw up today?" I ask, interrupting the flow.

She glares. "That's all you care about, what I eat and whether I throw up!" she shouts. "You don't care how I feel!"

I do care about her feelings, of course I do. But what I really care about is getting her well as fast as possible. Getting her through this nightmare.

I hate the demon. I fantasize about strangling it with my bare hands, squeezing until its forked tongue protrudes. But I can't picture that without also picturing my hands around my daughter's neck, because the demon wears her face and speaks with her voice.

Kitty cries until she falls asleep at one o'clock in the afternoon. Clearly she's not going back to school today. When she wakes up an hour later, she's a bit calmer. I sit with her as she drinks her milk shake, and eventually I ask, again, whether she threw up.

The look she gives me now is weary. "I tried," she confesses. "I wanted to. I went into the bathroom and stuck my finger down my throat. But I couldn't do it."

I'm not religious, but I send a prayer toward the ceiling. *Thank you, whoever and whatever. Thank you for watching over my daughter.*

One of the strangest things about this whole year is that despite all the trauma and drama, I have a hard time remembering that Kitty's ill. When she smiles or makes a joke, when I see a bit of the old Kitty, it's as if I suddenly mistrust the events of the last few months. *Things can't be that bad. Can they?* I'm a pessimist, the first to leap to the worst possible scenario; my lack of sunny positivity is a family joke. Yet these days I often find myself wondering whether we're making a big deal out of nothing. It's not denial; three months ago I was in denial. I know without question now that Kitty has anorexia, that her life was and still is in danger. And yet every time the demon emerges I'm surprised. *I thought we were past all that.* It's as if my own thinking has been compromised by Kitty's illness. As if I've caught a touch of anorexia myself.

If I look beyond what I want to see, I can easily chart the rise and fall of Kitty's distress. It jumps when she's stressed—like now, starting ninth grade in a new school—and when we hold the line around eating. It's as if the illness is a wild animal, snarling, backing slowly into a corner. Its outbursts are a sign of resistance. We didn't see the demon until we started refeeding her. In a way, it's a measure of our effectiveness.

For instance, the night after Kitty tries to make herself vomit at school is a bad one. We get dinner into her, and a bite or two of the bedtime snack, but then we give up. Jamie stays in her room, holding on to her, keeping her safe as she rages and cries, while I put Emma to bed.

Emma's room is dark and quiet, with two closed doors between her and Kitty's radiating misery. Yet I know Emma is hyperconscious of the drama playing out across the hall. I sit beside her on the bed, as I've done every night since she was a toddler. This is our talking time, in the dark, just the two of us. I want to help her process what's happening, but I don't want to make everything revolve around Kitty. So I try to follow her lead.

Tonight she wants to talk about the anorexia. "Is Kitty going to get better?" she asks.

"Yes," I promise, hoping it's true.

"Are you taking care of her?"

Will you take care of me? That's what I hear in Emma's anxious question. "Always and forever," I say.

We sit quietly for a few minutes. Then Emma says, "I can see the anorexia in my mind. It's like a cartoon person, but it's not funny."

"No," I say. "It's not funny."

"It's wearing all black and has spiky hair."

"Blond hair, like Kitty?"

"No, dark hair," she says. And suddenly I can picture it too, faceless. A walking black hole that sucks everything into its open, aching mouth. Including a lot of Emma's life.

My only consolation is that maybe watching Kitty go through this will somehow inoculate Emma against the possibility of an eating disorder. Craig Johnson, who directs the eating disorders unit at Laureate Psychiatric Hospital in Tulsa, Oklahoma, says that having a family member with anorexia nervosa makes a child twelve times more likely to develop it herself. In relative terms, the risk is still small, since only about 1 percent of girls and women develop the disease. But any extra risk is too much for me. I've heard of families with two anorexic daughters; a mother named Mary Ellen Clausen, who lives in central New York, started a nonprofit called Ophelia's Place after both of her daughters struggled with anorexia. I can't imagine what she's gone through—what their whole family has gone through. Then again, before anorexia, I could never have imagined what Kitty's going through now.

Back then, I wouldn't have thought it important to understand the inner reality of an eating disorder. People suffer in so many ways—it's not possible to get them all. Anorexia, I would have said, is one of many illnesses, and thank God it hasn't happened to my family.

I don't feel that way anymore, of course, because it *has* happened to my family. But self-interest is only part of the urge I feel to make people get it, give them a taste of what it's like to have anorexia. Only a small subset of the population is biologically predisposed to have an eating disorder. But we're all vulnerable in some way. I've had panic disorder for as long as I can remember, and the experience has shaped me profoundly. I've watched friends struggle with depression, bipolar disorder, anxiety disorder—the kinds of illnesses we all think happen only to other people. Advocates for mental health parity say that for every piece of parity legislation that's been introduced, there's a legislator with a spouse, a family member, or a close friend who struggles with some form of mental illness. We don't get it until it gets us. But one way or another, it gets us all.

The next day, I take Kitty for her weekly weigh-in. Dr. Beth schedules us as her last appointment of the day, and she often stays to talk with us long past closing time. As usual, Kitty's anxiety rises as the afternoon wears on. Getting weighed for her is a no-win situation. The demon wants her to lose weight, or at least not gain; the part of her that's separate from the anorexia wants to gain weight, both because she wants to please us and because she wants to get better. "I want my life back," is how she puts it. "I have no life now." If she doesn't gain weight, she suffers our disappointment, and her own. If she does, she suffers a cascade of anorexic thoughts and feelings, the wrath of the demon.

At the office, the nurse hands Kitty a cup and ushers her into the bathroom for the usual ritual. Then comes the moment of truth, when Kitty steps onto the scale, her back to the machinery, and waits for the nurse to nudge the metal weights into perfect alignment. I try to keep my face blank, though Kitty says she can always tell by looking at me whether she's gained or not.

Today the scale shows neither gain nor loss. My heart sinks, even though I know that metabolism is complicated and weight gain is not a linear process. But I need to feel like Kitty's moving forward, even at a glacial pace. Plus, some days I'm overwhelmed by the feeling of being way out here on our own. It's not just that no one is telling us exactly what to do, that we're more or less feeling our way through the dark and scary forest; we're actually going against the conventional wisdom. If we'd taken the accepted route, Kitty would be an inpatient now at a hospital an hour away. Instinct tells me that that wouldn't help her, that in fact it would harm her. But Jamie and I don't know what the hell we're doing. I'm not a doctor. What if my judgment is compromised? What if I'm just wrong?

Dr. Beth comes in with her usual smile. Tucking a strand of blond hair behind one ear, she looks over Kitty's chart and reassures me that by every objective measure, Kitty is improving. Her heart rate's up into the 70s; her pulse and blood pressure are good. Despite today's stagnant scale reading, Kitty has gained fourteen pounds in the last seven weeks.

We talk about Kitty's increasing anxiety, some of which is likely a by-product of refeeding. The psychiatrist bumped up Kitty's dose of fluoxetine a few weeks ago, because she was feeling more anxious, and now Dr. Beth wonders if the meds are part of the problem. "Try cutting back to the previous dose," she suggests—good advice that I suspect would never have come from the psychiatrist. In fact, as I later learn, study after study shows that antidepressants like fluoxetine don't help people with anorexia. Which doesn't stop psychiatrists from prescribing them.

Dr. Beth makes me feel like we're doing OK. So many of the doctors and therapists we've seen since this began have exuded some level of blame or anger or annoyance—toward us and toward Kitty. Even when their words are neutral—*Anorexia is no one's fault, it's a biological illness*—their body language, the look in their eyes, convey a subtle sense of criticism. It strikes me that both doctors and ordinary people project all kinds of judgments, feelings, and desires onto people with eating disorders. Since getting sick Kitty has been both admired and scorned for her perceived stubbornness, envied for her emaciation, belittled for her feelings. The praise she's received for her extreme thinness comes with a dollop of prurience, a sense that she's accomplished something both meaningful and shameful.

I don't believe anorexia is a response to environment, but I do wonder about its relationship with culture. Once you develop anorexia you become not just a person with an illness; you come to represent something here and now, in this time and place. You become the anorexic, your identity inextricable from the illness. Other diseases have carried a sense of stigma and judgment over the years—cancer, for instance, which was rarely mentioned or discussed when I was growing up. People with cancer felt a sense of shame and isolation, as if they were to blame for their illness.

But the stigma of anorexia, bulimia, and other mental illnesses goes beyond that. Even the way we talk about them is different. People with eating disorders lose their identity; they become *anorexics* or *bulimics*. We conflate them with the disease, as if whoever they were before the illness disappears when they're diagnosed. Whereas there's no one word to define someone with cancer or heart disease. A patient with lymphoma isn't a lymphatic; he or she retains a sense of individual identity. It's a small point, but it matters, because language shapes the way we think about the world. Calling someone "an anorexic" suggests that anorexia is all there is to her, that it *is* her and always will be, that there is no extricating the person from the disease.

Sometimes, while Kitty is at school or asleep, I take out our photo albums, filling my eyes with her face and body and essence before: Age eleven, standing in front of Lake Superior, pants rolled up, beside Emma, each of them holding up handfuls of rocks collected along the beach. Age three, on the dock of the house we rented in northern Wisconsin that summer, grinning beside her friend Cinda, a bulky orange life preserver around each of their necks. Age four, holding a newborn Emma, her blond hair falling protectively over the baby in her lap. Age nine, sitting at my mother-in-law's kitchen table, totally focused on a stack of homemade pancakes.

I won't mistake the disease for my daughter. I will remember Kitty as she was before anorexia and as she will be again when it's gone.

I know I'm hypersensitive about this. What I want is for people to treat Kitty as though she's not just another anorexic, one of the thousands who say the same things and look the same way and struggle with the same compulsions. I want people to see the girl beyond the disease, with her habits and charms and failings. *Her* idiosyncrasies, not anorexia's.

But Kitty seems to feel relief at meeting other kids with eating disorders. She comes home from Ms. Susan's first lunch group practically gushing. "No offense, but you guys don't know what it's like," she tells me. "Mom, they really get it."

I'm standing at the kitchen counter, scooping Häagen-Dazs into the milk-shake maker a friend sent over. "Honey, I'm so glad," I tell her.

Kitty leans against the doorjamb, staying outside the kitchen as

I prepare her food. "They totally get it," she repeats. "I can be myself around them."

I want to ask, *Which self?* But I'm afraid of what she might say, or imply. I don't want her to take on the identity of *anorexic*. Maybe it's inevitable. Maybe, in fact, it's already happened, and I'm trying to close the barn door after the horse has galloped off. Still, one of the reasons I look forward to our appointments with Dr. Beth is that she seems to see beyond the disease. She talks to my daughter as if Kitty is an ordinary teenager. She asks about school and friends, boyfriends and movies. She brings a feeling of joy into the exam room, the joy of ordinary life, which we all have been missing for months.

Over the next few days, Kitty brightens visibly. Maybe cutting back on the meds helped. Maybe it's the new lunch group. Or maybe it's the weight gain. She seems engaged with the world in a new way. Or, rather, an old way, one we haven't seen since last winter. She tells me she's going to join Latin Club; Latin's her favorite class, because she loves the teacher.

A few days later, as I walk Kitty up the hill to school, I ask, "How was Latin Club yesterday?"

Silence. Then she says, "I didn't go."

"Why not?"

Her eyes fill with tears. "Because they serve brownies at the meetings," she says. "And I would want one, but I'd be afraid."

"Afraid of what?" I think I know the answer, but I want to hear what Kitty says. Sometimes she seems incredibly unaware of how she's feeling and acting. I wonder how she sees things in moments like this, when the demon has subsided below the surface.

"If I choose to eat something I don't have to, then I'm bad," she explains. *If I choose to eat something I don't have to.* Anorexia is a prison sentence for a crime you didn't commit, a crime that fills you nevertheless with guilt and dread.

I look at Kitty, pride and sorrow welling up in my heart. Sorrow over the claustrophobic, obsessive world she inhabits, and pride at her astonishing candor. These dispatches from the land of anorexia take a kind of bravery few people understand.

"You could go to the meeting and not eat anything," I say, but she shakes her head, and I understand: Not yet.

The next day I get another lesson in just how hard things are for my daughter, when we go downtown to do errands. As we walk by a new Ben & Jerry's store, she says, "If I were required to have another snack today, I would want to have it in here."

I open my mouth to say "What?" and then close it again. I pick up on her cue. "You know, I've been reviewing your day's calories, and you need an extra snack this afternoon," I tell her.

I expect her to say no, despite the invitation she's extended. Instead, she pushes open the door and goes inside, where she spends five minutes deliberating about what to eat—not freaking out, not panicking, but deciding what she's in the mood for.

I have a good idea of how many calories Kitty's eating every day—between twenty-five hundred and three thousand—and so far today she's on track. I'm astounded by the fact that the harsh taskmaster that flays her with guilt and fear and misery could be rendered harmless by such a transparent charade.

But this charade only strengthens my instinct that Jamie and I are at war with the voice in Kitty's head, the one that tells her not to eat, that she's fat, that she's loathsome and worthless. We hear only a fraction of its awful words, but Kitty gets up with it in the morning and goes to sleep with it drumming in her ears. We sit in Ben &

Jerry's and I watch her dip her wooden spoon again and again into a dish of frozen yogurt. Her face is open and unguarded and, yes, happy. I'm struck by the power of words—in this case, my words, which have rendered the voice in Kitty's head mute and harmless. For the moment.

And I am amazed and grateful that this is so. All my life I've heard people say that love is powerful. This is the first time I deeply, truly believe it. Love can overcome the demon—for the moment. I know it will come back, in ten minutes or an hour or a day. The demon's voice will roar in Kitty's ears and spew out of her mouth and nothing we say or do right then will make it stop. But there will be other moments like this one, when our voices drown its insidious refrain. More and more moments, I hope, until, like the Wicked Witch of the West, the demon melts away.

I know that time is a long way off. I know the trouble is still now and the happy ending is yet to come. Earlier today I saw my doctor for a physical. When she walked into the room, I surprised both of us by bursting into tears. It felt good to cry; these days I am mostly numb and disconnected. I can't afford to feel pain because once it starts it might never stop, and then what good would I be to anyone? There will be plenty of time to process all this later. After Kitty's recovered. *When,* not *if.*

In fairy tales there is often a cleansing ritual, a symbolic expunging of dangerous magic. I want there to be a ritual for us. I want to walk through the house with a bundle of burning sage, a braided candle, a stick of incense. I want to wipe away the confusion and misery and suffering. But for rituals to work, you have to believe in them. And I don't. I believe in the marriage between the mind and the body, thought and feeling. I believe in the body's need to be nourished and the mind's ambivalence about doing it. I can't afford to feel powerless and helpless; that's a luxury, that kind of thinking, and it won't help Kitty one bit.

That night I sit with Kitty as she gets ready for sleep. Six months ago she would say goodnight and close her door, and that was that. Since the anorexia, we've resurrected our old bedtime routines. Now she lies on her stomach and hikes up her pajama top, and I put my hand against her back. I can still see the knotted rope of her spine, but now the vertebrae are covered with smooth flesh. Three months ago, I hated feeling the rude skeleton protruding through her icy skin. The claws of her hands. Touching her left me bruised and anxious.

With the tip of my index finger I trace letters against the warm skin of her back: I. L. O. V. E. Y. O. U. We started this ritual when she was learning to read, when putting letters together into words was a magic act she never tired of.

After a while I get up. "Don't go," says Kitty. "Don't leave me all alone."

"I won't," I say, easing myself down on the bed again. "You know I won't."

By the third week of September, Kitty's weight has plateaued. Jamie and I confer with Ms. Susan and raise her calories to thirty-five hundred a day. That's a lot of food.

Eating large amounts upsets Kitty's stomach—eating any amount seems to upset her stomach, actually—so we try to reduce the volume and make sure everything she eats is calorie efficient. Our kitchen becomes High-Calorie Central; Paula Deen is my new literary muse. We go through so many sticks of butter that I dream about unwrapping them in my sleep, peeling back the translucent paper, dropping them one by one into an enormous metal bowl.

Which leaves Kitty with a meal plan something like this:

Breakfast: a large bowl of nutty granola mixed with vanilla yogurt and raspberry jam
Snack: a high-calorie protein bar
Lunch: a large sesame bagel slathered with 3 to 4 tablespoons of almond butter; chips; a piece of fruit
Snack: a milk shake made with 2 cups of Häagen-Dazs ice cream and a little milk
Dinner: a large serving of whatever we're having; bread and butter; milk
Snack: three or four pieces of toast, buttered and sprinkled with cinnamon sugar; or a large (4 to a pan instead of 12) pumpkin chocolate chip or banana nut muffin

One of the challenges in refeeding Kitty is the fact that she feels no hunger. So she says, and I believe it. It's still there—coming out in her continuous and obsessive thoughts about food, her need to plan every bite—but her brain and her body have become disconnected when it comes to eating, which makes sense in a way. If starvation is a function of, say, famine or war, if there's no food available, then constant hunger pangs would be a pointless torment. Loss of appetite, in that case, is both a blessing and a self-defense mechanism.

Hunger is a function of a complex set of chemical interactions we don't yet understand, involving hormones like ghrelin, which is produced in the stomach and makes its way to the brain, rising before a meal to trigger eating. People with acute anorexia have high levels of ghrelin. Another hormone connected with hunger is leptin, made by fat cells, which tells the brain you've eaten enough, shutting down hunger. People who have lost weight have low levels of leptin, which pushes them to eat more.

We need hunger in the same way we need pain: a stimulus that makes us behave in ways that preserve ourselves and our species. Without hunger, eating is a chore dictated by the clock, a literally unpalatable task to check off a list. Eating without hunger can feel punitive, the introduction of foreign matter into a body that does not welcome it. It's easy to forget to eat without the relentless goad of stomach pangs, when food doesn't look or smell good.

And hunger does more than just get us to the table. It determines, in part, how we metabolize what we eat. In the late 1970s, Swedish researchers fed two groups of women—one Swedish and one Thai—a spicy Thai meal. The Swedish women absorbed only about half as much iron from the meal as the Thai women. When the meal was mushed up and served as a paste, the Thai women absorbed 70 percent less iron than they had before—from the same food.[*]

The researchers concluded that when we eat a meal that's unfamiliar or unappetizing, we don't get as much nutrition out of it as we otherwise might. Why? Because some of the digestive and metabolic processes don't take place in the gut. The smells, looks, and sensory gestalt of a meal we're looking forward to trigger a series of processes in the brain, which in turn tells the salivary glands to kick into high gear, producing more saliva, and the stomach to secrete more gastric juices, both of which help digest the food.

Maybe this explains, in part, why it's so hard for Kitty to gain

---

[*]   Harriet Brown, "Go with Your Gut," *New York Times* op-ed, February 20, 2006.

weight. Maybe refeeding is not just a matter of calories in, calories out; maybe the anticipation and experience of eating helps determine how much of the meal Kitty's body hangs on to. In which case this process is going to take a long time.

Physically, Kitty is making progress. Slow progress, but still. Mentally—that's another story. At Dr. Newbie's urging we start her on Zyprexa, a new-generation antipsychotic, and after two days she perks up, acting like herself again, with a certain alertness and outward-looking perspective that's been gone for months. She says she feels better too, that she still has all the anorexia thoughts but the guilt isn't as strong. Unfortunately, she develops a side effect called akathisia—jitteriness, agitation, and anxiety—and Dr. Newbie says we have to take her off the Zyprexa, that the anxiety will intensify to unbearable levels. When I tell Kitty, she protests, "But it makes the voice get quieter." The voice in her head, she means. The voice of the demon.

I'm frustrated enough to cry. This is the only medical intervention that's helped Kitty at all, and now she can't take it. No shortcuts; we'll have to do this the hard way.

When I look back even a month, though, I see how far Kitty's come. Dr. Beth agrees. At our weekly appointment, Kitty asks when she can stop trying to gain weight and go on a maintenance diet, and Dr. Beth says, "Now!" When she heads down the hall to get something, I follow her out.

"I thought Kitty had to gain another ten pounds or so to reach her target weight," I say.

"I think she can gain weight more slowly now," says Dr. Beth. "Maybe a quarter pound a week."

A quarter pound a week? I think about how long it took to get Kitty started gaining weight. I don't understand why Dr. Beth

wants us to slow down now that she's actually got some momentum. Why go back to prolonging the misery?

"I've seen people overshoot their goal, and that wouldn't be
good," she explains.

I want to ask, "Why not?" But I'm conscious, suddenly, of the
fact that I weigh thirty pounds more than the charts say I should.
Self-conscious. I don't want to hear Dr. Beth say, "Because I don't
want her to be fat like you."

To be fair, I have no idea if that's what she's thinking. What *I'm*
thinking is, Wouldn't it be better for Kitty to be a little "over"—
whatever that means—than to chance falling down the rabbit hole
again? We know the risks of her weighing too little; what, exactly,
are the risks of her weighing five pounds "extra"?

I don't say any of this, partly because I feel such self-consciousness.
Instead, I tell Dr. Beth that I think Kitty heard the words "You don't
have to gain *any* more weight" and ask her to clarify. When we go
back into the room, Dr. Beth tells Kitty she can up her activity
level a bit and stay at the same calorie count. "So your weight gain
will slow down," she says. This is still a mixed message; for the
last month we've been telling Kitty that she's going to feel better
when she's gained enough weight, that our goal is to get her there as
quickly as is practical and possible. We've told her to hang on, that
things are going to get better. Now she's hearing, more or less, this
is it. This is as good as it's going to get. I see the ambivalence on her
face: the anorexia thinks this is fabulous news—you can stay thin!
The part of Kitty that's not thinking like an anorexic is not so sure
this is a good idea.

I'm with her.

This will happen again and again over the course of the next
seven months: not just Dr. Beth but Dr. Newbie and every doc-

tor we see will be quick to tell Kitty that she can back off, not gain any more weight, based on the numbers on the chart. No one asks whether she still has anorexic thoughts and feelings. No one asks *us* what her behavior's like, how hard it is for her to eat. They tell her she's fine when we can see clearly that she's not.

Once more I think of Daniel le Grange's comment about how anorexia seems to infect everyone around the sufferer too. And I can't help but wonder how much the current angst about obesity and the general culture of fatphobia affects doctors' attitudes. Still, we're lucky to have our treatment team, even if I don't agree with everything they recommend. Today, for instance, toward the end of this appointment, Kitty asks if she can fast on Yom Kippur, two weeks away. I hold my breath, wondering what Dr. Beth will say.

What she says is just right: "That would not be a good idea for you, Kitty."

"But all my friends will fast, and I'll feel awful if I don't," says Kitty. "How about if I just eat lightly?"

"Nope," says Dr. Beth. Thank God.

In the end, the nagging sense of unease I have about Kitty's target weight is resolved in the best possible way: she begins to grow. By the end of September she's half an inch taller, which means her target weight goes up too. For the moment, anyway, we're back to straightforward refeeding. Spare no calories. Full steam ahead.

chapter seven

In Which We Take On the Insurance Company, and Lose

It wasn't simply that I chose not to eat; I was forbidden to.
Even thinking about forbidden foods brought punishment.
How dare you, this voice inside me would say. You greedy pig.

—ANONYMOUS ANOREXIA SUFFERER,
quoted in an online "thinspiration" video

Every family deals with anorexia in its own way, just as each family deals with—well—everything in its own way. One of the long-standing arguments for the screwed-up-psychodynamics theory is that by the time families get to treatment with an anorexic teen, they tend to look rather similar: resistant child, angry/worried/overwrought parents. Lots of tension, especially around meals.

Lots of frustration expressed on all sides, especially around meals and eating. Lots of criticism, also related to food and eating.

But this homogeneity is superficial. There's no better way to see what a family's really made of than to go through the process of refeeding. Anorexia and its horrors can highlight every little crack in the mirror of a family's self-image; it can also take a hammer and smash the whole thing to bits.

In their 1994 book *Helping Families Cope with Mental Illness*, psychiatrist Harriet P. Lefley and professor of social work Mona Wasow write:

> *Families [struggling with mental illness] . . . must deal with disrupted household routines; time investments in negotiating the mental health, housing, social security, and sometimes the criminal justice systems; impaired relations with an unsympathetic outside world; financial burdens; psychological and career impact on other household members, and difficulties in finding alternatives to hospitalization. . . . Families must learn to cope both with the patient's behavior and with their own reactions; to balance the patient's needs against those of other family members; to perceive when expectations are too high and too low; and to know how and when to set limits. They must deal with unwarranted guilt feelings, learn to handle their anger, tolerate the suffering of people they love.** *

I cringe at the label mental illness. Yet there's truth here. Janet Treasure, a psychiatrist at the Maudsley Hospital in London who

---

* Harriet P. Lefley and Mona Wasow, eds., *Helping Families Cope with Mental Illness* (Chur, Switzerland: Harwood Academic Publishers, 1994).

specializes in treating eating disorders, says that caring for a child with anorexia is just as stressful as caring for a child with schizophrenia or other serious psychiatric disorders.

I believe it. Taking care of Kitty has been the hardest thing our family has ever gone through. Harder than both girls' colicky infancies. Harder than my bout with postpartum depression after Emma was born. Harder than surviving the ups and downs of the freelance world, or the week Emma spent in the hospital with Kawasaki disease.

It's harder because the range of emotions is so much greater, and because the literal exigencies of this process are so complex. There's the denial at the start, followed by dawning comprehension, shock, and horror. There's shame and self-blame, guilt and doubt. There's anger and frustration. And then there's the sheer exhaustion, physical and emotional, of battling a force you can't physically touch and don't understand.

I know families who put a child into residential care because they need a break, and I don't think badly of them for it. "For a year and a half, anorexia consumed our whole family," one mother tells me. "We had a bit of breathing room when she was away. Time to think." I can't imagine sending Kitty away and being able to relax. But I also can't imagine dealing with the demon every day for a year and a half.

And then again, the fallout isn't entirely negative. There's a growing movement toward involving families more in the mental health treatment for their children, whether they're dealing with bipolar disorder, eating disorders, depression, or autism. The days of experts "fixing" a child—or attempting to "fix" the child—are over. This isn't to say that families should go it alone without professional help. But part of the pleasure as well as the burden of being a parent is engaging with your kids, no matter what's going on with them. Caring for Kitty now—despite the demon—feels more satisfying than watching her starve and not being able to do anything about it.

The events of the last few months have taught me a lot about our family's strengths and weaknesses. On the plus side, we've practiced attachment parenting from the start, and both Kitty and Emma seem to trust us. In times of trouble, they tend to turn toward the family rather than away. We know them, and each other, pretty well. We're a communicative family, and I think we do OK at expressing feelings and listening to one another. That was one of Hilde Bruch's critiques of "anorexigenic" families, families that produce (in her view) children who must resort to anorexia in order to express themselves. Bruch believed that families like ours shut down their children's true feelings and engender a kind of intimacy based on falseness and superficiality.

I'm ready to take the blame for anything I've done that might remotely have harmed either of my daughters. But on this point, I think Bruch was wrong. Both Kitty and Emma have been enthusiastically telling us how they feel and what they think from the time they learned to talk. For the most part, we've been listening. Not perfectly or all the time, but consistently and enough. More than many parents.

I sound defensive, I know. Like so many of my generation, I grew up in a household where children were supposed to be seen and not heard. My parents brushed off my feelings, telling me that if I just stopped thinking, everything would be all right. Maybe they didn't know what else to do; maybe that's what *their* parents had said to them. But I grew up determined to *listen* to my children, even if I didn't want to hear what they said.

Another of our family strengths is the fact that Jamie and I have very different temperaments. I'm quick—sometimes too quick—to take action and rush to conclusions; he's a think-about-it-from-all-angles kind of guy. I'm loquacious; he's more reserved. I like to—*need* to—talk things through, while he's more private. He processes situations slowly; I tend to leap first, ask questions later. I'm empathetic, sometimes overly so, while he maintains more of an emotional distance. At times these differences have proved problematic for us as a couple. But they've made us more resilient and resourceful parents.

For instance, when we started this process of refeeding Kitty—only seven weeks ago?—I researched anorexia, came up with the plan to do family-based treatment, got things rolling. Jamie was slower to come to terms with what was happening. He got frustrated and angry more often than I did. "Why can't she just eat?" he would ask me in the privacy of our room. "I just can't understand this disease." I didn't understand it either, but I didn't need to. I was focused on the next step, and the next. What did we have to do today? Tomorrow?

Now, however, we've switched roles. I'm the one who often loses patience first, who paces or frets when the demon emerges. I'm restless, always in motion; I clean and tidy obsessively and still have too much anxious energy at the end of the day. Jamie can sit with Kitty indefinitely as she weeps or rages. He's the calm and steady presence these days. On one of Kitty's bad nights not long ago, Jamie took her upstairs while I stood in the middle of the kitchen, overcome. I picked up a dirty plate, to load it into the dishwasher, and instead hurled it at the floor, where it smashed in a satisfying spray. It was so satisfying, in fact, that I broke three more. The only thing that stopped me was remembering that Kitty needs big plates. She'd freak out if I served her food on small plates, because it would look like she was eating so much more.

Jamie would never have broken plates on the kitchen floor.

On the other hand, he's less assertive about what and how much Kitty eats. He's hesitant to push for more and often holds back instead of actually dishing out the food and requiring her to eat. The concept of counting calories in either direction is strange to him; that and his natural reticence make him hesitant to plunge in.

If Kitty gets well, all the struggles and suffering will have had a purpose, and the hardest thing we've ever done will also become the most important and most satisfying thing. And if Kitty doesn't get well?

I can't, I really can't imagine that.

One morning in early October, when I collect the mail, I see an envelope from Kitty's school. I open it absently, thinking it's a progress report. Instead, Kitty's school picture stares up at me, taken the day she registered for school, nearly two months ago. It's shocking to come face-to-face once more with her huge, shadowed eyes, the exhaustion and despair written on her gaunt face. I slide the photo back into its envelope and bury it at the bottom of a dresser drawer. This is one school photo that's not going up on top of the piano.

But I'm also encouraged by this glimpse of how much progress Kitty's made in the last six weeks, progress it's hard to see on a day-to-day basis. Before anorexia, I tended to think about time in chunks—this week, this month, this season. This day. Now time has telescoped down into the intervals between Kitty's meals and snacks. Each takes on its own character and rituals. Midmorning snack, for instance, which these days often comprises several slices of toast with cream cheese. Kitty arranges them on a large plate and methodically cuts them into squares with a knife and fork. She spears them, one at a time, and slowly chews them. It takes her twenty minutes to consume three slices of toast. Which feels like a long time when I'm sitting at the table with her, buttering my own toast (I've learned the best way to keep her eating is to eat along with her), but which is only half the time it took her to eat the same snack two weeks ago.

Progress. I'll take it.

Each day has its rhythms, too. Eating seems easiest early in the day for Kitty, both physically and mentally. As the afternoon wears on she complains of stomachaches, indigestion. She bargains and pleads. The demon is far more apt to make an appearance between, say, five o'clock and bedtime than earlier in the day.

She's particularly resistant to the daily milk shake, asking why she can't have a smoothie instead. "Peaches and yogurt sounds delicious," she says, and I'm tempted, because it's such a pleasure to hear her say that any kind of food sounds delicious. But a peach smoothie is three hundred calories, tops, while a Häagen-Dazs milk shake is about a thousand. Kitty swears it's not the calories; she just prefers the taste of a smoothie, honest.

We tell her no, sorry, milk shakes are a must. I ask Dr. Beth to "prescribe" a daily milk shake, and that helps. A little.

For many kids, the descent into anorexia begins with restrictions that could be reasonable. Vegetarianism, for instance. I was a vegetarian for fifteen years; I'm certainly not wedded to the idea of eating meat. But I've heard too many stories about teens who go meatless (and often vegan) right as they're developing an eating disorder. Coincidence? I doubt it.

I'm convinced that Kitty's preference for smoothies over milk shakes comes from the anorexia, not from her natural tastes. But when, exactly, did the shift begin? I think again of the sixth-grade "wellness" class that inspired her to cut out desserts. I bet other kids in that class cut back on sugar for a day or two, but Kitty's probably the only one who stuck to her resolution for weeks and weeks. Was that the beginning?

Years ago, Walter Kaye discovered lower-than-normal levels of the neuropeptide galanin in the brains of people who'd recovered from anorexia. Galanin is a kind of amino acid made by the brain, and its role is to stimulate an appetite for fat. Low levels of galanin likely lead to an aversion to eating fat. I wonder how long the subjects in his study had been recovered. Six months? A year? Ten years? I wonder if levels of galanin ever recover. Or is it possible that people who go on to develop anorexia make less galanin in their brains from the start?

Will Kitty's tastes change back, once she's recovered? Will she ever dig in to a plate of sesame chicken with the same innocent pleasure? Will the eating disorder rob her of her original appetites? Or is that loss part of growing up in this culture—acquiring guilt and anxiety over every bite we put into our mouths? So many women eat the way Kitty does, avoiding fat and calories; do they do it out of a wish to be thin, or true preference?

A few years ago, researchers identified a fat receptor protein known as CD36, found on the surface of human cells and throughout the body, including on the surface of the tongue. Recent research done by Nada Abumrad, a professor of medicine at Washington University School of Medicine in St. Louis, suggests that some people may naturally have higher levels of CD36, which may lead to a taste (and even a craving) for fat. Maybe people like Kitty who develop anorexia are born with lower levels of CD36. Maybe the disease process of anorexia alters levels of these fat receptors. Or maybe anorexia masks Kitty's true tastes.

Whatever the cause, what I want to know is simple: Will she ever again eat the way she used to?

As October proceeds, Kitty goes to school most days, if not eagerly then at least willingly. She spends part of her sessions alone with Ms. Susan. She seems livelier, more interested in the rest of the world. She still complains about stomach pain every time she eats. But she does eat everything we put in front of her.

One day she comes home from school with news: one of her friends is joining the school gymnastics team, and she wants to join too.

I love seeing her excited about something. One of anorexia's most devastating consequences is isolation. But gymnastics? Everything in me says no. Gymnastics was part of how Kitty got where she is now—the emphasis on form and line and how she looked in a leotard. The hours of strenuous practice. The constantly sprained ankles and pulled tendons. The stress of competing in meets.

And something more: my sense that the coaches, however pleasant, however good with the girls, saw them as gymnasts rather than children and teens. What I mean is that they saw them as interchangeable elements of the team rather than as whole people. There wasn't much warmth, despite the fact that most of the girls, including Kitty, spent ten or fifteen hours a week at the gym, spent years training, practicing, and competing.

All last spring, as Kitty began to slide, her coaches never raised the issue of an eating disorder, not to her and not to us. When I called the head coach to tell her that Kitty was in the ICU, I asked if she'd ever known a gymnast with an eating disorder before.

"Of course," she said. "Unfortunately, it's fairly common."

"Did you know Kitty had a problem?"

The coach said cautiously, "I'm not surprised."

"Why didn't you say anything to us?"

Did they think we'd dismiss their concerns, get defensive? Did they worry that we'd pull Kitty off the team? Or maybe they didn't consider it a big deal. Maybe eating disorders are so common in gymnastics, they're not even worth discussing.

I really wanted to know. But the coach said nothing. "She won't be coming back," I said, and hung up.

"Just say you'll consider the high school team," begs Kitty now. That night Jamie and I talk it over, going around and around. My gut tells me it would be a mistake to say yes. She's still way too thin, and emotionally fragile. We haven't seen as much of the demon in the last ten days or so, but we have seen a lot of tears and anxiety. Jamie argues that maybe gymnastics will motivate her to recover. Plus, it's hard for him to say no to something she cares about so passionately. It's hard for me, too; I don't want to be the killjoy. Maybe I'm overreacting. Maybe I'm letting my own fear get in the way of her recovery. Or maybe the emperor truly has no clothes.

Eventually we come to a compromise: the high school season doesn't start for another month. We'll let Kitty go to the gym once or twice a week to practice with her friend, as long as she keeps gaining weight. And we'll ask Ms. Susan what she thinks of the idea.

Over the next few days, Kitty's anxiety becomes palpable. At dinner one night, the demon digs in its heels over a plate of chicken Parmesan. Not-Kitty pushes the plate away so it skids into the middle of the table, chicken and buttered noodles flying everywhere. "Why are you doing this to *me*?" she shouts, her voice rising to an eerie scream, dripping with rage and self-loathing. The demon's voice is relentless and reptilian, its vocabulary poorly developed but effective. I've heard this voice in my own head, though it's more like me talking to myself—a mean version of me, sometimes a downright cruel me, but still me. Whereas the demon in Kitty seems so *other*, so different from her.

This concept may not be as bizarre as it sounds. More than thirty years ago, psychologist Julian Jaynes suggested that consciousness is a function of neuroanatomy—specifically, of the corpus callosum, the fibrous band that connects the right and left hemispheres of the brain. [*] His theory was that thousands of years earlier, before the two halves of the brain evolved a connection, they functioned independently. He pointed to the many biblical and literary references to earlier peoples hearing voices or seeing visions, which they interpreted as messages or visitations from God or the gods. In fact, Jaynes believed, they were communications from the other side of the brain.

Maybe there's something to Jaynes's theory. In people with schizophrenia, who often hear voices, the corpus callosum is typically smaller and narrower than in those without schizophrenia. [†] I wonder if the demon might also be explained in terms of neuroanatomy. It certainly seems like Kitty's experiencing an altered state of consciousness when the demon is at its loudest. It would be fascinating to see what areas of her brain light up at those moments.

The next night we see a slightly different face of the demon.

---

[*]   Julian Jaynes, *The Origin of Consciousness in the Breakdown of the Bicameral Mind* (New York: Houghton Mifflin, 1976).

[†]   J. E. Downhill Jr. et al. "Shape and Size of the Corpus Callosum in Schizophrenia and Schizotypal Personality Disorder," *Schizophrenia Research* 42, no. 3 (2000): 193–208.

Kitty goes to her first gymnastics practice and comes home upset because she's lost her skills. She's thrust into that altered state where she spins around and around—in this case, over the fact that she's lost her conditioning, she can't do gymnastics, she's no good, it was the only thing she's looked forward to, it was the only thing she was good at and now she's not. On and on she worries and obsesses. This time, maybe because I'm paying attention, I hear the moment when her distress over gymnastics flips into anxiety about eating. She goes from back handsprings to breakfast in one breath, worrying that if I make her have cereal the next morning, the milk will upset her stomach and then how can she possibly drink a milk shake tomorrow because that will also upset her stomach.

"I'm serving eggs tomorrow morning for breakfast," I tell her, hoping to allay a bit of the anxiety.

"I'm afraid of eggs!"

"Why don't we talk about what's really upsetting you?" I say.

Out comes a gush of words. She says Jamie's mad at her because she needs him to sit in the kitchen with her at lunch, and now we all hate her, she's done nothing but cause us problems, she is stupid and fat and ugly. Oh, and why do I hate gymnastics when it means so much to her?

"I don't hate gymnastics," I tell her. "I hate the anorexia."

In a flash her tone turns from self-pity to rage. "Well, the anorexia is part of me," she says furiously, "and you hate the anorexia, so you must hate me!"

"No, I don't hate you, I love you," I say as calmly as I can, but it's like she's Helen Keller and I'm no miracle worker. She doesn't see me, she doesn't hear me, she's locked in, lost in her own terrible world, and I would give anything in my power right now to snap her out of it.

"Why do you hate gymnastics?" Kitty cries. Then she leaps from the table, grabs a pillow from the living room couch, and starts stuffing it into her mouth. I grab it and yank it out; I don't want her to make herself throw up.

"I don't hate gymnastics!" I yell. This is a lie. I do hate gymnastics, and gyms, and coaches, and leotards, and every last thing associated with the sport.

Kitty glares at me. "Gymnastics isn't to blame for my illness," she yells. "I am! I'm stupid and fat and ugly! I'm a horrible person and everyone hates me!" She hits herself in the head, hard, with her open palm. I grab for her arm but miss. She hits herself two or three more times before I get hold of her. She's much stronger than she looks—much stronger than she should be, and despite her frailty she could get away from me if she really tried. But she's not trying.

After what feels like an hour, but is probably three or four minutes, she collapses in my lap. "You want to take away the only thing I care about," she sobs.

"I don't," I say, stroking her hair. "But right now the most important thing is your health. That's what I care about."

When she is finally asleep, I sit in the living room, lights off, feeling like a failure. I said all the wrong things tonight. I made things worse, not better. I yelled at my daughter. I couldn't help her.

Now I understand what the Maudsley people mean when they say it's not helpful to cast blame. Blame makes you sit alone in the dark and feel like your skin has been flayed. Blame takes away your power and makes you into a small scolded child, when what you need is to get bigger. So big that you can reach down and swat away what plagues you. Big enough to stare down the demon no matter what form it takes.

It's self-indulgent to sit in the dark and feel sorry for myself when Kitty's the one who's got the demon inside her, who can't get away from it. Who feels, as she said tonight, like it's part of her, a notion that makes me sick to my stomach.

That's what most "experts" in this field seem to believe: once an anorexic, always an anorexic. That it's like alcoholism, something you have to manage, actively or not, for the rest of your life. The day she diagnosed Kitty, Dr. Beth told us Kitty would feel much better in a year. She said she knows people who had anorexia in their teens and twenties, got better, and left it behind. Who didn't feel it always lurking somewhere inside them. That was what I wanted to hear. But I wonder, now, if it was true.

I'm relieved when Kitty decides not to go to the gym later in the week. She says she's sore from the earlier practice. Instead, she volunteers with the Latin Club after school, and when I pick her up she's smiling. *This* is what I want for her—this kind of social and emotional connection with the rest of the world.

The next week the three of us meet with Ms. Susan to talk about the gymnastics team. I love this woman: after listening to Kitty talk about why she wants to join the team, she says, "There's a lot of stress that comes from competing. I don't think it's a good choice for you right now."

"But I love competing!" says Kitty. "It's not stressful!"

"You love it, but maybe it's not so good for you," says Ms. Susan. She points out that any sport where you have to be in a leotard or bathing suit isn't a good one for someone in recovery from an eating disorder, because it puts a lot of emphasis on the body, which is the last thing Kitty needs.

"You want me to sit around and do nothing!" Kitty snaps. I'm glad she's venting her frustration here instead of saving it for when we get home.

Ms. Susan talks about the need to find a sense of flow in life, about the intersection between what you're good at and what's good for you. She tells Kitty this is her chance to explore other interests, to think about what makes her feel calm and centered. She tells Jamie and me that our instincts are good and that we should trust them. I think I want to marry her. Or at least get this on tape so I can play it every day.

Ms. Susan speaks about using the anorexia as an opportunity for Kitty to go deeper, to look beyond the surface. For the rest of the session she talks to Kitty, and I really do wish I'd brought a tape recorder, because what she's saying feels true and right, and I don't think Kitty can hear it now. She's still too impaired, too much under the spell of the demon and its distractions. Daniel le Grange told me about a mentor of his who used to say that if you do intensive psychotherapy with someone with anorexia, you wind up with an insightful corpse, because without enough glucose the brain can't process or think properly.

Sitting in Ms. Susan's office, I can see that Kitty is on a path, as we all are, and that as much as I wish otherwise, anorexia is part of that path. I don't believe it has to define her, now or later. But I realize I've been thinking about the eating disorder as something to get through and leave behind, and it may not be that simple. Even if Kitty gains the weight, gets well, and moves forward, this will always be part of her history and her journey.

I can't see the future and I don't know what part anorexia will play in Kitty's life. If all goes well, if we're lucky, this will be it. But I also know from my own life how long-lasting the experiences of childhood and adolescence can be. The events of these years shape our lives in powerful ways. For better and for worse.

Anorexia will be one of those events for Kitty, even if she's never actively ill again. I think that's part of what Ms. Susan is getting at: Kitty will have to integrate the whole of this experience—all the feelings and events, the terrors and the lessons—into the rest of her life. It's a process that will take years.

After the session, when the decision about gymnastics has been made once and for all, Kitty *says* she's upset and angry. But she *seems* relieved. As if what she wanted all along was for us to simply say no. *Remember this,* I tell myself. Remember to look past what Kitty says and into what she feels. Because clearly, they're not always the same.

In the third week of October, Kitty gains another two pounds. She's now within eight or nine pounds of her target weight. Around the same time we also get the first bills for her treatment.

The state we live in does not have mental health parity, and the federal parity bill is still several years in the future. Which means that our insurance company covers only $1,800 a year of mental health expenses. Back in June, when I started looking for a therapist, I paged through our plan's provider list and wondered why I didn't see any mental health listings. It took a while to realize that they were listed under "behavioral health," a term that suggests that good mental health is merely a function of changing your behavior. It would be funny except for the deeper implication: that mental health is a matter of choice, and if you make the right choices, if you choose the "right" behaviors, presto! You'll be healthy.

This linguistic sleight of hand infuriates me, especially as I come to understand that we blew through our $1,800 "allowance" in the first month of Kitty's treatment.

Kitty's visits to Dr. Beth are covered—with the usual copay, of course—because she's a pediatrician, not a mental health provider. (Later I find out that Dr. Beth gets the same amount of money from the insurance company whether Kitty sees her once a year or every day, meaning that our weekly two-hour sessions are essentially freebies.) But everything else goes on the behavioral health balance sheet:

Weekly visits to Dr. Newbie
(whom the insurance company forced us to see): $220 each
Visit to a nutritionist: $100
The first therapist we tried: $150
Weekly sessions with Ms. Susan: $135 apiece

Apparently we've been on our own, financially speaking, since mid-August.

On the other hand, Kitty's five-day hospital admission, including two days in the ICU, was nearly all covered, all $12,000 of it. I suppose I should be grateful we don't have to pay for that, too, but I'm pissed. Because I really don't understand: Why is mental health care not covered the way physical health care is? We're creatures of body and breath, blood and bone, not disconnected minds in jars. The brain is an organ, same as the liver or the heart. Your heart takes care of getting oxygen to your cells; your brain takes care of how you move, feel, and think. When it comes down to it, what's the difference? Why does one bodily function deserve care while another doesn't?

Of course I know the real reason insurance companies don't cover mental health care: because they don't have to, at least in states like ours that don't have parity. Even in states like New Jersey, which has a mental health parity bill, insurance companies look for ways to weasel out of paying. They divide brain disorders into what they call biologically and nonbiologically based illnesses. In this ridiculously random categorization, schizophrenia is biologically based; eating disorders are not.*

The mental health profession unwittingly reinforces this kind of discrimination, especially when it comes to eating disorders, by maintaining that anorexia and bulimia are caused by psychodynamics. These "experts" who insist that eating disorders are psychological in origin play right into the hands of insurers, who use this to put eating disorders firmly into the "nonbiological" category.

Even if eating disorders *were* psychological, so what? They damage the body, sometimes beyond repair. They cause physical pain and suffering. People die from them. Do we somehow believe that people with mental illnesses deserve to suffer? That they don't deserve to get better? Because that's how we act. We act like it's OK for families whose children have autism or schizophrenia or anorexia to bankrupt themselves trying to get care for their kids or watch their children deteriorate because they can't afford treatment.

I plague our insurance company with complaints. I cry on the phone—out of frustration, mostly, but they don't know that. Eventually our behavioral health "consultant" grants us another $400—*$400*—for which I must kowtow at every opportunity.

---

* Each state sets its own laws about insurance, creating an inequitable and variable picture across the country. In 2008, a New Jersey woman named Dawn Beye sued her insurer for failing to cover her daughter's inpatient treatment for an eating disorder. That suit forced insurers in New Jersey to cover eating disorders as biologically based illnesses.

She now begins all our conversations by reminding me how generous the insurance company has been to give us this "extra" coverage, which frankly will take us through another week and a half and then dump us right back on the road to financial ruin. If Kitty winds up in an inpatient residential treatment center, then we're really screwed: one to two thousand dollars a day, of which our insurance will cover six days. *Six days*, out of, say, a forty-five-day admission. Thirty-nine uncovered days at the conservative estimate of $1,000 a day equals $39,000. Where would we get the money?

And we're in good shape compared with other families. I'm probably not going to lose my job because of Kitty's illness. If I worked elsewhere—at a law firm, say, or a 7-Eleven—I'd have been fired long ago or would have had my pay docked. We're lucky, relatively speaking, but the situation is still unfair. Besides, these months of guerrilla warfare against an enemy I can't see or understand have left me spoiling for a fight.

And so I make phone calls to the insurance commissioner, the president of our insurance company, our legislators, the local branch of the National Alliance for Mental Illness. I call Kitty Westin, who brought a lawsuit against her insurance company, Blue Cross Blue Shield, after her daughter, Anna, was denied treatment for an eating disorder and committed suicide. Westin settled out of court in June 2001, and part of the settlement was that BCBS in Minnesota must now cover eating disorders the way they cover broken legs and other undeniably physical ailments. After the settlement, several other big insurers in the state voluntarily changed their coverage too, afraid of similar suits they couldn't win. Westin, who created a foundation in her daughter's name, encourages me to push for legal action. "That's the only way things will ever change," she tells me.

The president of the insurance company doesn't return my calls, surprise surprise; neither do the legislators. I tell someone at the insurance commissioner's office about Kitty Westin, and he tells me we have no case. Minnesota has mental health parity laws; our state doesn't. Our insurers have fulfilled their legal obligations and then some. "So that's it?" I say. "We have no recourse? We're supposed to go home and be grateful we're not in debt for $100,000?" Pretty much.

The only thing left to do is file a grievance with the insurance company and ask for an appeals hearing, which they have to give us. Dr. Beth says she'll come to the hearing if she can. But the insurance company gives me only a few days' notice, and she can't rearrange her schedule.

So on the appointed afternoon I drive thirty miles to the company's brand-new world headquarters, which looks incongruous in its cornfield, on the outskirts of a small rural town. And at the appointed time I am ushered in to a conference room and seated at the head of a table full of people, none of whom introduce themselves. I've got ten minutes, so I talk fast. I roll out facts and statistics: average length of illness is five to seven years, average anorexia patient requires multiple hospital admissions, a third become chronic. I detail the high costs of treating chronic anorexia. I hand out copies of research studies and scientific papers, making the case that eating disorders are physiological, not psychological, and should be covered the way pneumonia and every other disease is covered. I recount an urgent, abbreviated version of Kitty's illness. I describe family-based treatment, contrast the thousands of dollars spent on Kitty's hospital stay with the relatively low cost of FBT, and suggest that covering a few thousand dollars of therapy now will save them money in the long run.

Once or twice I look up from my notes and see people nodding thoughtfully. I have no idea who they are. I've been told there are several doctors in the room, a "patient advocate" (though as far as I can see no one at this table is on my side), some administrators, and I don't know who else. I finish in exactly ten minutes, because an impatient-looking man near the head of the table is looking at his watch and I have the feeling he would take great pleasure in cutting me off midsentence. I stand up, collect my papers, thank the roomful of anonymous faces, and walk out on trembling legs.

The next morning—*fifteen hours later*—I get a letter from the insurance company saying they have "carefully considered" our case and have denied our appeal. Which means that the denial letter went out within an hour of my leaving the office yesterday. Considering that someone had to fill in the blanks on the form letter, print it, sign it, and mail it, that letter must have been ready to go before I walked into the room.

For all I know, that room was full of actors who populate grievance hearings for a living.

Either way, the whole thing was a sham. An exercise in futility. We'll find ways to pay for Kitty's treatment. But what about the families who can't, whose children go untreated because they can't take time off work to refeed them, whose insurance doesn't cover other treatments? Or the families who bankrupt themselves paying for two or three or five stints in residential treatment, who whip through their retirement funds, who take out second and third mortgages on their houses, who run up their credit cards and wind up so deep in debt it would take several lifetimes to dig out?

I don't have an answer. But I know right from wrong. And this is wrong. Very wrong.

{ chapter eight }

Watching Kitty

I keep both eyes on my man. The basket hasn't moved on me yet.

—JULIUS ERVING

In some ways, Halloween is the perfect holiday for anorexia: it's about collecting candy but not necessarily eating it. After the ritual acquiring of the candy, the traditional counting, organizing, and trading of the candy are an obsessive's dream come true: arranging seventy-five or a hundred candy bars and bags in concentric semicircles, their cellophane wrappers festive against the dark wood of the living room floor. Long before anorexia, Kitty and her friends would set out their candy according to their own mysterious hierarchies. They would line up the Snickers bars, the Milky Ways, the Oh Henry!s and Baby Ruths, the Skittles and packages of jelly beans, the little red boxes of raisins (always at the bottom of the heap). They'd pick them up, put them down, rearrange them, square them into neat rows. They'd bargain with one another, swapping the rejects for their favorites. Then they'd eat one or two and dump the rest back into a pillowcase or bag, to be stored in a kitchen cabinet, picked through over the next few months, and finally, a month before next Halloween, tossed out.

I wish Kitty wanted to go trick or treating, but I'm not surprised that she doesn't. I *am* surprised when she throws herself into putting a costume together with Emma, who wants to be Anne Boleyn. The girls spend all afternoon in Kitty's room with the door closed, improvising from the dress-up box, and emerge before dinner laughing and excited, with Emma in a long green cape and flowing white gown, her hazel eyes lined with dark pencil, her lips a glowing red. Her whole face shining with the pleasure of having her big sister pay attention to her.

And I'm even more surprised when Kitty announces that she wants to take Emma around. The three of us go out, leaving Jamie behind to hand out candy. Kitty walks behind Emma, holding up her trailing cape, encouraging her to tackle another block, and another. When we spot a couple of her friends, Kitty runs across the street to talk to them. "Why don't you walk around with them?" I ask. "Emma and I will be all right on our own."

"But I want to stay with you!" says Kitty, looping her arm through Emma's. This isn't the clinginess of anxiety or terror; it's the pleasure of being with people you love. We cover the last block arm in arm, like Dorothy et al. in *The Wizard of Oz*, and I feel a wave of gratitude. An hour from now Kitty might be sobbing on the couch, or the demon might be raging through our house. Or the rest of the night could be just as magical as this.

Anorexia is teaching me to live in the moment. When the moment is awful, as so many moments have been over the last months, I can't imagine how we're going to survive it. When the moment is sweet, like this one, there's nowhere else I'd rather be.

When we get home, Kitty asks if she can take over candy duty. I hear her at the door, talking to the children who ring our bell. "You must be Madeline!" she cries to a small girl from down the street. "What a great costume!" *This* is the Kitty we've known for fourteen years—outgoing, sparkling, kind. I haven't realized until now how much I've missed this side of Kitty, the part of her that's so good at reaching beyond the borders of her self.

Later, she sits on the floor with Emma and inspects each piece of candy with her, turning it over in her hand, setting it neatly into its appointed spot. She's tender with Emma, and attentive. The two girls lean their heads together—one blond and curly, one dark and straight. Kitty pulls her curls up into a ponytail and whispers in her sister's ear. Emma bursts out laughing, her face open and vulnerable. Despite everything that's happened, she trusts her sister, a fact that astonishes and humbles me.

That night, tucked into bed, Emma says, "I like my hair, my body, and my feet."

"Good," I say. "Because you're perfect just the way you are."

"But what if I had feetalimia?" she continues. "What if I thought my feet were too fat, and I cut off all the circulation to them, on purpose?"

I look at her in the light from the hallway. Eyeliner smudges each cheek, like the dark half-circles football players draw under their eyes. I worry about Emma, who doesn't say nearly as much as she feels.

"What if you did?" I say. "What do you think?"

She slides one leg out from under her blue-and-green biscuit quilt and considers it, turning it this way and that, looking at her pale toes, the slight swell of her calf muscle. Finally she says, "I think that would be ridiculous."

"Me, too," I say. I tuck her leg back under the quilt, smooth the fabric under her chin, kiss the spot on her forehead where her hairline dips into a heart shape. Emma has always had this knack of holding a mirror up to reality, showing us her own quirky, frank take on whatever's going on. She's only ten, an age when children are still literal thinkers and trauma can overwhelm their psyches. Plus, I haven't forgotten that Emma's more vulnerable to developing an eating disorder herself. So I'm not just amused by her analogy; I'm relieved. She gets it, and maybe that will keep her safe on both fronts.

Of course, I thought Kitty would be safe because she'd written a research paper on eating disorders, because she knew so much about them. Now I wonder if *knowing* can actually trigger anorexia in kids who are susceptible.

Keep Emma safe, I think—to myself, to the universe, to anyone who's listening.

From the beginning of this refeeding process, Jamie and I have been watching Kitty, day and night. We watch every bite she puts in her mouth and every bite she doesn't. We watch her in the bathroom after meals—that is, we require that the door be partly open if she uses the bathroom, and one of us hovers nearby, listening. We watch to make sure she eats, she drinks, she doesn't hurt herself. We check on her to make sure she's not exercising at 2:00 A.M. We watch because we've learned the hard way that the demon will exploit any moment of inattention or trust, like that day in the park when Kitty tried to throw away part of her protein bar. I'd guess there have been other moments we've missed.

On the whole, Kitty accepts our watching. On some level she seems to realize she's not capable of making good decisions, at least when it comes to food and eating. On some level, she still trusts us. Not just trusts us but *relies* on us to keep her safe.

One of the biggest criticisms of the Maudsley approach is that no teenager would willingly give up so much autonomy (or should be asked to), especially to her parents. And if you believe that anorexia is a choice, the last resort of a growing child who's been denied self-determination, then I can see how the refeeding process might seem like a further violation of a child's independence.

But I think this perspective fundamentally misunderstands the nature of anorexia. When I observe Kitty at the table I don't see a child who's expressing herself, who's exerting control over her environment. I see a child who's the prisoner of compulsions she doesn't understand—that no one understands—and that she can't control. I see a terrified hostage yearning for rescue. And there's no cavalry on the way. Only us.

If I need persuading (which I don't), the gradual shift that starts at the end of October—about three months into refeeding—convinces me we're on the right track. As eating has become easier for Kitty, Jamie and I have backed off a little in our scrutiny. If I'm sitting with her at the table, I might get up and stir something on the stove, leaving Kitty at the table for five or ten seconds. I'm still in the room with her, just not at the table. But one afternoon during snack, when I get up to get the newspaper from the living room, Kitty puts down her fork.

"You left," she says when I reappear. "Where'd you go?"

"I had to get something. I'm back now."

Kitty picks up her fork and resumes eating, turning the pages of her book with an apparent lack of concern. We say no more about it. But the next day I re-create the experiment. At breakfast I dish up her oatmeal, wait for her to stir in brown sugar and whole milk. After the first few bites I get up and begin rummaging in a cabinet, my back to Kitty for a few seconds. When I turn around, I see that she has indeed stopped eating. I give her an oblivious smile. "How're you doing?" I ask cheerfully, and she starts eating again.

Later that day, I pick Kitty up at school for an appointment with Dr. Newbie. After she climbs into the front seat, I hand her a protein bar. "You'll have to eat your snack in the car today," I say.

She tears open the paper wrapper and takes a bite as I pull into traffic. She chews for a second, swallows, and says, "You're watching me, right? I can't eat if you're not watching. You can see me out of the corner of your eye, right?"

"Yep," I say, my eyes firmly on the road. "I see every bite you take."

Over the next few days Kitty asks again and again whether we're watching, and I know what she's really asking: *You're making me eat this, right? I don't have any choice here. Do I?* She needs us to take the responsibility for her eating because the compulsion to *not* eat is still so powerful.

Which is why, I realize, more traditional treatments are not just ineffective—they're cruel. It's cruel to insist that a child in the throes of anorexia "take responsibility" for eating, and absurd to suggest, as many therapists and treatment programs do, that unless a person with anorexia "chooses" to eat, she can't recover. Kitty's reactions make sense to me now. What wouldn't make sense would be to turn my back on her. To have her life hinge on her doing something she cannot do.

Because I believe this with all my heart: *Kitty cannot choose to eat.* Not yet. The time will come when she'll have to do that, of course, when she'll have to maintain her weight and her health herself. And when that time does come, I think we'll know. She'll tell us, just as she's telling us now that she's not ready to go it alone. Just as she told us when she was ready to go away to camp, stay home alone, stay up a half hour later. All along she's been telling us, through words and action, what she needs in order to grow and become more independent. All we have to do is listen.

Kitty's spirits have improved as her weight has inched up. And I've learned I can occasionally head off the demon by refusing to acknowledge it. On Halloween night, for instance, Kitty asks if she needs a snack. She hasn't collected or eaten any candy. I say yes, she needs to eat two ice cream sandwiches. "Do I really need two?" she asks. "My stomach hurts." I hear the beginning of an edge in her voice.

"Yep, that's what you need," I say matter-of-factly, and turn away deliberately to talk to Emma. Kitty eats the ice cream sandwiches, and the moment passes.

This strategy doesn't always work. A few nights later Kitty erupts into a sudden rage when I bring out her bedtime snack. The plate flies across the room and breaks, a shower of yellow shards. When I jump up to get the broom and dustpan, she bolts out the front door, yelling, "I'm going to run away!" Jamie finds her down the block, on her bike in the dark, and half carries her back to the house, bike helmet and all.

I feel blindsided and stupid, shocked all over again. It's been a few weeks since we've seen the demon, and already I'm forgetting its claws and fangs, its flicking tongue. How quickly the face of anorexia came to seem normal to us, and now I see that the opposite is true too: on a superficial level, at least, we're slipping back into something resembling ordinary life. Not our old life, which was more fragmented, less organized, more spontaneous. The new normal includes shopping, cooking, and supervising three meals and two snacks a day for Kitty. It includes more time spent as a family, sitting at the table or in the living room, driving to doctors' appointments, playing board games, talking before bed. It has its pleasures, this new life. Kitty taking Emma trick or treating, for example— that's something she wouldn't have been willing to do last year, or able to do six months ago. Last year, of course, Kitty was hanging with her own friends; next year, I hope, she'll be doing that again.

I'm puzzled by the fact that the demon is still so close to the surface. When Kitty doesn't get quite enough to eat, or when she goes more than a couple of hours during the day without eating, her mood plummets predictably. But she's nowhere near as thin as she was three months ago; in fact, her weight is now within a normal range for her height. That is, someone her height who had never had anorexia might be healthy at this weight, though clearly, Kitty has a ways to go. She's been eating three thousand to thirty-five hundred calories a day for weeks now, but both her physical and emotional well-being are still intensely frangible. She has no equilibrium point; she swings from feeling good to falling apart with frightening fluidity.

When we started refeeding Kitty, Jamie and I told each other and her that food was her medicine, that it would cure her, body and mind. I still believe that. But I thought we'd see change more quickly. Before we began, Kitty ate very little, but she was chipper, competent, tireless. She practiced three hours a day at the gym, and, as we later discovered, spent hours at night in her room on conditioning exercises. I understand now that hyperactivity is a hallmark of anorexia; back then, I thought Kitty's stamina meant that she *was* getting enough food. Some people need less sleep than others; I wondered if some people need less food.

I can see now how my own attitudes toward food and eating blinded me to reality. I am the miser who expects his dog to not just survive but thrive on little or no food, only in my case it's not cheapness that informs this skewed perspective but my own ambivalence about food. I can't remember a time when I didn't feel conflicted about eating. The message I've gotten all my life, from a variety of sources, is that food is dangerous. *Enjoying* food is dangerous, because it might lead to eating too much, and the goal is to eat as little as possible and still survive. Because the worst thing you can be in this culture is fat.

Like every parent, I want to save my children from pain and suffering, especially the pain and suffering I've experienced. So when Kitty announced she would eat no more desserts, I thought *Good for her* instead of *What's going on?*

I go back to Ancel Keys's Minnesota Experiment, this time focusing on what happened to the volunteers toward the end of the study, after twelve weeks of refeeding—about where we are now with Kitty. The volunteers still struggled with stomach pains and constipation, exhaustion and swelling. They ate vast quantities of food—five or six thousand calories a day—but most continued to feel tired and weak. "We were rather surprised," wrote Keys, "at the slow rate of overall recovery, including recovery in the psychological aspects." [*]

Researchers interviewed the men one more time, eight months after they'd started refeeding. Most had gained back all the weight lost and were more or less back to normal. Keys commented that both psychological and physical recovery from starvation "required many months of unlimited good diet." [†]

I feel a little better knowing that the volunteers recovered—eventually. That the punishment starvation inflicts on a human being, body and mind, can be overcome in time. More time than I'd like, maybe, but it can happen. It will happen.

Meanwhile, because of Kitty's continuing stomach pain, Dr. Beth schedules her for an endoscopy and a colonoscopy, to make sure there's no underlying disease. The worst part about the test is that Kitty has to fast for about thirty hours. Dr. Beth agrees that the fasting is unfortunate, but says we have to make sure there's nothing else going on. "I had a nineteen-year-old patient with stomach pain once who turned out to have colon cancer," she tells me. "Not that I think Kitty has cancer. But we need to rule it out."

The tests are scheduled for a Monday, so Kitty doesn't have to fast on a schoolday. Not that she would mind. She says she likes the way fasting makes her feel: clean and light and virtuous. She says she hasn't felt hungry in many months, since long before the diagnosis. As Sunday wears on, her mood improves; mine deteriorates. After everything we've been through, I can hardly bear to watch her not eat. It feels wrong on every level.

The next morning, the nurses let me hold her hand as they insert

---

[*]   Keys et al., 917.

[†]   Ibid., 906.

the IV and start the anesthesia. "You know," she murmurs sleepily, "it's going to be hard for me to say I'm hungry when we get home."

I hear what she's saying under the words: *I will be hungry. I am hungry. Please feed me. Please take care of me.*

I smile. "No problem," I say. By the time they wheel her out of the waiting room, she's asleep. And thankfully, the tests show no cancer, no Crohn's disease. Nothing to worry about. I never thought I'd be grateful that my daughter "only" has anorexia.

When we get home I make Kitty a coffee milk shake, put on a Harry Potter movie, and sit beside her on the couch as she drinks. At her weigh-in later that week, she's down a pound—not surprising, given the long fast, but still upsetting. Her progress has been meandering—up two pounds, down one, stay the same for two weeks, up a quarter. It's taken three months for her to gain fourteen pounds, but five of those came in the first three weeks. So she's basically gained three pounds a month. At our appointment later that week, Dr. Beth says she'd rather have Kitty gain the weight slowly; she says we shouldn't worry, things are moving in the right direction. We have to be patient but steady, keep doing what we're doing.

"Well, I hate what you're doing," Kitty interrupts her. She folds her arms. "I don't *want* to gain weight," she says.

I glance at Dr. Beth, who after all spends most of her professional life dealing with adolescents. Her face is watchful, nothing more. "I know," she says to Kitty, then turns to me and asks, "Any questions?"

I do have questions, actually, but I already know they have no answers. How do we tell the difference between anorexia and, say, ordinary teenage behaviors? The full-fledged demon is unmistakable. But what about moments like these, which we see with increasing regularity? Maybe they're like the rumblings of a dormant volcano that's about to erupt again. Or maybe they represent emotional progress. I've noticed how anorexia and the refeeding process sent Kitty back to infancy in many ways. As she recovers, she seems to be moving forward, recapitulating the developmental stages of childhood. Right now it feels like she's hit age two.

I remember Kitty in the hospital, too weak to sit up, let alone resist, and take this stubborn crankiness as a good sign. Maybe we can teach Kitty to stick up for herself, stop worrying about pleasing others and figure out what makes her happy. Maybe, in an odd way, anorexia's giving us all a second chance. And what parent hasn't wished for a do-over somewhere along the line?

Over the next few weeks, Kitty's weight gain stalls, and her mood continues to deteriorate. Dr. Beth suggests cutting out dairy to see if that helps with the stomachaches. The trouble is, it's awfully hard to get in enough calories without the daily milk shake, the lasagna, the macaroni and cheese. And it feels like the very act of restricting anything—even for medical reasons—reinforces the anorexia.

I realize how much ground Kitty's lost one afternoon in mid-November, when she appears in the kitchen to ask what she's having for her bedtime snack, six hours from now. "Why do I need to eat anything for snack?" wheedles Not-Kitty. "I ate so much today already. I feel really fat. I think I'll skip dinner and snack tonight."

Standing at the sink, wrist-deep in soapy water, I say nothing. That's the best way to deal with the demon.

"I won't eat," persists Not-Kitty. "You can't make me."

No, I can't, I think. I can't physically put food in her mouth, make her chew and swallow. I wouldn't do that even if I could.

"No school until you eat," I say, not turning around.

"I don't care," says Not-Kitty. This shocks me as much as anything. Part of her goal of going to Columbia and then to law school has been not missing any school—and, of course, excelling at it.

It would be best to say nothing. Best not to argue with the demon. But I open my mouth and out come words I haven't planned on saying: "You'll never get to be a lawyer if you die from anorexia."

I think this is the first time I've mentioned the idea of dying from anorexia to Kitty. No, I know it's the first time, because I've been careful to stay positive and hopeful. *She's* said the word a few times, as in "I'm going to die if I have to eat one more bite!" And of course there was the night she said at the dinner table that she wanted to go to sleep and never wake up. But this feels different. Something about the juxtaposition of the illness with Kitty's hopes for the future strikes home, for her as well as for me.

For the rest of the day, Kitty eats. Quietly. Unhappily. More slowly than usual. But she eats, afternoon snack, dinner, and bedtime snack. And no more is said, for the moment, about not going to school.

The next afternoon is, if anything, worse. The demon takes over at the lunch table and the rest of the day is a disaster. Trying to figure out why, I sit down and calculate calories—something I've stopped doing, thinking we had the hang of it. I write down as much as I can remember of her recent meals, ingredients and quantities, and realize, in horror, that for the last week, she's been taking in fewer calories than I thought—more like twenty-five hundred a day than three thousand. I can't believe we let this happen. No wonder she's been antsy and anxious; twenty-five hundred calories is nowhere near enough for her right now.

Then another thought strikes me: I wonder if she's grown? Or is growing? At her next weigh-in I ask the nurse to measure her, and sure enough, Kitty's nearly an inch taller. Now the whole picture begins to make sense: just as Kitty's body began to need more calories, for growing, we inadvertently cut back. Those two processes, plus the physiological and psychological effects of restricting, combined to strengthen the demon within her.

Ms. Susan agrees. She says restricting—even the tiniest amount—quickly takes on a life of its own for someone with anorexia. Starvation over a period of time creates actual neural pathways in the brain. And now even the most minor echo of starvation—a slight reduction in calories, nowhere near the danger zone—reactivates those pathways, brings back the emotions and obsessions of true starvation. The reason lies in the brain's malleability—what researchers are beginning to refer to as its neuroplasticity. Psychiatrist Norman Doidge, author of the book *The Brain That Changes Itself*, compares the brain to a snow-covered sledding hill. Because snow is soft and easily shaped, the first time you sled down the hill, your sled carves a path. Each time you go down after that, your sled tends to run along the same path, digging it deeper and making it harder to steer your sled elsewhere. It's the softness of the snow, ironically, that creates a rigid, well-defined pathway. Doidge argues that it's the same with the brain: the brain's very flexibility, its ability to create new neural pathways, also makes those pathways hard to break away from. Each time Kitty restricts, no matter how slightly, it's as if she's sledding down that hill again, wearing the old groove ever deeper in the snow.

Neuroplasticity doesn't cause eating disorders, of course; it's just part of what makes them so tough to overcome. In Kitty's case, I suspect a confluence of events last spring pushed her into full-blown anorexia: a growth spurt, restricting, and a prepubertal hormonal shift. And it's going to take time, and many thousands of calories, to reverse.

In any case, I know what we have to do, and I know, now, that we can do it. We push Kitty's calories back up to three thousand a day. I buy a big bottle of Maalox and start making milk shakes again. We pull out the Ensure Plus from the basement. We carry on.

By Thanksgiving week, Kitty's gained two more pounds. She's calmer, though still fragile, still quick to fall apart. Dr. Beth wonders if Kitty could use some individual therapy right now. I think it's a good idea. Of course we've used up all our mental health benefits. But the amazing Ms. Susan calls our insurer and extracts extra "transitional" funding, enough to cover about six weeks of individual therapy. All I have to do, she says, is call Melanie, our behavioral health "consultant," and make nice.

I very nearly don't manage that, because the first thing Melanie says when I call is "You've used up all your benefits," making it sound like I'm the grasshopper from Aesop's Fables, blithely romping through summer, failing to prepare for the winter ahead. Her attitude reminds me of the *last* round of health-care debates, when the buzzword was *choice*, as in "Make wise choices about how to spend your health-care dollars." Whatever the hell *that's* supposed to mean. Should we *choose* not to treat Kitty's anorexia because, gosh, we'd use up too many health-care dollars? Or should we choose instead to not have Emma's broken arm set? Or maybe we're supposed to choose not to get sick or hurt at all.

I know I shouldn't argue with Melanie. I know she is the gatekeeper and I need to have a good relationship with her. "If my daughter had diabetes, you wouldn't just cut off the benefits part-way through her treatment," I say.

"Your employer chooses the plan," she says. "It's not our fault if your employer buys a health plan that doesn't cover this."

True enough. But I work for a small company that doesn't have to give me *any* health insurance. I'm lucky to have this plan—and I didn't get any choice about it. Jamie and I work hard, pay our bills on time, and pay plenty for our insurance, such as it is. Our daughter is sick, with an illness neither she nor we caused, an illness that requires care. An illness with a high mortality rate. An illness that could take her sanity and her life.

What we need is help. What we get is the message that we're unreasonable, freeloaders or criminals, or worse: negligent parents who are to blame—and therefore must pay the price—for our daughter's illness.

In the end, despite my argumentative comments, we are granted six more weeks of therapy with Ms. Susan. It won't be enough. It won't even be close to enough. But it's the best offer we're going to get from the insurance company. We'll take it. But I refuse to be grateful.

chapter nine

Crusts and Crumbs

Hunger is a country we enter every day,
like a commuter across a friendly border.

—SHARMAN APT RUSSELL, *Hunger: An Unnatural History*

Years ago, when I was pregnant with Emma, I had to decide whether to have amniocentesis. I was old enough that there was a fair risk of Down syndrome and other chromosomal abnormalities, but I was pretty sure I wouldn't have an abortion, no matter what I learned about the child I was carrying. I wasn't keen on the idea of the test, which in itself can cause miscarriage. But my obstetrician encouraged me to have it.

"It gives you time," she said. "Time to let go of the fantasy of the perfect child. You have to grieve the child you're not going to have before you can embrace the one you are having."

I had the amnio, which was normal. And I've thought of her analogy often these last few months. Jamie and I have had to let go of a certain image of Kitty in order to focus on how she is right now. I think about parents whose children have cystic fibrosis, spina bifida, sickle cell anemia, any of the thousands of ailments that will never get better and will never go away, that make a child's life painful, one way or another, and may ultimately end it. We're lucky, really; Kitty has a chance to make it through, to come out whole on the other side.

But that doesn't make things any easier. The obstetrician was right; this is a process of grieving and letting go, acknowledging that the fantasy not only isn't happening right now but will never happen. Intellectually, I get it; emotionally, I'm lagging way behind.

I can see, now, that I've been going through Elizabeth Kübler-Ross's famous stages of grief. *Denial:* then, when I thought Kitty couldn't have anorexia because she hadn't lost a lot of weight, when I tried to talk the doctor out of transferring her to the ICU; and now, when I believe (because I want to) that Kitty's fine and that we can slack off on watching, observing, recalculating. *Anger:* breaking a stack of dishes on the kitchen floor; pulling out clumps of my own hair, as I've done more than once; yelling, when I know it's not her fault, when I know that she's in pain. *Bargaining:* If I give up my life, stop seeing friends, do nothing but shop and cook and sit with her, she'll be all right. *Depression:* not sleeping; crying a lot; feelings of despair, guilt, hopelessness. *Acceptance:* nope; I'm not accepting this; not yet; maybe not ever.

·　　　·　　　·

Two days before Thanksgiving, Kitty comes home from Ms. Susan's lunch group distraught. She tells me she's figured out what "the problem" is. "I'm doing this for you, not for myself," she says.

"Doing what? Going to lunch group?"

"No," she says irritably. "Eating. I'm eating what you tell me to. So I'm doing it for you, not for me."

Slowly the story emerges. She's pretty much the only one in the group whose family is doing FBT; many of the other girls have been in and out of hospitals and residential treatment centers for years. But all Kitty can see is that they're somehow "doing better" than she is. "They seem like they're so much more insightful than I am, Mom," she says.

Ms. Susan warned me that competitiveness can be a problem in eating-disorders groups. I'm beginning to see what she meant.

"So what are you saying, Kitty?" I ask her. "You *want* to go away?"

In fact, that is what she's saying. I can't help but wonder if this has something to do with her weigh-in today. She weighs more than she's ever weighed in her life by about ten pounds. In fact, she's only about four pounds under her target weight. Could this all be a ploy by the demon, a last-ditch attempt to claw its way back?

"Kitty, you're doing so well right now," I begin. "It seems to me that we'd be going backward to send you away now. We've got momentum going. Why would you want to throw that away?"

"I knew you'd think it was just the eating disorder talking!" she cries. "But it's not!" She pauses, then says, "Maybe I would lose a little weight at first if I went away. But I'd make so much emotional progress!"

We are talking to the demon, and it's scary, because on one level what Kitty says makes perfect sense. She is a people pleaser, eager to do what other people want her to do. But real emotional insight and growth typically comes *after* physical recovery. That's how FBT is structured, and for good reason. Starving doesn't make you more insightful; it just makes you sicker. The demon is so very clever, taking a little bit of truth and twisting it into a lie. Right now, Kitty *does* have to do what we want her to, at least when it comes to eating. There will be plenty of time for her to become more independent later, when she's recovered.

When Kitty realizes that we're not going to send her away, she switches gears. If we're not going to send her to a treatment center, maybe we can support her emotional growth here at home.

"We've been trying to do that all along," I say carefully. "What do you have in mind?"

What she has in mind, it turns out, is to skip our traditional Thanksgiving celebration with friends, stay home, and eat dinner—alone—with another girl from the lunch group, Shelly, who's just been released from the hospital.

I stare at Kitty. I want to say, *Where the hell did this come from?* Except I know where it came from—the demon, that's where. The demon, who wants Kitty on the outside looking in. The demon, who will take every chance we give it to starve our daughter.

I get that this is a tough holiday for anyone struggling with an eating disorder. All the more reason to spend it with the people who love you, who care about you, who want you to get through it and get over it. And I get that teenagers crave autonomy. But starving at home with another anorexic for Thanksgiving? That's the illness speaking. Not my daughter.

Anorexia wants Kitty to be as separate as possible from us, because we are its enemy. Anorexia wants Kitty to be isolated, with only the company of others who are ill, so that it can continue to sink its claws and teeth into her. I look my daughter in the eye and say, "Sorry, but you have to come with us to Thanksgiving dinner." She storms off, crying, and after a while Jamie goes in to sit with her, to try to calm her so she can eat the rest of her food and go to bed.

She's grumpy with us for the next few days, worrying about Thanksgiving. The day itself, at the home of our close friends Harry and Lisa, goes smoothly. Kitty sits next to me at the table and eats what I serve her—turkey and cranberry sauce and roast potatoes, bread and butter, pumpkin pie. After dinner she wants to go home. I tell her we're not quite ready, that she can take her book upstairs to a quiet room if she wants to get away from the hubbub of nine children, six adults, and several dogs. But instead of going upstairs, she follows me around the house, standing so close to me that I can feel her breath on the back of my neck. I try to draw her into the conversation, but she stays quiet. I try to ignore her, but I can feel her silent pressure bearing down, and it irritates me. At one point I tell her she's standing way too close, and could she please go sit on the couch? When I turn back to the conversation, she takes hold of my upper arm and pinches, hard.

"Ow!" I cry, and look at her. Not-Kitty looks back at me through a studiously neutral mask.

"I'm sorry," she says. "I didn't mean to do that."

I rub my arm and stare into my daughter's face. Kitty didn't mean to do that. The demon did.

We go home.

The next week, Jamie and I accompany Kitty into the session with Ms. Susan. It's time for a family check-in. In traditional FBT,

Emma would come to the session too. But Emma begs not to go, and I don't have the heart to force her.

Kitty is eloquent on the subject of wanting to take control of her eating once more. She tells Ms. Susan what she's told us: that she feels her recovery won't count somehow unless she does it herself and not us, that she wants to go away to a treatment center, that she wants us to back off.

Ms. Susan turns to us. "Are you ready to give Kitty back control over her eating?" She barely gets the words out when both Jamie and I say no, she's nowhere near ready. Susan turns back to Kitty.

"Your parents say you're not ready," she says. "You're still under your target weight. I think if you want some control back we should talk about very small steps, and make sure they're working before we move on to anything more."

Together she and Kitty come up with an idea for a first step in that direction: Kitty might eat lunch at school once a week instead of coming home. "Could you arrange to eat with someone specific?" asks Susan. "What about the guys?" Kitty's been spending time with a couple of guy friends, Martin and Garth. I find it interesting that as she recovers she chooses to hang with them more than with female friends. Neither Jamie nor I picks up any sexual tension; it's more camaraderie, doing things together. Friendships among girls at this age tend to focus on talking about feelings and emotional interactions and, increasingly, boyfriends. Kitty's avoiding those kinds of conversations right now. She's not really in a place where she wants to spill her guts to other people, and I can't blame her. Plus, there's the added bonus of how much high school guys eat.

We agree that Kitty can try eating lunch at school once a week with Martin and Garth. "Or I could eat with Shelly," she says.

"If Shelly even eats lunch," says Ms. Susan conversationally.

"Eat with the guys," I say firmly.

Then Jamie, who tends to be quiet in therapy sessions, starts to talk. As the fall has progressed, I've been spending more time at work, and he's been in the trenches with Kitty. He's the one who makes the peanut butter and honey sandwiches at lunch; he makes the daily milk shake, and sits with her as she drinks it. Now he brings up something that's been troubling him for weeks: Kitty's tendency to leave food on her plate. Sometimes it's sandwich crusts; sometimes, though, she crumbles food and spreads it around on the plate.

"It upsets me when you do that," he says, and Kitty immediately bursts into tears, burying her face in one of Ms. Susan's overstuffed pillows. "It would be a lot easier for me to say nothing," he continues. "But I'm trying to take care of you, and I need to bring up the difficult things."

I am moved, as I have been so often this fall, by his willingness to not just show up but stand up for our daughter. It's hard to say these things to Kitty right now. It's hard to watch her fall apart. I think it's especially hard for him, because he comes from a family of enablers and avoiders. He's the kind of man who doesn't seek out conflict. Our roles here have flipped; I'm usually the confrontational one, always up for challenging the status quo. But I find it so painful to articulate what I'm seeing these days that I've retreated into silence more and more. Kitty's lucky to have him for a parent, though she may not feel that way right now, or for the foreseeable future. About either of us.

The day after our session, Kitty seems much calmer, more relaxed. After school she works on a jigsaw puzzle with Emma and me, though she says she doesn't like puzzles. She's nicer to me, giving me a spontaneous hug in the kitchen as I make tea. Most of all, she's clearly making an effort to eat more of what's on her plate. We measure her progress in crusts and crumbs, and keep going.

December is busy, as usual. There are school concerts and neighborhood potlucks and holiday parties, and every one of them involves food. This year we attend as few as possible: Emma's violin concert, my office holiday party. Kitty hits a couple of rough patches: finals are looming, and Ms. Susan thinks some of Kitty's anxiety comes from the pressure she puts on herself to not just do well in school but do perfectly. On her advice we pull Kitty out of school two weeks before the end of the semester and have her guidance counselor let her teachers know she will not take finals for medical reasons. Immediately Kitty seems more relaxed, better able to eat.

"People with eating disorders don't tend to do well with stress," Ms. Susan reminds us for the hundredth time.

No. Well. Neither do their families, at the moment.

The second rough patch has to do with sleep—or rather, the lack of it. Kitty's had insomnia on and off since last spring. The psychiatrist has tried a variety of medications, none of which have helped. In early December, Dr. Newbie prescribes Ambien. It's not particularly helpful; Kitty falls asleep fast but still wakes up several times during the night. And she's groggy in the morning, even though I'm giving her only half a dose.

After a couple of days on Ambien, Kitty's still not sleeping well. She complains of anxiety, says she can't concentrate or read. One evening she starts to hallucinate, rolling her eyes, backing away from some invisible threat. I don't give her an Ambien that night. The next day I call a friend who's a psychiatrist, who tells me that Ambien can cause paranoia and a psychosis-like state, especially in children. Why didn't the psychiatrist mention that when she prescribed it? Or the pharmacist, when we filled it? Someone should have told us to watch out for a reaction like this. Shouldn't they have?

I toss the Ambien. Better living through chemistry isn't the answer here. Alas.

Our days take on a semblance of normality, one that includes the regular, predictable landmarks of three meals and two snacks a day. But by mid-December, Kitty's weight hasn't budged; after nearly five months of refeeding, she's still ten pounds below her target, in part because she continues to grow.

I've spent time recently on a couple of online forums for families with eating-disordered children—one that focuses on the Maudsley approach, and another, bigger site that's more general. It's a relief to know we're not alone, that other families are doing what we're doing, and succeeding at it. But it seems like other people's children gain weight much faster than Kitty.

I realize how much like an anorexic I sound—competitiveness is a hallmark of the illness. The truth is, I want this to be over. For fourteen years my daughter has been a daily part of my life, and I miss her. I miss the small moments most. Occasionally we'd walk arm in arm to the grocery store or park, our legs moving in sync, and Kitty would give a little skip so we'd be off beat with each other—her right leg moving with my left leg. I'd skip again to put us back in sync, and then back and forth we'd go, hopping and adjusting until finally we were standing on one spot jerking and hopping and laughing so hard we couldn't breathe.

I miss her clear-eyed way of looking at the world. It's funny: before Kitty was born, my biggest fear about becoming a parent was having another person in the house, seeing everything I did. I felt abashed at the thought of a child who would see me at my worst, most disheveled, crankiest. I worried that this baby would grow up to be a child who judged me harshly. Who held my heart in her two hands and found it unlovable. But all my self-consciousness and worry fell away once she was born, because she wasn't a faceless watcher, she was Kitty, who was known and loved and loving. Parents and children are hardwired to love each other. But I liked Kitty. I like her.

And I want her back. I want her healthy and well so we can keep getting to know each other. So we can think about other things, travel and plan and be spontaneous in ways we can't right now. And I don't understand why it's taking so long for her to gain weight.

Though I do, really. Her goal weight has gone up since August because she's grown, and I think there's more to come. So we're aiming at a moving target. And she's become more physically active over the last month or two, with Dr. Beth's encouragement. She's started taking a weekly class in Israeli dance. And she's spending more time with the guys.

One December afternoon, Martin rings the doorbell to see if Kitty wants to hang out. She's working on a milk shake, and I offer to make him one. "Thanks!" he says enthusiastically.

He *doesn't* say, "Oh, I really shouldn't, I'm too fat." He doesn't say, "My butt's too big already!" He doesn't say, "Do you have any frozen yogurt instead?" He sucks up the milk shake in under two minutes, then turns to Kitty.

"Yo, hurry up with your ten-million-calorie milk shake!" he says.

I hold my breath, waiting for Kitty to snap or fall apart. Instead she giggles, finishes the last of the shake, and jumps off the couch. "I'm ready," she says, and off they go. And that's it. Not that they don't talk, she and the guys—they just talk about different things. And they do things. They take apart bikes and ride them. They play foursquare in the street outside our house. They do homework together. They go to the movies.

We couldn't have arranged anything better if we'd tried. Which comforts me, and reminds me that I'm not in charge, thank goodness, of every aspect of my daughter's life. That she's a resilient, savvy kid who's good at finding what she needs a lot of the time.

We still have to be vigilant. Her irrationality about food is matched by her hyperactivity. She'll push herself way beyond the comfort zone physically and then pay the price. One evening, right after dinner, Jamie takes her rock climbing, an activity they've done together since Kitty was four. She comes home a mess, refusing the bedtime snack, rocking back and forth on the sofa, literally wringing her hands.

"Kitty, I love you," I tell her, holding a pumpkin chocolate chip muffin on a plate. "And I expect you to eat this snack."

She turns her face away from the plate and keeps rocking. "You don't understand," she chokes out. "You don't understand how hard it is." And then: "Please love me no matter what!"

"Of course I do," I say. But something has tripped the switch again. I think back over what she ate today, and realize that dinner—fish, broccoli, squash with butter and brown sugar—wasn't especially high-calorie. It was a good meal, a nutritious meal; but maybe Kitty's metabolism is so sensitive right now that we need to match every "extra" outgo of calories with an equal intake. Or, clearly, more; she's been stuck at the same weight for six weeks now.

A few nights later, we replay the same scene. It's not the demon, exactly—more like its shadow falling over Kitty. She sits at the table, refusing to eat, and I sit with her, trying to project patient firmness. "Part of me wants to eat, but part of me doesn't!" she says. I'm impressed that she can articulate this so clearly; if only saying it out loud made that shadow disappear.

For my part, I've learned to stay on-message, as politicians say. No matter how articulate Kitty is, it's best for me to keep on reiterating the basic truths. So now I remind her, for the hundredth time, "Food is your medicine. You just have to eat."

"I can't, I can't," she says, sobbing.

"You can," I tell her. "You'll feel better."

Later that night I sit beside her as she falls asleep, looking at the glow-in-the-dark stars on her bedroom ceiling. And as I lie there it's as if a movie starts to play on the dark screen of my mind. I see Kitty in the ICU, her eyes closed, her arms limp at her sides. I see the long, snakelike tube sliding up her nose, disappearing into her body. I see a faceless nurse, her body radiating anger and irritation, unable to tell the difference between my daughter and the disease. I touch the skin on Kitty's back, which is smooth and warm, flesh over bone; but I feel the ridge of her shoulder blade, sharp enough to cause a bruise. I see her sticklike arms and legs, her shrunken features. I shake my head, put my fingers in my ears, chant silently: *No no no.*

What's that corny expression? "Do you curse the darkness or light a candle?" I'm groping for the candle, but I can't find the matches, and my hands are shaking so badly that no matter how many times I try, I can't strike a spark. I'm hoping that the act of groping itself will somehow bring on the light.

That's how I feel right now. Other times, I feel sure we're on the right track, that Kitty will be OK. And still other times, the knowledge and reality of what she's going through takes up every bit of space inside my body. The pain of it washes through me like blood, flares when I breathe. My skin feels tender and hot and bruised; my brain feels swollen and slow. Those times I literally want to jump out of my body. Like Kitty, I want someone to make it stop.

And Emma does too. Emma, who calls me from school the next day, sobbing, saying she can't stop thinking that we're all at home, dead, and she's supposed to save us and can't. Ten-year-old Emma, who feels powerless and overwhelmed and scared just as we do. Who cries at the dinner table later, saying she's not hungry, she can't eat.

A shaft of pure ice lodges in my chest when I hear this. Anorexia's heritability—meaning how much of it is caused by genetics rather than environment—is hard to pinpoint. The ongoing Genetics of Anorexia Collaborative Study, sponsored by the National Institute of Mental Health, is creating a repository of genetic information about people with eating disorders and their families. "We now know that [eating disorders] occur when there is a perfect storm of events that include genetic vulnerability and a culture that is promoting thinness through dieting and exercise," says Craig Johnson, director of the Eating Disorders Program at Laureate Psychiatric Hospital in Tulsa, Oklahoma, and one of the study's principal investigators.[*]

Emma is clearly at risk. Her sister has anorexia; her great-aunt, my mother's sister, had bulimia for many years. Anxiety, perfectionism, and eating disorders overlap and coexist in ways that aren't yet clear but are undeniable.

Knowing all this, I wish there was a way to prevent her from falling down the rabbit hole. We can't change her biology; all we

---

[*] Interview with the Associated Press, February 21, 2007.

can do is wait and watch for signs of trouble. At least now we know what to do if we see them. At least now we know we not only can do something—we have to.

New Year's has never been one of my favorite holidays. The collective frenzy of self-criticism, the communal fantasies of starting over (this time for real) with whatever it is we wish we were doing differently—none of it appeals to me. As a friend once said, "We do exactly what we want to do." Yeah. When it comes to behavior, talk is more or less irrelevant; it's what we actually do that matters.

I will admit, though, that I can't wait for this year to officially end. I know time is an artificial construct and nothing will change when the clock hands hit midnight. Still, this year I need the feeling of a new beginning, even if it's an illusion. I need to believe that next year will be a better year for us, that it will contain the tipping point I've been waiting for, the moment when we glimpse the demon's back, retreating, when the fog clears from Kitty's eyes and everything goes back to normal.

Alas, this is magical thinking, and I know it. Life isn't a play, with a predictable arc, clear moments of conflict and resolution. Life is muddled and disorderly, proceeding in fits and starts. There's nothing linear about it.

I think by now we've at least seen all of the demon's tricks, but, as usual, I'm wrong. On New Year's Day, Kitty struggles with lunch and cries so hard afterward that she throws up. She begs us to believe that she didn't do it on purpose, that it was, as she says, "an accident." She says she's sorry she violated our trust, which suggests that there was an element of intention.

But I don't know what to believe. Kitty sobs herself to sleep, napping for an hour or so; when she wakes up I give her an Ensure Plus, to make up some of the lunch calories, and she drinks it without complaint. Later that afternoon, she eats cookies and milk for her snack, then announces that she's going to the bathroom upstairs; do I want her to not flush the toilet after? Because this is so uncharacteristic I say, yes, don't flush the toilet. She comes out of the bathroom saying, "I'm sorry, I didn't mean to, I don't know why I did," and I run for the bathroom, bracing myself for the worst. I look into the toilet and see not vomit but an unidentifiable object, floating in the water.

"I've never done it before, I don't know why I did," Kitty cries outside the bathroom door. Eventually she tells me she'd spit the last bite of cookie into the toilet. My knees go shaky with relief. "Now you won't trust me," she sobs. "How can I win back your trust?"

"I trust you," I say (which is not a lie: it's the anorexia I don't trust). But I'm on my guard. And a few days later, it happens again. Kitty has come to work with me, for something to do during winter break. We eat lunch together—chicken salad, potato chips, milk, and, for her, a Hershey's bar. When she gets up to throw away her garbage, I have a feeling, like the feeling I had the day in the park, and I say, "Give it to me."

She hands it over wordlessly, pulling the napkin off the top of the pile to reveal half the chocolate bar, which she proceeds to eat without fuss. Afterward, she says, "I don't know why I did that."

"I know why," I tell her.

She says, "Because you always know."

I say, "Yes, and you want me to know. You want to make sure I'm paying attention, that I'm watching and taking it all in. You want to make sure I'm taking care of you."

She stares at me for a long minute. The look on her face is one of relief.

That night, as I'm making her bedtime snack of two pieces of buttered toast with cinnamon sugar sprinkled on top, she asks if both pieces need cinnamon sugar.

"No, but they both need butter," I say. "Do you want to butter them yourself?"

"No, you do it," she says, but as soon as I've buttered both pieces she says, with despair in her voice, "Oh God, I should have done it myself, I had a chance to get away with eating much less."

"You know I would have been watching," I tell her firmly. "You wouldn't have gotten away with anything."

I hand her the plate and we sit down on the couch. She looks up at me. "I love you Mommy," she says. "You always know just what to say."

And that's the last of the demon's tests. For a while.

It's coincidence, really, that just after New Year's I set out to buy a calorie counter. Kitty's weight has been stalled for nearly seven weeks; obviously we need more information. I'm unprepared for the embarrassment I feel, walking into a bookstore and asking for the calorie counters. I'm sure the bookseller thinks I'm embarking on a New Year's diet. I want to say, "It's not for me, honest! It's for someone who needs to *gain* weight!"

Instead, I slink upstairs to the nutrition section, where I stand in shock, gaping at shelf after shelf of diet books. There are at least a hundred different diet books here, and their names range from the pathetic to the absurd: The Prayer Diet. The Coconut Diet. The Paleo Diet (raw meat? really?). The Slowdown Diet, the Fat Flush

Diet, the 3-Apples-a-Day Diet. The After-40 Diet. The Starch Blocker Diet. The Big Flavor Diet. The Real Age Diet (mine would be around seventy-five by now, I fear). The Soy Zone Diet, The Acid-Alkaline Balance Diet, the Super Foods Diet. The Potatoes, Not Prozac Diet. The Warrior Diet. The Uncle Sam Diet (hot dogs, hamburgers, apple pie?). The 5-Day Miracle Diet.

Losing weight has become our national obsession, our holy grail. I watch part of a talk show one afternoon at the health club, without sound. The segment covers new diet drugs, and the on-screen graphic shows a three-dimensional model of the brain with lots of animated capital A's swarming toward one particular spot in the brain and being magically repelled. The drug purportedly brings about weight loss by chemically suppressing appetite. Judging by the looks on the hosts' faces, this is excellent news.

The cultural assumption seems to be that there's something wrong with wanting to eat. Appetite is something to be fended off, with willpower or chemically. We're locked in a war with our own hunger, which is the primal force that sustains us. Of course the talk shows and magazines aim mainly at women, who make up the vast majority of those with weight issues. We're socialized to fear our appetites, whether they're for food or sex or power. We're taught from birth to make ourselves small and dainty, to not take up room. Can this kind of acculturation cause anorexia? I don't think so. Can it trigger someone who's vulnerable? No doubt about it.

Kitty's anxiety waxes and wanes over the first week or two of the new year. She's much more relaxed before school starts, and we briefly consider homeschooling her for the rest of the year.

But homeschooling would be so isolating. Jamie thinks it's good for her to go to school and see people, and I have to agree. Though social interactions are fraught for Kitty right now, they're also, sometimes, energizing. Ms. Susan asks her one day to think back to an earlier time, a time in her life before anorexia, and remember what made her happy then.

"Other people," Kitty says promptly, and it's true. It's always been true. Even as a toddler, when other kids her age would play next to each other, not connecting, Kitty wanted to interact.

Some social situations aren't so good for her, though. Like Ms. Susan's eating group. Lately, Kitty's been coming home from group upset; a few times she's balked at eating a snack or dinner afterward. The last straw is the night Kitty comes home from the group, refuses her bedtime snack, and cries for an hour: she's the fattest girl in the group, she's the only one who's doing it this way, why can't she be like everyone else. She says again that she wants to go to an inpatient program, it would be so much easier if we weren't involved with this; we make everything so much harder.

Kitty is the only teen in the group whose family is doing FBT; the other girls (and they are all girls) are struggling to eat on their own. I wonder how many of their families have been told that's the only way to do it. I wonder how many have been scared off by one of the main criticisms of family-based treatment—the idea that most families can't handle it, that you have to be a very special family to pull it off. I don't think so. Our family is as flawed and dysfunctional as the next. We make a lot of mistakes. We get mad, we get sad, we get frustrated. If we can help Kitty through anorexia, other families can do that for their children too.

"Sometimes parents are just too afraid to actually challenge and disrupt the behaviors at the level they need to, and to do so consistently," says James Lock, professor of child psychiatry and pediatrics and director of the eating-disorders program at Stanford University. "Sometimes the parents' relationships may interfere with their ability to work together to do this. Sometimes other mental illnesses like severe OCD or depression can interfere. Sometimes there are other needy children in the family, so it's difficult to focus on this issue. There may be people whose parenting style is such that they just can't do it. It wouldn't sit with their way of being a parent."

I can see that last idea reflected in our own family. For me, some of the hardest moments this year have come while we watched Kitty's illness unfold. FBT appealed to me because it's all about *doing* something, which fits with my parenting style. James Lock believes most families have the capacity and the impetus to do FBT. "It's really not rocket science," he says. "Families just have to accept that it's going to be hard. There's going to be a lot of pushback. They'll be on, 24/7, until the behavior is disrupted."

He's right, of course. But I wonder what he or any other doctor imagines goes on at home in between therapy sessions. I wonder if they can have any idea of how hard it really is.

In any case, our path at the moment is clear. I call Ms. Susan and tell her that Kitty will be taking a break from the lunch group, though she'll keep doing individual sessions. Maybe she'll go back to the group at some point. Or maybe, by the time she can see clearly again, she won't need to.

Without the overt triggers of the group, Kitty's eating goes a bit more smoothly. But there's still drama to spare at our house. One day in mid-January, when Jamie has a job and I have to go to work and Emma goes to a friend's house, Kitty stays home alone for part of the afternoon. Her anxiety spikes, and she spends much of the evening in tears, which prompts Emma to make a rare outburst. "I'm sick of you always crying!" she shouts at her sister. "All you do is cry!"

Kitty immediately goes into paroxysms of apology. She makes a halfhearted attempt to run away, fumbling with the front door until Jamie leads her gently upstairs. I feel furious at Emma because I know that it will take hours to calm Kitty down again. I make Emma apologize, which she does, sullenly, and then runs to her room and bangs the door shut.

I sit at the kitchen table, tears of self-pity stinging my eyes. So much of the time now I feel like a bad parent to one or both of my daughters. I'm more or less checked out at work, doing just what's necessary; I'm lucky my boss is understanding. I'm sick of shopping and planning meals and cooking. I'm sick of thinking about food all the time. I've become obsessive about food myself, always checking calorie counts, always calculating in my head: Is this enough? How can I get more calories into this? I'm sick of it all. If I never cooked another meal, I'd be quite happy.

The truth is, I'm wrung out. Used up. Exhausted. I don't know if I can hang on until Kitty's better. How long will it be? We're only five months into this—many families spend years fighting the demon. I don't know that I have it in me. I really don't.

I sit at the kitchen table, where we spend so much of our time now. I've run my finger over every nick and dent in its chrome rim, memorized the patterns of black and white dots on its Formica surface. I've scraped oatmeal and ice cream, fried onions, bits of lettuce—every kind of food imaginable—from the space where the two halves of the table don't quite meet. I sit there for an hour, until Jamie wordlessly turns out the kitchen light, helps me out of the chair, and guides me up the stairs to bed.

When this is all over, I'm putting this table out on the curb. Let some other family use it. We're getting a new one.

And it's only two or three days later—can that be true?—that we have a really good day, a stellar day, the best we've had in eight months. Kitty comes to work with me, and we spend a peaceful morning sitting side by side, each of us engrossed in her own task. Eating her pumpkin chocolate chip muffin after lunch, she asks, "Did you do something different with the recipe this time? It tastes much better than usual."

I want to leap onto my desk and do a little dance because Kitty isn't worrying about what's in the muffin; she's enjoying it. She likes it! It tastes good to her! She still insists that she never feels hungry, that she hasn't felt hunger since sometime last spring. But this must be a first step. Eating as a sensual experience. Eating as pleasure. Not only that: what's different about these muffins is that I made them with butter instead of oil—an entire stick of butter, a fact I judge it best not to share with Kitty right now, because that would trigger her guilt and anxiety over eating. She doesn't need to know.

Critics of FBT would disagree with me here. They'd say I'm being dishonest, that I'm lying to my daughter. That I'm sneaking butter into her food, violating her trust, destroying any chance of an authentic relationship with her.

But I'm not lying to her, or sneaking anything; I'm taking care of her nutritional needs as I see them, which is precisely what she needs from me and what I've promised her. Most people don't know what's in the food they eat. I don't give Kitty a list of ingredients for everything I make because (a) she doesn't need to know, and (b) it would derail her eating, which in turn would (c) impede her recovery. Besides, it's Not-Kitty who freaks out at the thought of eating butter. And I don't owe Not-Kitty, or the demon, a thing.

Don't ask, don't tell. And don't confuse what we're doing now for pathology, or for a permanent arrangement. Right now, my job is to know what Kitty needs and provide it; her job is to eat what I put in front of her. If she recovers—*when* she recovers— we'll renegotiate.

That night, when Emma asks for her favorite bedtime snack, Kitty says, "Can I have toast with jelly too? That sounds good." She'd eaten enough earlier in the day, so I make toast with jelly for both of them, and they eat it together at the table, giggling and licking strawberry jam off their fingers.

Later, as I sit on the edge of Emma's bed to say goodnight, she says, "Kitty had a good day, didn't she? When I heard her say she wanted toast with jelly, it made me feel really good." She closes her eyes, settles herself, then says sleepily, "I know tomorrow might not be a good day, but today was. That's still really good."

As usual, Emma nails it. It's so easy to focus on the anguish and misery; it's harder, somehow, to acknowledge the positive, maybe for fear of jinxing it, bringing the nightmare back down on our heads. The nightmare will come back; we'll have plenty of opportunities for endurance. But today was a good day. Today was a *good* day.

"Yes," I tell Emma. "Yes, that's still really good."

{ chapter ten }

The Happy Ending

One cannot think well, love well, sleep well,
if one has not dined well.

—Virginia Woolf

If you'd asked me twelve months ago to come up with five words to describe Kitty, here's what I would have said:

Graceful. Poised. Verbal. Smart. Independent.

The words I'd choose now, in April, ten months after her diagnosis:

Brave. Anxious. Smart. Honest. Scared.

So much has changed over the last year. And so much will change, I hope, over the next few months. Things aren't nearly as awful as they were last summer or early fall; Kitty has made progress, physically and psychologically. So why do I feel upset? I mean, I know why I feel distress; this whole year has been distressing beyond anything I could have imagined. But why *now*? Why do I lie awake nights, my stomach churning, my thoughts grinding around and around the same obsessive track? I should be feeling better, now that we're seeing more and more good days.

I catch myself thinking this—I should feel better!—and hear the words I've repeated to Kitty many times over the last year: *There are no shoulds. There's only what is.* It astonishes me, as it always does, that thinking a thing does not make it true, that feelings are, by comparison, so slow, so awkward, so necessarily painful.

Now that Kitty's getting better, my thoughts are reaching forward, toward the possibility of real recovery, real life. But my feelings are still stranded in last year's quicksand of terror and anxiety. It makes a kind of evolutionary sense. When you're in the midst of crisis, the past and the future fall away, allowing you to focus only on the task before you: this meal, this evening, this doctor's visit. Adrenaline carries you from moment to moment, deferring the shock, keeping you moving, changing, doing. But as soon as the emergency abates, you have time to sit down and think, to worry and contemplate and obsess. To feel the moment of impact— whether it's cancer or anorexia, an accident or a crime—again and again, the slow waves of pain beating against the shore of your self.

There are more good days, but still plenty of bad ones.

Best of all, we see glimmers of the old Kitty. In late February, she goes on what's more or less her first date, to the freshman formal at school. The boy is someone she met through a friend—not a serious boyfriend, but not Martin or Garth, either. I'd worried that shopping for the dress would be traumatic, as Kitty no longer fits into a size 00. Her body has changed; she's still thin, but she's got a shape now. On our shopping trip, she tries on a strapless dress that brings out the green flecks in her hazel eyes. "You look great!" I say, and instantly wish I'd kept my mouth shut. Kitty's illness has sensitized me to how many comments we all make about other people's appearance. In Kitty's case, even the most well-intentioned compliment can trigger an anorexic reaction.

Today, though, my slip goes unnoticed. Kitty, admiring herself in the dressing-room mirror, says only, "I think so too."

On the night of the dance, the boy slips a corsage onto her wrist, and though Kitty rolls her eyes and pretends to be annoyed, she poses for Jamie's photo, her eyes shining, her smile full and real and dazzling. After they leave to walk up to the high school, Jamie and I look at each other in amazement: Kitty has had a Normal Adolescent Experience, and so have we, for the first time in months. Maybe ever, actually. Anorexia has robbed both her and us of the beginning of her adolescence. And while we can never get that time back, we can move forward. Kitty is growing up.

We celebrate Kitty's fifteenth birthday a day early, since Jamie will be out of town on the day itself. She picks the restaurant—Japanese—and we order takeout, so she can eat at home, followed by carrot cake from her favorite bakery. There's plenty of cake left over, and my plan is to serve her another piece for a snack the next day. But at breakfast that morning she says, "I have a favor to ask."

"Anything, birthday girl," I say.

"Can I please not eat cake on my birthday?"

She asks so plaintively that I say of course. But this "gift" makes me feel sad. I remember going to the bakery with Kitty when she was five, spending half an hour leafing through a catalog of decorations while she tried to decide whether she wanted a gymnast or a horse decorating her cake, how many icing flowers would fit on top and what colors they should be.

I wonder if she'll ever look forward to a piece of cake again.

A few weeks later, in early March, Kitty goes to Boston for a weekend with her Israeli dance troupe. Two months ago, a trip like this would have been unthinkable, because we wouldn't be there to watch each bite she put into her mouth. We talk ahead of time about how it will feel for her to eat on the trip and acknowledge that she probably won't eat quite as much as usual. We pack her lots of snacks and tell her we want to know how things go, whatever happens.

Despite my nervousness about the trip I feel more relaxed, that first night, than I've felt in months. So relaxed that Jamie and I fall asleep at ten and don't hear the phone ring—Kitty calling to say goodnight. The next morning she calls at eight. "The eating isn't going so well," she says tearfully. "I'm not having any fun." I talk to her for a while, trying to soothe her with my voice the way you'd gentle a spooked horse. We hang up and I call the group leader, who tells me not to worry; she sat next to Kitty this morning and watched her eat a nice bowl of fruit for breakfast.

Now I'm panicking. A bowl of fruit contains maybe a fifth of Kitty's usual breakfast calories. I remind myself that she's doing well, that she wanted to go on this trip, that it's only two days out of the hundreds we've been refeeding her. Two days, it turns out, filled with emotional phone calls from Kitty, whose anxiety climbs as her eating diminishes. She's relieved and exhausted when she gets home late Sunday night, and she goes right to bed. And I'm proud of her: she managed. Not ideally by any means; she's a long way from being able to take care of herself. But the fact that she wanted to go, and went, despite the difficulties, feels positive.

Ms. Susan thinks so anyway. "As I've told you many times, I think people with eating disorders should make their lives as stress-free as possible," she tells us at Kitty's next session. "On the other hand, there's a lot to be gained from learning to cope with stress and anxiety, from coming away from the experience of being bored and anxious and learning to manage those feelings."

Dr. Beth agrees. For months she's encouraged Kitty to spend time with friends, join a club, hang on to as much real life as possible. Now she tells me, "I think Kitty's going to be in that one-third who make a complete recovery and just go on with their lives."

She smiles as she says this. All year we've been drawing on Dr. Beth's steady encouragement. These words, coming from her, mean more than any dry pronouncement or study. She doesn't know the future, of course; no one does. But she does know Kitty, and she knows us. And I know she wouldn't lie.

I've described the demon in great detail to Dr. Beth because I want her to understand what Kitty's going through. And she seems to, as much as anyone can: she's never been punitive or angry; she's maintained her empathy for Kitty, spent many hours talking with her, reassuring her, cheering her up.

But I also want Dr. Beth to know what refeeding entails because I know she has other patients with anorexia; in fact, I've talked with other parents, at her request, explaining FBT and encouraging them to look into it. And when those families try FBT, I want Dr. Beth and other pediatricians to prepare them for what they might encounter along the way. I've heard stories about kids who bang their heads on the wall until they break their own noses and black their eyes. Who leap out of moving cars or jump from second-story windows. Who kick and pinch and bite their parents—behaviors so completely foreign to their ordinary personalities that their parents panic, understandably, lose faith in themselves, believe their children are too sick to stay home. Behaviors that come from the damage starvation wreaks on the body.

But if parents know what's within the realm of possibility, they can prepare themselves, mentally and physically, do a better job of keeping their children safe. That's where pediatricians come in: they can reassure families who go through this that, yes, these behaviors are part of the recovery process, they will go away; your child's not crazy in any permanent or overarching way.

Pediatricians are nearly always the first doctors to mention the word *anorexia* to a family. They're the ones who describe the disease, who sketch out treatment, who refer families to shrinks and therapists and nutritionists. I don't understand why insurance companies insist that only psychiatrists can diagnose and treat eating disorders; pediatricians are the ones who have relationships with parents and kids. The pediatrician is like the first-base coach, keeping up a steady stream of chatter and reassurance, whereas a shrink is like the designated hitter, brought in late in the game to knock a home run over the fence.

I know who I'm going to trust.

Pediatricians are best positioned to help a family. The trouble is, they get little to no training in how to treat eating disorders. Unless they're unusually motivated and responsive, like Dr. Beth, they know only what they were taught in medical school, which often consists of Hilde Bruch and not much else. When a child is as sick as Kitty was last summer, pediatricians usually recommend sending her away for residential treatment at a for-profit chain like Remuda

Ranch or Renfrew, or to an eating-disorders center like Sheppard Pratt in Baltimore.

Places like Renfrew and Remuda boast sky-high recovery rates—but those are short-term rates, often measured on the day they leave. Kids usually *do* gain weight at residential centers, but they rarely gain enough; typically they're sent home when they reach 90 percent of "ideal body weight." Which is about where Kitty is now. So I know that 90 percent of ideal body weight does not constitute recovery. It's an improvement; it's medically stable. But it's too low to promote true psychological healing. The demon is still very much in the picture at 90 percent. When teens leave residential care, they nearly always lose weight. Unless there's someone at home who's willing to take on the task of making sure they eat and keep gaining weight, they backslide very quickly, losing ten or twenty hard-won pounds in a couple of weeks. "Recovery" over; back to anorexia as usual.

Which is not to say that residential care is never helpful; sometimes it can literally save a child's life. But it's usually a stopgap, a kick start to recovery, rather than recovery itself. Real recovery takes months, maybe years. It takes the regular application of food, lots of food, to break the self-reinforcing cycle of restricting, to alter the neurobiology that perpetuates the disease, to retrain the brain.

There hasn't been a lot of research on anorexia, but what little there is clearly shows that for kids eighteen and under, FBT nearly always constitutes the best shot at recovery. The trouble is, there are very few FBT therapists in the United States today. Which is why families in our small city often drive three hours each way for treatment in Chicago. Or do what we've done—put together a treatment team that's open to FBT but not particularly knowledgeable about it.

And that's also why, in 2008, James Lock and Daniel le Grange created the Training Institute for Child and Adolescent Eating Disorders and began offering workshops and supervision for therapists who want to become certified in FBT. It's the only way to make sure that therapists who say they offer FBT are actually doing it correctly. Le Grange has seen too many variations on the theme, including a therapist who, at a conference, encouraged parents to physically restrain young patients and force-feed them—a practice that's diametrically opposed to both the spirit and the letter of FBT. Her words appalled him so much that this dapper, soft-spoken man stood up and publicly corrected her. At least people like that can't say they practice FBT anymore.

As I write, the institute has certified nineteen FBT therapists; many more are going through the several-years-long process. Five years from now, there should be more FBT therapists around the world. Still not enough, unfortunately. But a start.

In early April we raise Kitty's calories to four thousand a day, and she gains another four pounds. She's also grown another inch, so she's still below her goal weight. But she weighs twenty pounds more than she's ever weighed in her life. She gets her first period. In the second half of April, her weight seesaws—up two pounds, down two—even as she grows another inch. This drawn-out process feels torturous. I wish we could speed things up, but I'm not sure Kitty can physically eat any more. I wonder if I'm going to spend the rest of my life thinking up ways to get more calories into her.

She's no longer at the bottom of the rabbit hole, but rather climbing her way laboriously up through the darkness. I want to reach down and pull her to the surface quickly, cleanly, in one motion. That's always been my instinct with my daughters—to spare them as much of the world's pain as possible. Of course I know I can't do that, most of the time—and that, in fact, I shouldn't. Without pain, they won't grow and change and become who they truly are. Kitty's life is her own and has been from the moment she was born. I respect that. I get it. I know she has to go through recovery at her own pace. It's just hard to watch her suffer.

Meanwhile, Kitty's made a couple of new friends this spring, girlfriends she goes shopping with. Girls who have nothing to do with the world of eating disorders. She's taken up scrapbooking. She's been kinder to Emma, too, typing up an essay for her one night, helping her adjust the water in the shower another. Little things, but they mean a lot to Emma.

The outbursts, when they come, are often triggered by subjects other than food these days—usually school. Kitty's taking a full load this semester, with one study hall before lunch so she can come home and eat. It's a stretch. One night she falls apart while studying after dinner, saying she can't do her homework, she can't concentrate, she's falling behind and can't keep up. She wrings her hands, says her chest feels tight with anxiety, rocks back and forth in her desk chair, and nothing I say can comfort her. So I sit with her for an hour, until she's calmed down enough to go back to studying. A month ago, an outburst like this would have lasted the rest of the night. Progress? I think so.

Another night, faced with a doughnut for her evening snack, Kitty begs for something different—a yogurt, toast, anything. I stand in the playroom, wondering what to do. Should I insist on the doughnut? If I don't, am I pandering to the anorexia? If I give in to her fear, does that set her back? How much of her preference is "normal"—whatever that means, at this point—and how much is eating disordered?

The answer to that last question comes quickly, as the demon's twisted words begin spilling from my daughter's mouth. "You're trying to make me fat!" she says. "This is disgusting. I feel greasy just looking at it. I can't eat this, it makes me feel sick."

On and on she goes. I stay calm, as I've learned to do, until she looks up and says, with real fear in her voice, "I'm afraid I'm going to be built like you!"

I stand there, the plate in my hand, my heart hammering in my throat. I'm glad in a way she's said it, because I've felt her thinking it for months now. I've seen it in the way her eyes sweep down my body and then her own, the pucker of anxiety that appears between her brows. Shame steams through me, hot and bitter, scouring away every other thought and feeling, leaving me immobilized in the face of my daughter's judgment. *It's good that she's expressing her feelings,* I tell myself mechanically. I take away the doughnut and bring out a plate of cookies, and Kitty eats, not meeting my eyes, then goes silently to bed.

That night in bed, I wonder if all daughters think that at some point. *I don't want to look like you.* Girls rebel against their mothers; it's part of how we figure out who we are. We push away from the flesh and blood that carried and bore us so we can move toward our own future, ourselves and not just another version of our mothers. We reject our mothers, body and spirit and soul, so we can find ourselves. I know all this, I really do, but still Kitty's words rise up in the space between us. And they hurt.

·   ·   ·

At Dr. Beth's the next day, Kitty's weight is the same as it's been for four weeks, *and* she's grown a bit. Four weeks of four thousand calories a day and she hasn't gained an ounce. In fact, if you consider the height change, she's lost weight. And she's still eight or ten pounds shy of her current target.

How is it possible that Kitty can eat that much food and not be gaining weight? Except for trying to make herself throw up back at the beginning (and, luckily, not succeeding), Kitty hasn't done any purging; I know, because we've stayed with her in the critical hour after every meal and snack. It's not unusual for someone with anorexia or bulimia to throw up, use laxatives, or overexercise compulsively to get rid of the calories consumed. Last summer Kitty did hundreds of sit-ups in her room each night; that was purging. Since then we've kept a pretty close eye on her bathroom and exercise habits. But maybe we're missing something. Dr. Beth suggests another possibility: maybe Kitty's energy is going toward growing taller at the moment rather than gaining weight. Or maybe all of these are true to some extent.

I think, for the thousandth time, about what a mystery anorexia is. How many times have I heard the expression "Calories in, calories out"? It's usually offered in the context of dieting—that is, if you want to lose weight, eat fewer calories or burn more. But this, it turns out, is a gross oversimplification, and not necessarily true. Gina Kolata, a science reporter for the *New York Times*, explored some of the paradoxes of human metabolism in her 2007 book, *Rethinking Thin*. She wrote about a study done by Ethan Sims of the University of Vermont, who turned Ancel Keys's Minnesota

Experiment on its head: Sims made volunteers fat in order to understand the physiological changes involved in gaining weight and keeping it on.

Sims expected to find a variation on the "calories in, calories out" theme; he confidently hypothesized that by letting his volunteers eat as much as they wanted, he could quickly and easily make them fat. And they couldn't cheat and jog off the calories because they were prisoners in the Vermont penal system whose actions were closely monitored.

Sims did make his volunteers fat, but it was a lot harder than he expected. The process took four to six months and required feeding some of the men a staggering ten thousand calories a day. When Sims did the math he discovered that each man gained weight at a different rate, despite the fact that they were eating the same number of calories. Not only that: the men who had been thin before the study began needed almost twice as many calories to maintain their higher weights as they had to sustain their ordinary lower weights.

Sims's experiment highlights the fact that each person's metabolism has a kind of set point, a natural range. Trying to alter that range—making a thin person fatter, or a fat person thin—takes nearly superhuman effort and blows the calories in, calories out theory right out of the water.

Maybe one of the effects of anorexia is to reset a person's metabolism to an unnaturally low range. Which might explain why it's so hard for Kitty to gain weight, despite eating large numbers of calories. And why even a very minor dip in calories seems to make her fragile and volatile.

The next morning, as she gets ready to leave for school, I ask if she has her midmorning snack with her. "I always pack it," she says. I tell her I want to see it. I'm not in the habit, these days, of checking up on her. But my intuition is rarely wrong. And it's not wrong this time: Kitty says she forgot to pack it, just this once. She pops a protein bar in her bag and runs out the door. But will she eat it?

I want to lie down and weep with weariness. Our friends have been commenting on how good Kitty looks, how much happier she seems. "She's doing so well!" they say, and I want to say yes, but she still wrestles with the anorexia every single day. Yes, but if we let up for a few days, she'd go right back down the rabbit hole. Yes, but she's not safe yet. Nowhere near it. Before, the illness was visible on her face, in her body. Now only Jamie and Emma and Kitty and I know the real distance between how she looks and how she feels. "You must be feeling so much better!" they say. I muster a smile and say as little as possible, because I have neither the energy nor the heart to tell them the truth.

If you fall ill with pneumonia, the treatment is fairly straightforward: a course of antibiotics. And so are the signs of recovery. You're recovered from pneumonia when you feel better, when there's no fluid in your lungs, when your blood count returns to normal. Three simple measures.

But when are you recovered from anorexia? I mean *really* recovered, not the 90 percent of ideal body weight that insurance companies and many doctors hold up as a goal. Some doctors talk about weight restoration as a mark of recovery—getting a child back to the weight she was before she started restricting. The trouble is, teenagers are still growing. They're supposed to put on weight even after they stop growing vertically. So the healthy weight for an eighteen-year-old is unlikely to be the same as it was for that same child four years earlier.

The whole question of target weight is complex and much debated. Experts in the field often refer to body mass index, BMI, as a measure of restored health. But BMI is a crude measure, a simple ratio between height and weight. It says nothing about a person's body type. Athletes score high on the BMI chart because muscle weighs more than fat and tissue; you can be "normal" on the BMI chart and still lack enough fat and mass. Kitty, for example, now has a BMI of 18.8, which puts her—barely—into the "normal" category for her age on the BMI chart. By this one standard, she'd be considered recovered. But it's clear to both Jamie and me that she's not.

Dr. Beth says the best way to gauge a child's weight is to plot her height and weight since birth, find her natural growth curve, and aim to get her back on it. It's sensible advice, especially compared with the gobbledygook of BMI charts and percentiles of ideal body weight. It's not always enough, though. Kitty at thirteen was still on her growth curve. She didn't fall off it until she lost five pounds, last April or May. And Kitty now, having gained twenty-five pounds, weighs far more than she ever did, and still has five or six pounds to go. For her it's less a question of weight restoration than it is a question of weight correction.

Carolyn Hodges, a nutritionist and director of the Sol Stone Center in Elmira, New York, suggests that each person has a kind of magic number, a weight that signals true recovery for her. "Below that body weight, the thought process is very obsessive," she explains. "I've seen this in several patients. Above that weight, they are much less obsessive; one to two pounds below, they will be very obsessive."

We've noticed this with Kitty. And it's not all about weight gain, especially for teenagers. There have been times over the last nine months when the number on the scale has stayed the same but Kitty's grown taller, putting her further from her target weight. Every time, her mood has deteriorated and she's seemed sicker again.

Another measure of recovery often suggested for women is menstruation. When body fat drops below a certain level, menstrual cycles stop. The problem is, this happens at a different point in the process for everyone. One teen may lose her period at 90 percent of her goal weight, while another may continue to have it even at 75 percent. Some women with anorexia never stop menstruating.

Maybe I'm deluding myself, but I have a sense that I'll know when Kitty is really well again. I probably *am* deluding myself, because even the experts don't seem to have a good grip on who is and isn't recovered. This has ramifications not only for the patients themselves but for the ongoing research, much of which compares people who are actively ill with recovered anorexics. Often, the criterion for recovery is "being weight restored for a year." But it all depends on what you mean by weight restored, doesn't it? Who's measuring, at what age, and how much growth has taken place? Pediatricians and doctors seem inclined to lowball weight. They're often all too willing to settle for keeping a kid on the edge of normal; I suspect this is because everyone's so obsessed with obesity in children these days. Doctors, especially, have internalized the notion of "thinner is better." Whereas I think for a child like Kitty, having an "extra" five pounds is insurance against relapse.

Physically she looks healthy and strong, if still on the thin side. She's developed more of a womanly shape. Her hair, which fell out in clumps all last summer and fall, is now shiny and long. Her eyes sparkle, her face is nicely full; she's alive again.

She still says she feels no physical hunger; she says she can't remember the last time she felt hungry. It's been well over a year.

Does she truly feel no hunger, or does she just not connect the physical feelings with the idea of appetite? I think of people with brain injuries, who, if given a math problem, say they don't know how to solve it even as their hand writes the correct answer; they've suffered some crucial disconnect between speech and motor movements. I wonder if it's that way for Kitty, if malnutrition has broken the connections between body and mind, and, if so, if they will ever be healed. I wonder if Kitty will ever feel hunger again, ever feel comfortable with her own appetite, or if eating will forever remain a necessary but unpleasant chore.

Emotionally she's still volatile, still prone to anxiety attacks about everything from homework to friends to how she looks. But she smiles more these days; she laughs. After months of ignoring the three-year-old across the street, Joe, she now makes a fuss when she sees him. One day in early May she tells me she feels happy some of the time now—a huge improvement over ten months ago.

She's come along in other ways as well. She sees Ms. Susan by herself, and she seems a little more open, more willing to talk about the eating disorder. One day she says she's trying to keep the eating disorder in check by not "talking e.d." Two months ago, she didn't have the self-awareness to make a comment like that.

By mid-May she's eating her afternoon snack alone in her room every day, at her request. Once a day, at least, she seems able to marshal her inner resources and overcome the inner compulsion not to eat. I'm pretty sure she's actually eating it because in the last month she's gained another four pounds, which puts her close to her goal weight.

And I think that compulsion to not eat is growing weaker. She hasn't talked as much about needing us to watch her, though she still asks me to measure out her portions at breakfast and dinner.

One morning I ask whether she'd like cereal or granola for breakfast. "Granola," she says, and then, with real anguish, "Oh, no, I could have had cereal and it would have been fewer calories!"

"Not true," I say at once. "I would have served you more cereal so you got exactly the same number of calories."

So the anorexic thoughts are still with her. But they are—dare I say it?—beginning to lose their power.

On Mother's Day, we do not go for a family bike ride, as we did so disastrously last year. We stay in, because it's raining, and Kitty and Emma put on a treasure hunt for me, complete with clues hidden all through the house and coupons for foot massages and breakfast in bed. We laugh. We play Scrabble. We spend hours reading together in the living room. We eat Japanese takeout for dinner and ice cream for dessert.

We do not say the word *anorexia* all day.

More ups and downs follow in the next few weeks, as they have all year. Kitty comes home from school one day and reports that a girl in her Latin class brought in a cake shaped like the Parthenon, and that she ate a piece. She actually ate a piece of cake that we did not serve her or insist she eat. That we didn't even know she was eating.

"Are you proud of me?" she asks.

I grab her hand and squeeze it, feeling how solid and warm and strong it is, feeling the tingle of electricity that passes between one human being and another. To anyone else, this would be a non-event. But she knows, and I know, that the paradigm is shifting. The demon is in retreat.

It hasn't disappeared entirely. There are still days when Kitty balks at eating, when she castigates herself and, once, lies to me about drinking an Ensure. She has panic attacks, which she never had before. Her relationship with food is still fraught, though it's better. So much better.

I don't believe in fairy tales, but still, I want a happy ending. I want the child I knew before. Before starvation and longing, before guilt and terror. Before these interminable months of heartbreak and misery and woe.

One night I dream that I'm in a big Victorian house, searching for Kitty. I run up and down steep flights of stairs and finally find her taking a dance class on the second floor. From outside the room I signal her frantically—*Come here, get out of the class*—but she ignores me. I vault a railing, grab her, and yank her angrily out of the room. I'm furious in the dream, and getting angrier by the second.

"What did you eat for dinner last night?" I bark. Not-Kitty smiles, a nasty, insincere smile, and says nothing. I shake her by the shoulder. "You didn't eat dinner last night, did you?" I shout. "What did you have for breakfast?"

Not-Kitty leers at me. "A teaspoon of air," she says prettily. I wake with my heart pounding, my arms trembling as if I really was shaking her.

I want a happy ending, but life isn't that clear-cut. It's only when we look back over a period of time that we see—or think we see—an orderly shape emerging from the chaos of everyday living. Except for death, the only endings we get are the ones we impose on ourselves and the world.

So maybe it's enough for me to say that Kitty could have died but didn't. That all year she's been unspeakably brave; she has done the most terrifying thing imaginable to her, over and over and over. That if there's no happy ending, there's no unhappy one either.

·   ·   ·

And then one morning in June—just about a year after Kitty's diagnosis—I answer the phone at work and hear her voice sing out, "I'm hungry!" I'm speechless. But I don't need to say anything, because Kitty's so excited. She knows what this means as well as I do. She says she can't wait for me to come home for lunch—can she drink a can of Ensure now? I tell her of course, I'll come home early. I'll bake cupcakes in her honor. I tell her, *I'm so happy for you.* What I want to tell her: *Thank you for telling me. Thank you for sharing this moment with me, after all we've been through. Thank you for not hating me, for still trusting me.*

Now I could weep with gratitude. But I don't. I turn off my computer, grab my car keys, head for home. For now, this is as close as we're getting to a happy ending.

Relapse, Recovery, Renewal

Fall seven times, stand up eight.

—JAPANESE PROVERB

As I wrote this book, I became conscious of how many times I mentioned Mother's Day—how much a part of this story Mother's Day has been. It happened to be Mother's Day when our family took the bike ride that alerted us to trouble, when Kitty shared her anxieties for the first time. Mother's Day was the beginning and so became a landmark, a measure of time gone by and progress made, or not made.

It's fitting in a book like this, about a family's struggle with a child's mental illness. So many narratives on this subject wind up focusing on mothers, and not in a positive way. Every serious illness that affects a child affects his or her whole family, whether the illness is cancer or AIDS, cystic fibrosis or depression or an eating disorder. Every family that goes through such an illness is changed by it. Every family that comes through that fire presents a different face to the world and to one another.

We live at a time and in a culture that seems obsessed with establishing cause and effect, and in some ways that's good, feeding the spirit of inquiry that fuels scientific progress. If Alexander Fleming hadn't become curious about what made a dish full of *Staphylococcus* turn blue and why the bacteria beside it were disappearing, we wouldn't have penicillin. But sometimes our urge to know, to assign blame and responsibility, backfires. Families aren't petri dishes, and the millions of events and interactions that make up a family's collective life are not easy to categorize. Bad things happen in families, certainly; so do good things. So do many things that are neither bad nor good but just are.

Nearly every family whose child must deal with a mental illness knows the experience of being dissected and analyzed, taken apart with an eye toward judgment and blame. The thing is, the experience of being judged also changes a family. It makes parents feel defensive. It makes parents behave in ways they might not ordinarily. Blame and judgment change the dynamic nearly as much, sometimes, as the original illness.

When anorexia chose Kitty, it also chose me, and Jamie, and Emma. It chose our family; it called into question many of our deeply held beliefs and traditions. It challenged our assumptions, our way of being with one another. When it built walls between us, we put in doorways. When it let grief into our house, we opened every window and shooed it out. When it called us names—*jailer, torturer, liar*—we answered *mother, father, sister.* Kitty was the one diagnosed with anorexia. But it happened to all of us.

After that terrible year of refeeding, things got better—for Kitty and for the rest of us. She took up her life again. She spent time with friends, acquired and then de-acquired a boyfriend, found a new sport. She seemed happy some of the time, and when she wasn't, her sadness or anger or angst seemed like normal teenage emotions to Jamie and me.

It took us longer to recover. For months I burst into tears for no reason. I flinched at any mention of eating disorders. My panic attacks, which had been under control for years, started up again.

One night I dreamed that Kitty was sitting next to me on our living room couch. One of her arms had turned into a kind of flipper grafted onto her shoulder, with three fingers attached to it. Her other arm was crooked at an odd angle, fingers dangling uselessly, just the thumb cocked and moving. In the dream a disembodied voice said, "Isn't it great—they were able to save part of both hands!" My screaming woke Jamie, who put his arms around me and said maybe the dream represented my anxiety that Kitty was not fully recovered, that something was still wrong. True enough. But far worse than the damage to Kitty's arms and hands was the voice telling me I should feel grateful, even happy, about something I could view only with horror.

I will never be grateful for anorexia or its legacy.

At times the shadow of the demon did seem to pass over Kitty again. That December, for instance, when she'd been at a healthy weight for six months, we took a ski trip to the Porcupine Mountains, on the edge of Lake Superior in Michigan's Upper Peninsula. It's gorgeous country and very isolated; the only place to eat was our hotel, which served mediocre food, and the rustic ski lodge, which served snacks.

We spent the first two days on the slopes. By midafternoon on the second day, Kitty's mood had begun to slide. She became apologetic and guilt-ridden; she had an anxiety attack about getting into college, two years away. She came off the slopes in tears.

When I suggested a cup of hot chocolate, she accused me of having a one-track mind. "Every time I'm upset you think it's all about food!" she said. "You think my whole life is all about what I eat and don't eat. I'm sick of it." She stormed across the lodge's great room and flung herself into a chair by the fire, her back to me.

She was right, of course; I did associate her mood with her food. I sat by the window and thought back over what she'd been eating for the last week—or at least what I'd seen her eat. It seemed to me, watching skiers come down the slopes through the floor-to-ceiling windows, that I'd seen Kitty start to restrict. Nothing major—just choosing, say, a plain baked potato over French fries, fruit for dessert, fish instead of meat. I hadn't seen her eat cheese in a while. Was this normal eating, or was I inventing a problem? Was my anxiety a sign that I was one of Hilde Bruch's overcontrolling mothers after all?

I crossed the room and sat on the arm of Kitty's chair. With her back to me, she said, "I'm really not trying to restrict," and it was this more than anything else that made me realize the truth. I bought a Hershey's bar and a mug of apple cider and insisted that she eat and drink. That night at the hotel's dinner buffet, I nixed the broiled fish she wanted in favor of shrimp scampi with a side of French fries and a slice of pie. She was furious, stabbing at the food with her fork, complaining more or less continuously that her stomach hurt, that I was making her eat too much, that this was my problem, not hers.

The next day she was fine: self-possessed, making jokes, helpful. She came back to the lodge a little early, saying she was tired, and without any nudging on my part ate a large protein bar and drank a carton of milk. *Remember this*, I thought: the more she eats, the more willingly she eats; the less she eats, the harder eating becomes. There appears to be a self-reinforcing quality to both the act of eating and the act of restricting. I told myself to trust my instincts, that even if I couldn't articulate the symptoms, I'd come to recognize the altered state Kitty got into with even the slightest bit of undereating, whether it was intentional or not.

There were other incidents like this, and I wondered whether time would help or whether, maybe, Dr. Beth was wrong. Maybe Kitty was going to have to be vigilant about what and how much she ate for a while. Maybe forever.

By her junior year of high school, she was stopping by Dr. Beth's herself for weigh-ins every couple of weeks. She would get on the scale and have a nurse record her weight and call us with the number. Keeping her weight up still seemed to present a challenge, especially because Kitty, ever the athlete, had discovered a new sport, cycling. And she was good at it: in her first year she won a couple of national championships in her age group. As she put on muscle, we adjusted her target weight up, to make sure she wasn't losing body fat as she gained muscle mass.

"Why can't you take up embroidery instead of sports?" I asked her one afternoon, smiling to show that I was joking. But I wasn't, not really. In 1986, Walter Kaye did a study showing that people with anorexia need more calories than usual for months after weight restoration; eventually, he believes, their systems return to normal. In the meantime, Kitty's hypermetabolic state combined with cycling meant that she had to keep on eating about thirty-five hundred calories a day just to maintain her weight.

Something else troubled me, too: Was Kitty's drive for competitive athletics good for her, or was it a sign of ongoing pathology? Was she biking to purge calories, or because, as she said, it made her feel good? She saw her athleticism as part of who she was—the most important part, to her, at least for now. Jamie and I accepted that. But we still wished she'd expand her passions. Before anorexia, her dream was to go to law school. When I asked her about that now, she shrugged.

Most of the time, she ate with enthusiasm and hunger and pleasure; most of the time, except for our nightly family dinners, she ate on her own, like a normal teenager. When her weight dipped a pound or two, we offered support as tactfully as possible. I might walk into the kitchen as she made lunch—she still came home for lunch, by her choice—and say, "I think you need another slice of turkey on that wrap," or "How about if I make you a couple of grilled cheese sandwiches?"

How far should we push Kitty? We weren't sure. I thought we were in Phase 2 of family-based treatment, where parents gradually return control of eating to the teenager. That's what we were trying for anyway. And Kitty's weight was good; her BMI was around 20, solidly on her growth curve, and it stayed steady over her last two years of high school. But she still seemed vulnerable in ways that surprised us. She still sometimes seemed too close to the edge.

But we were the only ones who felt that way. Dr. Beth invited me into the exam room at the end of Kitty's sixteen-year checkup. There she told me that Kitty was in a good place, she was ready to move on from the anorexia, but that my continuing anxiety over Kitty's eating was "inappropriate" and holding her back.

Over the next few days I thought hard about what Dr. Beth said. Was she right? Was I hanging on to the anorexia in a way that was holding Kitty back? Kitty's relationship to food still felt tense and controlled to me. Both Jamie and I noticed that she still shied away from foods she used to love, like pizza, cheese, chocolate. She *said* they upset her stomach; it seemed a bit too coincidental that they all contained fat. She was often emotionally volatile; then again, she was a teenager. Her weight was good for her height but not high. She told me she was having regular periods.

Her urge to exercise still felt excessive to me, especially when I discovered by accident that she'd added running to her workout routine, after we'd agreed she wouldn't run. When I confronted Kitty about it, she said running helped her deal with stress, that it wasn't part of an eating disorder, it was just who she was. That she wasn't doing it to burn calories.

I believed her. But I didn't believe anorexia. And I didn't know who we were talking to.

In some ways it was easier to know what to do when Kitty was in crisis. Things were black and white then: the hospital, the medical emergency, the physical manifestations of malnutrition all inspired a sense of urgency. In Phase 1, all our efforts focused on getting Kitty to gain weight. Now the goals were more complex and more individual.

Maybe Dr. Beth was right. Maybe I did have issues about letting go. I couldn't tell anymore. My anxiety boiled down to a feeling that Kitty wasn't there yet—wherever *there* was.

In my anxiety about being anxious, in my wish to respect Kitty's growing independence, I argued with Jamie. Kitty was still nervous about getting weighed; she wanted to know a day in advance, so she could, as she put it, "prepare herself mentally." Jamie thought this was suspicious and wanted to be able to pop her on the scale randomly—not in a punitive way, just to do the occasional spot check. I said I could understand her anxiety; after all, we put a lot of emphasis on her hitting the right number on the scale. I was trying hard to let go of my anxiety, as Dr. Beth had suggested. I didn't want to be one of those neurotic mothers who couldn't let their child grow up.

I won the argument; we gave Kitty advance warning when we were going to weigh her. In retrospect, I wish I'd lost.

Every parent worries when a child strikes out on her own. We're not like birds, who push their fledglings out of the nest. We worry about who will be there to comfort our child, to help her learn to take care of herself. And when that child has special needs, whatever they are, the process of becoming independent is that much more fraught. The stakes are that much higher.

Kitty graduated from high school a semester early. She'd been accepted at a small midwestern university for the fall, and she wanted to spend spring of her senior year living in Colorado, training and racing with the rest of her cycling team. She said she knew lots of people in the area; she could cook, do laundry, hold down a job in a bike shop. She couldn't wait to be independent.

She was close to her new, slightly higher target weight, a couple of pounds shy, and said she could reach it on her own. "I've left anorexia behind, Mom," she told me. And I wanted to believe her. I wanted Dr. Beth to be right about Kitty being one of the lucky ones who recover completely, go on with their lives, never look back.

So she went off to Colorado, with certain conditions: She had to stay in close touch with us. And she had to find a doctor's office where she could be weighed, and where the nurses would send us the weight, at least every two weeks.

At first things went well. Every time we talked I asked if she'd found a doctor's office for weigh-ins, and every time she said, "Not yet." And every time we hung up, Jamie and I muttered to each other about making some calls and finding a doctor for her. Setting it up.

But the truth is, Kitty was eighteen, and part of the point of this gap semester was for her to become more independent. So we didn't make any calls. The weeks passed, and she said she was doing well. But I noticed that she sounded a little fragile on the phone—a little more high-strung, more prone to tears. "Are you eating?" I asked, over and over.

"Yes, Mom," she said in an exasperated voice.

"What did you have for breakfast?"

"I can handle it, Mom!"

Around Mother's Day I went out for a weekend visit, at Kitty's request. When I got out of the airport taxi, she was standing at the door, waiting for me. And even from the curb I could see why she wanted me to come out. I went to her, put my arms around her newly bony shoulders. I wanted to weep. I wanted to lay my daughter down as if she were made of china and take care of her. I looked into her eyes, and I saw that she knew what had happened. She was aware. Now I was too.

That weekend, we talked and talked. Kitty said she knew she'd lost a little weight, but she was on top of things, she could turn it around. I thought it was more than a little—it had to be at least fifteen pounds. How in the world did she lose fifteen pounds in less than two months?

I took her out for Thai food and she ate with gusto. I relaxed a little. But for the rest of the weekend, I watched her restrict without even knowing it. It was little things, like not putting butter on bread, eating salad with no dressing, eschewing anything with cheese. She was too full for pie, she said, eating half a peach instead.

My last morning, I told her what I saw: that whether she intended it or not, whether she thought I equated everything with food or not, she was not eating enough, or enough of the right foods. We talked through some meal possibilities, things she could cook or buy easily. "I know I can do it, Mom," she told me, and I wanted so badly to believe her.

A month later, we brought her home, another ten pounds lighter, and began again the work of loosening the demon's claws.

Over the last four years, I've talked to many families who have gone through some version of our story: their child recovered from anorexia at twelve or thirteen or fourteen and then relapsed at college or living independently for the first time. Every teen has to learn to take care of herself; inevitably, they make mistakes along the way.

"I just wanted to be normal," Kitty told me on her first day home. "I didn't want to have to think about food or anorexia. I just wanted to live like a regular person and not always be worrying about how much I was eating."

I could understand her longing to leave anorexia behind, to not worry about it, to be "normal." I told her if she had diabetes, she'd have to test her blood sugar every day; at first it would be a pain, but she'd get used to it. It would become just one of the things she had to do, like brushing her teeth. It would become part of "normal" for her. Nearly all of us have some aspect of our lives that we have to track like this.

One of the worst moments this time around came when Kitty confessed that three years earlier, she'd sewed weights into a bra, and wore it every time we weighed her. That's why she needed to know ahead of time before a trip to Dr. Beth's. Jamie was right about the weigh-ins all along.

I didn't even know she could sew.

She said she'd sewed five or six pounds of weights into the bra, which meant she was never even close to the target weight we set. Which explained why she so often seemed too close to the edge. And, maybe, how she lost so much weight so fast.

It was harder, this time around, to separate Kitty from the illness, harder to tell the demon's voice from her own. Kitty was eighteen, not fourteen, more sophisticated, more grown-up, both more and less aware of the fact that she was ill, of the distortions the illness imposed on her thoughts and actions. Last time, I'd worried that going through the refeeding process would damage our relationship irrevocably. It didn't, a fact I knew only from overhearing Kitty tell the mother of another girl with anorexia, "You need to do what my parents did. They saved my life."

This time around, she was stronger and more resourceful; so was the illness. This time even more than the last, Jamie and I had to block our ears to the demon's imprecations, stay calm, and keep feeding our daughter. I thought of Ulysses tied to the mast so he couldn't change course, seduced by the song of the Sirens. The metaphor seemed apt, only instead of Sirens we heard the voice of the illness: *I could recover much better somewhere else. You're making it harder, not easier. I can take care of this myself; give me another chance!* We considered sending Kitty to some kind of residential program. Cost was an obstacle, but even more than money was the knowledge that what she really needed was food and the patient scrutiny of people who loved her. Who *knew* her better than anyone else. Who weren't fooled, or at least not as often, by the demon's tricks and manipulations.

Many parents of teens with anorexia—especially older teens—are accused at some point of hanging on to the disease too long. Of not wanting to let go of their adolescent. Of missing the feeling of being needed, or the attention they got from doctors, or . . . fill in the blank. In my experience, this is rarely if ever true. Everything I know about eating disorders—that they're anosognosic, ego-syntonic, that they cloud the mind and alter the body's chemistry—is still true now that Kitty's over eighteen. The essential nature of the illness doesn't change once your child crosses the magical age line.

This is a big part of what makes family-based treatment more challenging for families with older teenagers. We're more vulnerable to the criticism of being overly controlling, because eighteen-year-olds in this culture are supposed to go off, be independent, take care (more or less) of themselves. FBT goes against the cultural grain even more for an eighteen-year-old than it does for a twelve- or fourteen-year-old.

And yet I've come to learn, through hard experience, that people with eating disorders as well as other mental disorders aren't always (or even usually) best suited to make choices about their recoveries or lives. I know this is a statement that will make some sufferers angry; they'll say, as Kitty said to me, that I'm not respecting them. That I'm pooh-poohing their feelings, sweeping them all into the box labeled eating disorders. That's not my intention at all.

In December 2007, the NYU Study Center caused a firestorm of protest with a public awareness campaign about childhood psychiatric illnesses and learning disorders. The concept was that mental illnesses hold children hostage; a series of "ransom notes" were designed to raise awareness of the realities of mental illness. For instance, one note read, "We have your daughter. We are forcing her to throw up after every meal she eats. It's only going to get worse. . . . *Bulimia.*" Another: "We have taken your son. We have imprisoned him in a maze of darkness with no hope of ever getting out. Do nothing and see what happens. . . . *Depression.*"

The campaign kicked up so much backlash that NYU withdrew it after only a week. I think one reason it hit such a collective nerve is that it challenged our culture's deeply held notion that we're in control. My mother-in-law, who suffered from mild depression, used to say, "When I feel myself beginning to be depressed, I just talk to myself. I say, You're not going to let that happen again." I'm glad that strategy worked for her. But we can't always control how we think or feel or behave. The take-yourself-in-hand line of thinking is cruelly ineffective for eating disorders as well as for many other mental illnesses, and especially for children, whose ability to reason, think deductively, synthesize information, and make judgments continues to develop until they're in their midtwenties.

As I write this, Kitty has just started college, a semester later than planned. She's not fully recovered from this relapse but she's made good progress and is working hard. Jamie and I agonized over whether to send her. She wanted to go and demonstrated that she was capable of gaining weight on her own. When she was fourteen, there was no question of letting her go anywhere until she was fully recovered. At eighteen, the process of recovery becomes by necessity more collaborative—up to a point. It's one thing to allow for some autonomy, to anticipate some bumps in the road. It's quite another to sit back and watch the demon take hold once more. That we're not prepared to do. We've built as much support as we can into her college experience; now we will wait, and watch, and be ready, knowing that the longer the demon lives inside her, the more comfortable it gets. The more entrenched the eating disorder, the harder it will be for her to achieve true recovery.

Kitty knows that if she doesn't continue to recover, we'll bring her home to finish the work here. Because the essential question remains the same now as it was four years ago: Do we want her to have the life she was meant to have, full of color and hope and joy? Or are we willing to settle for the gray half-life that comes from living with the demon?

The rest of the world may think we're being overprotective. We know the truth: we are saving our daughter's life, if not literally, then in every way that counts. We'll do whatever it takes to make sure Kitty gets well and stays well, whether she's eighteen or thirty-eight. That's what families do.

{ acknowledgments }

A **veritable and virtual** army of generous people helped us help our daughter. To all of you, I'm forever grateful. Beth Neary and Susan Neff are my heroines; I don't know what we would have done without you. Thanks to Ellyn Satter, who keeps me in her heart; the feeling is mutual.

A million thanks to the friends and neighbors who fed us, walked with us, listened to us, supported us. In particular, Joan Laurion and Barbara and Bob Koechley traveled places none of us wanted to go; the fact that we didn't have to go there alone made all the difference. Many thanks as well to Asja and David Young, Bobbie Johnson, Elaine and Dave Glowacki, Gale Petersen, Joan Fischer, Judy Woodburn, Kay and Nick Cahill, Laurie Zimmerman, Lisa and Harry Webne-Behrman, Margaret Krome and Steve Ventura, Melissa Schulz, Nancy Holyoke, and Pamela Reilly. Thanks to Scott Klug for being the kind of boss who puts families first.

And thank you to Daniel le Grange, Jim Lock, and Walter Kaye for answering my questions at length and ad nauseam, for your work on eating disorders, and for your compassion toward patients and their families. Eternal gratitude to Jane Cawley, my cochair at Maudsley Parents (www.maudsleyparents.org)—friend, colleague, adviser, and fellow traveler. Keep those videos coming.

Thanks as well to Cris Haltom for helping later, and to Laura Collins, who wrote the book that got us started.

As always, I owe a lot to Miriam Altshuler, agent and friend. Who would have predicted where we'd end up twenty years ago? To Nancy Miller, for believing in this book before it existed, and to Mary Ellen O'Neill, who championed the book from the beginning—thank you from the bottom of my heart.

My early readers offered invaluable feedback. Pam Reilly, Kasey Brown, and Shander Bawden, you're the best! I'm also grateful to Ilena Silverman at the *New York Times Magazine*, who helped me shape the article that led to the writing of this book.

Thanks to my research assistants, Lin Lin and Simone Becque, who helped me collect and organize hundreds of studies so I could find exactly the statistic I wanted when I wanted it—a miracle.

The Vermont Studio Center, Edenfred, and the Corporation of Yaddo gave me residencies where I was able to step outside my life and think and write. I am grateful beyond words for the gifts of time and space and creative camaraderie.

Thanks to my husband, Jamie, for his thoughtful, unwavering support; I'm so lucky to have you in my life. To Emma, for her powers of observation and her capacity for empathy; you once told me that no one ever talks about how hard anorexia is on the parents and sisters and brothers. Now, I hope, they will.

{ resources }

Web sites

Maudsley Parents
www.maudsley parents.org

National Eating Disorders Association
www.nationaleatingdisorders.org

Books

Brumberg, Joan Jacobs. *Fasting Girls: The History of Anorexia Nervosa*. New York: Vintage Books, 2000.

Collins, Laura. *Eating with Your Anorexic: How My Child Recovered Through Family-Based Treatment and Yours Can Too*. New York: McGraw-Hill, 2005.

Keys, Ancel, Josef Brožek, Austin Henschel, Olaf Mickelsen, and Henry Taylor. *The Biology of Human Starvation*. Minneapolis: University of Minnesota Press, 1950.

Lock, James, and Daniel le Grange. *Help Your Teenager Beat an Eating Disorder*. New York: Guilford Press, 2005.

Russell, Sharman Apt. *Hunger: An Unnatural History*. New York: Basic Books, 2005.

Treasure, Janet, Ulrike Schmidt, and Eric van Furth. *Handbook of Eating Disorders*. 2nd ed. Chichester, England: John Wiley & Sons, 2003.

Vandereycken, Walter, and Ron van Deth. *From Fasting Saints to Anorexic Girls: The History of Self-Starvation*. New York: New York University Press, 1994.

Selected Articles and Studies

Allan, Rosemary, Reena Sharma, Bhumika Sangani, Philippa Hugo, Ian Frampton, Helen Mason, and Bryan Lask. "Predicting the Weight Gain Required for Recovery from Anorexia Nervosa with Pelvic Ultrasonography: An Evidence-Based Approach." *European Eating Disorders Review* 18, no. 1 (2010): 43–48.

Arkell, James, and Paul Robinson. "A Pilot Case Using Qualitative and Quantitative Methods: Biological, Psychological and Social Outcome in Severe and Enduring Eating Disorder." *International Journal of Eating Disorders* 41, no. 7 (2008): 650–56.

Attia, Evelyn, and Christina Roberto. "Should Amenorrhea Be a Diagnostic Criterion for Anorexia Nervosa?" *International Journal of Eating Disorders* 42, no. 7 (2009): 581–89.

Attia, Evelyn, and Timothy Walsh. "Behavioral Management for Anorexia Nervosa." *The New England Journal of Medicine* 360, no. 5 (2009): 500–506.

Barboriak, Joseph, and Arthur Wilson. "Effects of Diet on Self-Starvation in the Rat." *The Journal of Nutrition* 102 (1972): 1543–46.

Bardone-Cone, Anna, Katrina Sturm, Melissa Lawson, D. Paul Robinson, and Roma Smith. "Perfectionism Across Stages of Recovery from Eating Disorders." *International Journal of Eating Disorders* 43, no. 2 (2009): 139–48.

Casanueva, Felipe, Carlos Dieguez, Vera Popovic, Roberto Peino, Robert V. Considine, and Jose F. Caro. "Serum Immunoreactive Leptin Concentrations in Patients with Anorexia Nervosa Before and After Partial Weight Recovery." *Biochemical and Molecular Medicine* 60 (1997): 116–20.

Cordero, Elizabeth, and Tania Israel. "Parents as Protective Factors in Eating Problems of College Women." *Eating Disorders* 17 (2009):146–61.

Couturier, Jennifer, and James Lock. "What Is Recovery in Adolescent Anorexia Nervosa?" *International Journal of Eating Disorders* 39 (2006): 550–55.

Crow, Scott, James Mitchell, James Roerig, and Kristine Steffen. "What Potential Role Is There for Medication Treatment in Anorexia Nervosa?" *International Journal of Eating Disorders* 42, no. 1 (2009): 1–8.

Dellava, Jocilyn, Peggy Policastro, and Daniel Hoffman. "Energy Metabolism and Body Composition in Long-Term Recovery from Anorexia Nervosa." *International Journal of Eating Disorders* 42, no. 2 (2009): 415–21.

Ehrlich, Stefan, Roland Burghardt, Deike Weiss, Harriet Salbach-Andrae, Eugenia Maria Craciun, Klaus Goldhahn, Burghard F. Klapp, and Ulrike Lehmkuhl. "Glial and Neuronal Damage Markers in Patients with Anorexia Nervosa." Special issue: *Biological Child and Adolescent Psychiatry* 115, no. 6 (2008): 921–27.

Ehrlich, Stefan, Leonora Franke, Nora Schneider, Harriet Salbach-Andrae, Regina Schott, Eugenia M. Craciun, Ernst Pfeiffer, Ralf Uebelhack, and Ulrike Lehmkuhl. "Aromatic Amino Acids in Weight-Recovered Females with Anorexia Nervosa." *International Journal of Eating Disorders* 42, no. 2 (2009): 166–72.

Fessler, Daniel M. T. "The Implications of Starvation-Induced Psychological Changes for the Ethical Treatment of Hunger Strikers." *Journal of Medical Ethics* 29 (2003): 243–47.

Garner, David M. "The Effects of Starvation on Behavior: Implications for Eating Disorders." *Handbook for Treatment of Eating Disorders.* New York: Guilford Press, 1997.

Goode, Erica. "Anorexia Strategy: Family as Doctor." *New York Times,* June 11, 2002.

Greenleaf, Christy, Trent Petrie, Jennifer Carter, and Justine Reel. "Female Collegiate Athletes: Prevalence of Eating Disorders and Disordered Eating Behaviors." *Journal of American College Health* 57, no. 5 (2009): 489–95.

Guisinger, Shan. "An Evolutionary Explanation for Anorexia?" *Psychological Review* 110, no. 4 (2004): 745–61.

Katzman, Debra K., Bruce Christensen, A. R. Young, and Robert B. Zipursky. "Starving the Brain: Structural Abnormalities in Cognitive Impairment in Adolescents with Anorexia Nervosa." *Seminars in Clinical Neuropsychiatry* 6, no. 2 (2001): 146–52.

Kaye, Walter. "Neurobiology of Anorexia and Bulimia Nervosa." *Physiology & Behavior* 94 (2008): 121–35.

Kaye, Walter, Cynthia M. Bulik, Katherine Plotnicov, Laura Thornton, Bernie Devlin, Manfred M. Fichter, Janet Treasure et al. "The Genetics of Anorexia Nervosa Collaborative Study: Methods and Sample Description." *International Journal of Eating Disorders* 41 (2008): 289–300.

Kaye, Walter, Guido K. Frank, and Claire McConaha. "Altered Dopamine Activity After Recovery from Restricting-Type Anorexia Nervosa." *Neuropsychopharmacology* 21 (1999): 503–6.

Kaye, Walter, Julie Fudge, and Martin Paulus. "New Insights into Symptoms and Neurocircuit Function of Anorexia Nervosa." *Nature Reviews Neuroscience* 10 (2009): 573–84.

Kaye, Walter, Harry Gwirtsman, Ted George, Michael H. Ebert, and Rosemary Petersen. "Caloric Consumption and Activity Levels After Weight Recovery in Anorexia Nervosa: A Prolonged Delay in Normalization." *International Journal of Eating Disorders* 5, no. 3 (1986): 489–502.

Klump, Kelly, and Cynthia Bulik. "Academy for Eating Disorders Position Paper: Eating Disorders Are Serious Mental Illnesses." *International Journal of Eating Disorders* 42, no. 2 (2009): 97–103.

Lambe, Evelyn. K., Debra Katzman, David J. Mikulis, Sidney H. Kennedy, and Robert B. Zipursky. "Cerebral Gray Matter Volume Deficits After Weight Recovery from Anorexia Nervosa." *Archives of Pediatric Adolescent Medicine* 54, no. 6 (1997): 537–42.

Lask, Bryan. "Anorexia Nervosa—Irony, Misnomer and Paradox." *European Eating Disorders Review* 17 (2009): 1–4.

Le Grange, Daniel. "Family Therapy for Adolescent Anorexia Nervosa." *Journal of Clinical Psychology* 5 (1999): 727–40.

Le Grange, Daniel, and Ivan Eisler. "Family Interventions in Adolescent Anorexia Nervosa." *Child & Adolescent Psychiatric Clinics of North America* 18 (2008): 159–73.

Le Grange, Daniel, James Lock, Kathryn Loeb, and Dasha Nicholls. "Academy for Eating Disorders Position Paper: The Role of the Family in Eating Disorders." *International Journal of Eating Disorders* 43, no. 1 (2010): 1–5.

Lear, Scott, Robert P. Pauly, and C. Laird Birmingham. "Body Fat, Caloric Intake, and Plasma Leptin Levels in Women with Anorexia Nervosa." *International Journal of Eating Disorders* 26, no. 3 (1999): 283–88.

Lilenfield, Lisa, Stephen Wonderlich, Lawrence P. Riso, Ross Crosby, and James Mitchell. "Eating Disorders and Personality: A Methodological and Empirical Review." *Clinical Psychology Review* 26 (2006): 299–320.

Lock, James, William Stewart Agras, Susan Bryson, and Helena C. Kraemer. "A Comparison of Short- and Long-Term Family Therapy for Adolescent Anorexia Nervosa." *Journal of the American Academy of Child Psychiatry* 44, no. 7 (2005): 632–39.

Lock, James, Jennifer Couturier, and William Stewart Agras. "Comparison of Long-Term Outcomes in Adolescents with Anorexia Nervosa Treated with Family Therapy." *Journal of the American Academy of Child Psychiatry* 45, no. 6 (2006): 666–72.

Lock, James, and Daniel le Grange. "Can Family-Based Treatment Be Manualized?" *Journal of Psychotherapy Practice and Research* 10 (2001): 253–61.

Mahaut, Stéphanie, Yvan Dumont, Alain Fournier, Rémi Quirion, and Emmanuel Moyse. "Neuropeptide Y Receptor Subtypes in the Dorsal Vagal Complex Under Acute Feeding Adaptation in the Adult Rat." *Neuropeptides* 44, no. 2 (2010): 77–86.

Mayer, Laurel, Christina A. Roberto, Deborah Glasofer, Sarah Fischer Etu, Dympna Gallagher, Jack Wang, Steven B. Heymsfield, Richard N. Pierson Jr., Evelyn Attia, Michael Devlin, and Timothy Walsh. "Does Percent Body Fat Predict Outcome in Anorexia Nervosa?" *American Journal of Psychiatry* 164, no. 6 (2007): 970–72.

Robin, Arthur, Patricia T. Siegel, and Anne Moye. "Family Versus Individual Therapy for Anorexia: Impact on Family Conflict." *International Journal of Eating Disorders* 17, no. 4 (1995): 313–32.

Sachdev, Perminder, Naresh Mondraty, Wei Wen, and Kylie Gulliford. "Brains of Anorexia Nervosa Patients Process Self-Images Differently from Non-Self-Images: An fMRI Study." *Neuropsychologia* 46 (2008): 2161–68.

Sim, Leslie, Jason H. Homme, Aida N. Lteif, Jennifer L. Vande Voort, Kathryn M. Schak, and Jarrod Ellingson. "Family Functioning and Maternal Distress in Adolescent Girls with Anorexia Nervosa." *International Journal of Eating Disorders* 42 (2009): 531–39.

Steinhausen, Hans-Christoph. "The Outcome of Anorexia Nervosa in the 20th Century." *American Journal of Psychiatry* 159, no. 8 (2002): 1284–93.

Steinhausen, Hans-Christoph, Maria Grigoroiu-Serbanescu, Svetlana Boyadjieva, Klaus-Jürgen Neumärker, and Christa Winkler Metzke. "The Relevance of Body Weight in the Medium-Term to Long-Term Course of Adolescent Anorexia Nervosa." *International Journal of Eating Disorders* 42, no. 1 (2009): 19–25.

Treasure, Janet. "Getting Beneath the Phenotype of Anorexia Nervosa: The Search for Viable Endophenotypes and Genotypes." *Canadian Journal of Psychiatry* 52, no. 4 (2007): 212–19.

Wagner, Angela, Howard Aizenstein, Vijay K. Venkatraman, Julie Fudge, J. Christopher May, Laura Mazurkewicz, Guido K. Frank et al. "Altered Reward Processing in Women Recovered from Anorexia Nervosa." *American Journal of Psychiatry* 164, no. 12 (2007): 1842–49.

Wagner, Angela, Phil Greer, Ursula F. Bailer, Guido K. Frank, Shannan E. Henry, Karen Putnam, and Carolyn C. Meltzer et al. "Normal Brain Tissue Volumes After Long-Term Recovery in Anorexia and Bulimia Nervosa." *Biological Psychiatry* 59, no. 3 (2006): 291–93.

Wagner, Angela, and Walter Kaye. "Altered Insula Response to Taste Stimuli in Individuals Recovered from Restricting-Type Anorexia Nervosa." *Neuropsychopharmacology* 33 (2008): 513–23.

Wagner, Angela, Matthias Ruf, Dieter F. Braus, and Martin H. Schmidt. "Neuronal Activity Changes and Body Image Distortion in Anorexia Nervosa." *NeuroReport* 14, no. 17 (2003): 2193–97.

Weltzin, Theodore E., Madelyn H. Fernstrom, Donna Hansen, Claire McConaha, and Walter Kaye. "Abnormal Caloric Requirements for Weight

Maintenance in Patients with Anorexia and Bulimia Nervosa." *American Journal of Psychiatry* 148, no. 12 (1991): 1675–82.

Zucker, Nancy, Molly Losh, Cynthia M. Bulik, Kevin S. LaBar, Joseph Piven, and Kevin A. Pelphrey. "Anorexia Nervosa and Autism Spectrum Disorders: Guided Investigation of Social Cognitive Endophenotypes." *Psychological Bulletin* 133, no. 6 (2007): 976–1006.